Sexual Politics and Popular Culture

Sexual Politics
and
Popular Culture

edited by
Diane Raymond

Bowling Green State University Popular Press
Bowling Green, Ohio 43403

Contents

Preface

Feminists have long maintained that "the personal is the political," that is, that the domain of personal relationships is inescapably charged politically. Thus, for feminist theory, any view which bifurcates these two worlds is *a priori* suspect and flawed.

In an atypical understatement, Kate Millett wrote in *Sexual Politics* that "coitus can scarcely be said to take place in a vacuum." Though at the time she wrote *Sexual Politics* in 1969, sex's "political aspect" may have been neglected, today one can scarcely avoid—in scholarly work *or* popular media—attending to sexual politics.

Our bodies are capable of a range of sexual practices and sexual pleasures, none of which are "natural" or "essential." Sexuality is both public and private. It includes but is certainly not limited to "sex."

[A]lthough of itself [sex] appears a biological, and physical activity, it is set so deeply within the larger context of human affairs that it serves as a charged microcosm of the variety of attitudes and values to which culture subscribes. (Millett 23)

Sex is indeed "charged." And we need not limit ourselves to "coitus" or even sexual practices in general to be addressing issues of sexuality and sexual politics. If one defines politics as more than a system of elected officials and formal proceedings and instead thinks of politics as including all those strategies designed to maintain a system, then "sexual politics" must include questions of gender roles and socialization, questions about what is 'natural,' violence, the family and its alternatives, pornography and censorship, the nature of desire, homosexuality, and mothering. In this sense, sexual politics—like politics in general—is concerned with *power*.

As Foucault has noted, our discussions of "sex" are concerned "less with *a* discourse on sex than with a multiplicity of discourses produced by a whole series of mechanisms operating in different institutions." (33) Thus, our discourses on sex are all "highly articulated around a cluster of power relations." One need not ascribe any crude intentionality or even posit some unitary driving force in order to accept this analysis.

One assumption that all the contributors to this volume share is that there is no essential "sex" or "sexuality" to which such discourses refer. What is generally called 'sex' is a highly mediated cultural phenomenon, directly experienced only by immediate participants, not usually directly available to witness by others. Our desire for knowledge about sexual practices, then, is not satisfied primarily by immediate access to the behaviors

i

but through the mediation of 'discourse.' Indeed, as Foucault reminds us repeatedly, sex is historically subordinate to sexuality.

Further, this "desire for knowledge" coexists with a need to regulate sexual practices; hence, normative categories emerge which serve to judge and also manage sex. 'Sex' enters the public domain as a topic to be talked about or visually or verbally represented; one thinks in this context of the forms of pornography, but it may also occur in various forms of 'erotica'; in mainstream films which teach us about love and romance; in sex manuals which tell us what to do and how; in the ever-popular Gothic romance; in the confessions of the famous or fictitious in newspapers and paperbacks; in the sex "quiz" of the women's magazine; in our popular preoccupation with the 'self' and its "full development"; in medicine's definitions of what is healthy and what is not. Such a list only scratches the surface of our "discourses" on sex, but it underlines Foucault's claim that "what is peculiar about modern societies . . . is not that they consigned sex to a shadow existence, but that they dedicated themselves to speaking of it *ad infinitum*, while exploiting it as *the* secret." (35)

Each of the essays in this collection is in some way concerned with power and sexual politics in the domain of popular culture. Each—whether it looks at film, language, literature, advertising, music or television— explores the sets of messages which serve to express and reinforce ideology. Though virtually all of these essays owe much to recent scholarship in feminist theory and in literary criticism, there is no one methodological perspective which unites them. Rather, one hopes that the differences among these essays will help to stimulate further discussion of the themes here.

The volume's organizational framework is, to some extent, arbitrary. The fact, for example, that the book opens with a section called "Theoretical Perspectives" is not meant to suggest that essays in later sections ignore theory. Further, several of these essays tackle a number of themes, and it would be overly simplistic to imply that the groupings here are anything but crude. For example, given our definition of "political," any of these essays might appear in the section called "Sexuality and Politics." Further, though the collection is organized in terms of "themes" in popular culture, one might have alternatively arranged the essays according to their medium.

These essays do offer important perspectives on methodology as well as on key themes—sexuality and desire; the family; politics and sexuality; and images of women. With the exception of Suzanna Walters's essay, reprinted from *Social Text*, each essay is original to this volume; and each opens new and exciting terrain in popular culture analysis. Our contributors are from a number of different disciplines: political science, philosophy, literature, history, and communications. Yet, like much of the best popular culture analysis, these essays not only avoid the jargon of the narrowly specialized practitioner but also cross and blur disciplinary boundaries in their approaches to these themes.

Works Cited

Foucault, Michel, *The History of Sexuality*, Volume I, trans. Robert Hurley. New York: Vintage Books, 1980.
Millett, Kate, *Sexual Politics*, Garden City, New York: Doubleday and Co., 1969.

Theoretical Perspectives

The Politics of "Meaning-Making": Feminist Hermeneutics, Language, and Culture

Nancy M. Theriot

Since the new wave of feminism brought women's studies into the university, feminist scholars in all fields of study have been interested in demystifying or deconstructing dichotomies such as public/private, individual/community, nature/culture, and masculine/feminine; and have also been critical of the "objectivity claim" of the sciences and social sciences. With this in mind, it is not surprising that there has been a "turn to theory" within feminist scholarship over the past five years and that poststructuralist theory has been influential among feminist critics. Although poststructuralism has been criticized by some as apolitical and as reducing everything to language, I will argue that a feminist hermeneutics based on poststructuralist methodology is inherently political and is specifically concerned with the interaction between language and "reality" and between language and subjectivity, two relationships important both to women's studies and to culture studies in general.

I want to begin by saying that my interest in poststructuralism comes from my frustration with the inadequacy of traditional historical methodology to accommodate significant questions in women's history. The interplay of private and public, body and culture, woman and femininity is beyond traditional historical imagination. Likewise, the relationship of sexual politics and women's sense of self is outside of traditional historical questioning. Finally, I have been alternately amused and infuriated by the refusal of traditional history to recognize history as the creation of historians instead of some unproblematic reflection of "what was." From the beginning of my work in women's history I have been drawn to literary criticism, philosophy, social psychology, and the sociology of knowledge for ways to conceptualize my question.[1] My reading of feminist and more general scholarship in these areas leads me to suggest: first, that a feminist hermeneutics, embodying a poststructuralist theory of meaning, is the basis of much feminist scholarship whether or not the vocabulary of poststructuralism is employed; and second, that a feminist hermeneutics offers a new way of approaching traditional problems in culture studies. My purpose in this essay is to outline a poststructuralist feminist hermeneutics and to suggest, more briefly, how it could be an enlightening methodological perspective for culture studies in general.

4   Sexual Politics and Popular Culture

By "feminist hermeneutics" I mean an interpretive strategy for understanding gender which posits meaning-making as political activity within the arena of language undertaken by historically situated actors. The first step to unravelling this admittedly complex definition is to explore the effects of the modifier, "feminist," on hermeneutics. Perhaps the only characteristic shared by modern hermeneutic critics is the assumption that there is an active relationship between the knower and the object of knowledge. In fact, this assumption forms the basis of the hermeneutic criticism of the "objectivity claim" in the social sciences.[2] A "feminist" hermeneutics rests on this assumption, and therefore claims that the feminist knower, like all other knowers, investigates/interprets/knows from a specific standpoint.[3]

A feminist standpoint is an "outsider position" in at least two ways, one fairly straightforward and the other more subtle. Most basically, a feminist standpoint is an interpretive position sensitive to the ways "otherness" is constructed and maintained. Groups and individuals defined by the discursive and non-discursive practices of society as outsiders—as bad, abnormal, insane, criminal, or "other" in any way—have a different vision of reality than those defined as inside. Not better, not more accurate, not more true; but different. Woman has been defined as "other," as "not-man," in both Western and non-Western traditions. Woman is the quintessential "other," always defined in relation to the one, the human norm, the man. While definitions of femininity and masculinity have changed over time, the two have been posed as opposites of unequal value, which, according to poststructuralist thinking, is one of the ways language works to structure experience. Woman contains not only "not-man," but everything man wants to see as not-quite-self, not-quite-human; the underside, the repressed, of "man" is "woman." The feminist standpoint is the position of woman-as-other. From a feminist standpoint, one is sensitive to the discursive and non-discursive practices that create and "normalize" woman's otherness.

Women's studies scholarship over the past twenty years has been written from a feminist standpoint, from the standpoint of woman-as-other. Feminist scholars from various disciplinary perspectives have pointed out the social and economic structures responsible for women's "otherness," and have been critical of dominant discourse about "the nature of reality" or "the way things are," whether it be in the writing of past historical characters or in the writing of contemporary scientists and social scientists. However, women's studies scholars also write from a feminist standpoint that is an outsider position in a more subtle sense than the position of woman-as-other. By demonstrating the social construction of "woman" and "feminine," feminist scholars illustrate how subjectivity and knowledge are political creations—how both are unstable, always changing, and mutually affecting. In making woman's otherness a subject of investigation, in de-stabilizing and de-naturalizing woman's otherness, feminist scholars who study gender stand to one side of their own subjectivity.

By deconstructing the category "woman," a category to which they belong, feminist scholars call into question the idea of unified self. "Femininity" or "true womanhood" is not simply an ideological and socioeconomic creation; it is a creation that women embody; it is an essential part of female self-hood; it is a creation that no woman can totally escape. Feminist scholarship goes beyond the standpoint of woman-as-other because it leads to the conclusion that identity itself—one's own subjectivity—is a creation in flux, and that knowledge about the "nature of woman" and "the nature of man" is a political creation that affects/determines one's subjectivity. This is one of the major ideas in Foucault's *The History of Sexuality*.[4] Without adopting poststructuralism as a methodological position, much current feminist scholarship rests on the poststructuralist assumption that neither knowledge nor the identity of the knower is fixed or true— that the act of interpretation, the act of knowing, mutually constructs the knower and the known.

A feminist hermeneutics from the standpoint of woman-as-other leads to questions about the forced category of female otherness, but a poststructuralist feminist hermeneutics leads to questions about how women lived (and live) our otherness, how female-ness is transformed and lived as femininity, how the word becomes flesh. A poststructuralist feminist hermeneutics recognizes that feminine identity is based on a "naturalized" idea of female body—"naturalized," made to seem normal and unquestionable, by the discursive and non-discursive practices that support the social, economic, and cultural power structure. A poststructuralist feminist hermeneutics makes questions involving subjectivity, ideology, body, and the politics of otherness askable and approachable by focusing attention not on otherness *per se* but on the ways in which otherness is created, maintained, and resisted. Language must be a central component in such a critique. Feminist hermeneutics, from a poststructuralist standpoint, is an interpretive strategy which assumes that meaning-making is a political activity within language by historically situated actors.[5]

"Meaning-making" as "political activity" is an on-going process of making self and world understandable, reasonable, known. I am suggesting that we abandon the concept of meaning as a noun—absolute, fixed, ahistorical, discoverable/knowable (or not) by objective investigators—and instead focus on meaning-making: meaning as a verb, an activity.[6] If meaning is not fixed, then meaning-making is a *political* activity; there are always competing meanings of events, activities, experiences, the "self"—with superior social/economic power determining which meanings are dominant. We can only capture meaning as a snap-shot of motion, a temporary freeze in the action. Analyzing meaning requires turning the snap-shot into a moving picture and identifying the relative power of the actors.

Meaning is not found, but made; and meaning is made *within language* by historically situated actors (which includes historical interpreters). Human activity in response to the material conditions of life—human animality itself—is mediated by language.[7] All human activities and experiences—from building bridges and fighting revolutions, to eating food, clothing ourselves and reproducing—are understood, known, made meaningful within language. Language structures perception of self and world, and all new experiences and activities are made sense of by taking them in, turning them over, comparing them to what has been, and finally integrating them and altering the what-has-been—all within the structure of language. This is not to say that everything is reduced to language or that everything is an idea. It is to say that meaning-making, by which self and world are made comprehensible, is a language-structured activity. "Reality" and "the body" are still "out there" and have existence independent of language; but *knowledge* of reality and the body (self) is language-structured.

The discourses that structure how we experience reality are not "representative," that is, language does not "reflect" reality or the self; instead, language is part of a historically situated struggle. Meaning-making is political activity because the discourses describing reality come out of (and help create) non-discursive practices and structures—such as the state, various institutions of professional authority, and the family—which maintain power relationships such as gender, race, class, and national hierarchies. There is a reciprocal relationship between discursive and non-discursive practices, between the institutions and activities which structure power relationships and the dominant discourse which serves to "naturalize" power's version of reality. Meaning-making in the arena of language is essential in creating, maintaining, and legitimizing power relationships, and those relationships are reproduced, challenged, and altered within language. Change in either area affects the other, and change in either area is reflected in the other. While the political activity of meaning-making depends on non-discursive structures, it is in discourse that we find the actual contest over meaning.

This concept of meaning-making is a powerful tool for understanding gender because it offers a new way of seeing some of the problem areas of feminist theory and women's history. Woman is defined as "other" on the basis of her female body, a material "reality" that is "out there" but never known outside of the social context that defines it as "other." This "otherness" is time/place specific, and its changing definition is a product of discursive practices within specific socioeconomic and cultural structures. The meaning of female body is contested in religious and scientific discourses that are controlled by men, within social, economic, and cultural institutions that are likewise male-dominated. Women have a "voice" in these discourses only by framing their arguments within the rules of the discourses. Whether objecting or adjusting to "otherness," women's subjectivity is created by the discourse of otherness; no woman can stand totally outside of it, and each woman's experiences are made meaningful within it and opposed to it.

Seeing gender from this poststructuralist feminist standpoint leads to a re-conceptualization of a central question in feminist theory: the nature of woman's otherness. This question is usually thought of as a dichotomy. Either there is an essence, "woman," different from the essence, "man," or there are no differences except in the naming—the socially produced difference. Either women have a special insight into the natural world and environmental issues and are inherently more nurturing and peaceloving than men, or women's maternal, peaceful "nature" is due entirely to cultural forces. Either difference is inherent or it is created.

I want to refuse the either/or and say "yes" to all of the above. Certainly women and men are biologically different, and the same. As material "reality," male and female bodies are both alike and different. But the different/same bodies are not known as such except through culture, through the discursive and non-discursive practices of historically specific societies. Differences and similarities are "out there," independent of naming them, but we recognize and experience only the sexual differences and similarities that are named. Difference between the sexes is the result *not* of essential body difference and *not* of cultural definition, but of both. Furthermore, it is impossible to experience ourselves outside of the cultural meaning of difference. We can refuse the sexual dichotomy on political and intellectual grounds, but no one can stand entirely outside of it. We "know" our *selves* as women and men, not as simply "human." This means, however, that our subjectivity, our identity *is different* according to sex. What we have "made" of different bodies *is* different selves, different not only "in name" but different in fact. It may be that women are indeed more connected to the earth, more able to care for others, and more interested in peace than men because of the way woman-as-other is experienced at this time. Following Foucault, the cultural feminists who assert woman's difference in the way I have outlined above may be "taking on" the subjugated position of woman-as-other and speaking from that experience of difference. This may be one way woman-as-other sounds when she asserts herself as subject, in Western society in the late twentieth century.

The cultural feminist position has been criticized as essentialist, as reproducing the fallacy of male/female difference rather than opposing it, as reasserting the woman/nature connection rather than challenging it. However, critics of cultural feminism also reproduce a dichotomy which feminist theory must deconstruct: the mind/body split. In theorizing woman's otherness as only a matter of naming, these critics fail to recognize the embodied-ness of all selves—that selves are named-bodies. If cultural feminists incorrectly literalize woman-as-other, and therefore fail to see gender as historical, their critics incorrectly disembody women's otherness, and therefore fail to see that it is as embodied selves, as engendered bodies that women have a history. Furthermore, in their claim that sameness rather than difference is the essence of the male/female relationship, critics of cultural feminism fail to recognize that sameness is just as socially constructed as difference, just as much the product of the discursive and non-discursive practices of society.

Both cultural feminist and their critics miss important dimensions of woman-as-other because neither group fully historicizes woman's otherness and neither group recognizes *itself* as historically specific. A feminist

8   Sexual Politics and Popular Culture

hermeneutics that assumes meaning-making as political activity within language by historically specific actors shifts the focus of investigation from woman's otherness *per se*—meaning as a noun—to the ways in which otherness is created, resisted, altered, and experienced—meaning as a verb. This involves, for example, analyzing the ways in which the discursive and non-discursive practices of a given society work together to "know" woman-as-other; the ways in which women's experiences of themselves are pre-figured, constructed, by a society's "knowledge" of woman; the ways women have resisted and altered a given definition of "woman"; and the ways gender overlaps other "outsider" categories—the obvious ones: race, class, and ethnicity, and the less obvious ones, such as physical or psychological "abnormalities" and "criminal" behavior—in the maintenance of the power structure.

One way to investigate meaning-making as political activity is to look at changing definitions of behavior or events, the groups responsible for the changes, and the people who are affected by the changes. As an example I offer the nineteenth-century and contemporary abortion controversy. In the nineteenth century abortion was criminalized due to the successful efforts of physicians to change the meaning of quickening—the woman's experience of fetal movement. Previously, quickening signified a change in the status of the fetus: from non-child to child. The law and religion, both male establishments, as well as women, outsiders to these establishments, viewed abortion before quickening as inoffensive and abortion after quickening as a breach of maternal feeling. In no case was the woman held criminally responsible, whether before or after movement. Around the middle of the century, male physicians, armed with new scientific knowledge that there was little difference between a pre-and post-quickening fetus, argued that abortion was murder from the moment of conception. This new way of knowing changed the meaning of quickening, and therefore of early abortion. The meaning change was a necessary prerequisite to criminalizing abortion; and the ideological battle took place in medical journals and popular magazines before it got to the courtroom. As outsiders of both legal and medical discourse, women were in no position to set the terms of the debate or to participate fully in the redefinition of abortion. However, women were not silenced on the problem of unwanted pregnancy. Faced with criminalization of a birth control method once popular with all classes of American women, some women began to argue for "voluntary motherhood" and a woman's "right to self" within marriage. These women wrote of abortion as a "crime against womanhood"—the murder of a child conceived due to the lust of the father.[8]

The history of legal changes regarding women and children in the nineteenth and early twentieth centuries is full of similar examples of struggles over definitions, over the meaning of behavior, with women on the outside of the official discourse. The point is: the meaning-struggle does not simply reflect "reality," it creates reality. Furthermore, the reality that is created is not simply a legal fiction, it is also an experience. The cultural dialogue about an event, experience, activity determines how people "live" it. A woman who believes she is murdering her baby experiences abortion differently than a woman who believes she is eliminating a non-viable fetus from her body. The event itself has no inherent meaning; instead, the meaning is created, through struggle, within language, and the meaning both determines the availability of the event and prescribes how the event will be experienced.

The late twentieth-century struggle over abortion rights also illustrates the interrelationship of language and "reality," but with women more actively involved in the public discourse, though still outside of the State and professional power structures. Since the abandonment of the quickening doctrine, abortion has become an issue of publicly contested meaning-making which involves the State, the medical profession, various religious groups, and women's organizations in a struggle to determine abortion law. Both sides in the meaning-struggle have had to frame the issue within the dominant discourses of law and medicine. Either demanding that the State outlaw abortion or that the State make no restrictions on abortion, each side has defined abortion within the legal/medical meaning structures in such a way as to insure total criminalization or total allowance. This partially accounts for the lack of subtlety in the meaning struggle.

Opponents of abortion use the term "right to life" as opposed to "anti-abortion" to designate their position, and they are adamant about the naming of their movement. Proponents of abortion rights (and I include myself in this group) are just as serious about calling themselves "pro-choice" instead of "pro-abortion." When referring to each other, each group calls the other by the name the other disdains. The naming is very important because the two positions are not simply different points of view on abortion. Abortion signifies a different act for the two groups: killing a baby or exercising control over one's body. To accept the right to life position is to equate abortion with murder, while to accept the pro-choice position is to define abortion as a woman's reproductive option.

Public opinion has been hard on both sides because "right to life" and "pro-choice" signify meanings of abortion that many Americans hesitate to embrace: either murder or just another birth control technique. In order to frame abortion within legal discourse, however, these two meanings are necessary. To criminalize abortion the only legal argument that opponents can make is that the fetus is a live human being, abortion is murder, and the state has a duty to protect the unborn's right to life. On the other hand, proponents' argument against restriction rests on the right to privacy and the understanding of the fetus as a sometimes unwanted set of tissues in a woman's uterus; proponents, therefore, must argue against all restrictions on women's private right to choose how to use our bodies. Because abortion is now part of a public legal discourse, the arguments on both sides must be posed within that structure.[9] Likewise, just as in the nineteenth century, the meaning of abortion and of women's relationship to the fetus must be established within the discourse of organized medicine. New knowledge/

techniques having to do with the viability of the fetus outside the uterus and extra-uterine fertilization are and will continue to be significant in establishing the meaning of abortion—and the availability of abortion. Thus far women have had much less input in the medical discourse on reproductive technology than they have in the legal discourse.

To view the nineteenth-and twentieth-century abortion controversy as a struggle over meaning is to see language and "reality" as interrelated, such that meaning is created within language in historically specific situations of power imbalance, and the meaning-making both reflects and constructs the power imbalance. Put another way, ideology (expressed in language) and the socioeconomic structure are interdependent; one is not caused by the other or prior to the other, but both constitute each other in struggle.[10]

From this theoretical perspective, subjectivity also is created, given meaning, by the interaction of discursive and non-discursive practices. There is no "natural" human, or natural man or woman; our identities are created by our experience in a specific socioeconomic structure, made meaningful and naturalized within language. There is no "pure" experience; as soon as we acquire language we filter experience and self through its lens. As power struggles of gender, race, and class take place and are visible in the socioeconomic realm, the contest over meaning takes place and is visible in the ideological realm of language. And the contest over meaning is essential to the struggle.

Again I turn to the nineteenth century for an example of the relationship between language and subjectivity. For nineteenth-century white middle-class women, the social construction of femininity involved a struggle over the meaning of domesticity and women's reproductive capacity. In fiction and non-fiction, in medicine and law, in reform societies, labor organizations, and churches—women and men defined femininity as maternal, home-oriented, and moral. Although both groups agreed on the basics, there was considerable disagreement about how femininity might be lived. Throughout the century there was women's discourse on femininity, in popular fiction and non-fiction, that created possibilities for feeling, thought and action beyond male prescriptions of female propriety. Eventually, women who saw themselves and were seen as totally proper and feminine could destroy property in saloons, successfully demand a sexual "right to themselves" within marriage, and argue that women should vote in order to bring domestic skills and feminine morality to the mess of politics. Within the women's discourse on domesticity, the conditions of women's lives (legal, social, and economic subordination) were made meaningful in such a way as to create the possibility for strong, self-assertive female subjectivity.

Women's sense of self, their sense of female identity, changed radically over the course of the nineteenth century, and that change, that new meaning, was worked out within language. I want to be very clear that I am not saying language and subjectivity are divorced from the social situation or are somehow in a separate realm. I am saying the opposite: it is the historical situation of which the self is a part that is the project of meaning-making. It is through constant re-conceptualization that takes place within language, that change or activity is possible. Over the course of the nineteenth century, several generations of women re-conceptualized femininity in response to a constantly changing historical situation; and that re-conceptualization made different behavior possible. But the re-thinking, the re-forming of femininity was always bound by sexual inequality; the new concepts were formed within the outlines of the dominant male discourse.[11]

My interest in poststructuralist theory comes from the kinds of questions I want to ask as a feminist historian. Beginning from a feminist poststructuralist standpoint and positing meaning-making as a political activity allows me a new range of interpretive possibilities, especially regarding body, subjectivity, and the relationship of "outsiders" to the dominant discourse. I believe that such a methodology can also be useful to scholars "making meaning" in areas of culture studies other than gender. American Studies has traditionally been concerned with meaning. But the field has also been criticized for taking a naive, non-political approach to meaning. Too often in American Studies scholarship, symbols and myths have floated around disconnected from social and economic context, and ideas have been described as representatively "American" with no regard to gender, class, race, or ethnic differences. It is impossible to fall into these interpretive dead-ends if we take a poststructuralist approach to meaning because the methodological assumptions include a suspicion of unities, a sensitivity to difference, and the belief that language (symbols, myths) is both reflective and constructive of the "real world." A feminist hermeneutics applied to American culture studies cautions us against the search for a unified "American mind" and instead gives us a way to see how "difference" operates in meaning-construction; it leads us away from a static notion of meaning and toward an understanding of the politics of language. By abandoning the search for "what things mean" and instead pursuing "how things mean," we prepare ourselves to see the politics of meaning-making: the political struggle within language that reflects and creates both subjectivity and reality.

Acknowledgment

I want to thank my colleagues at the University of Louisville with whom I have discussed these ideas. Especially helpful were discussions and conversations with the "Theory Group"—Ann Taylor Allen, Julia C. Dietrich, and M. Nawal Lutfiyya— and with Susan Griffin, with whom I worked on an interdisciplinary team-taught course. An earlier version of this essay was presented at the American Culture Association Conference in St. Louis, 1989.

Notes

[1]Critiques of traditional history that argue, as I will here, for a new emphasis on language are numerous. Most helpful to me were: Joan Wallach Scott, *Gender*

and the Politics of History (New York: Columbia University Press, 1988); Joan Wallach Scott, "History in Crisis? The Others' Side of the Story," American Historical Review, 94(1989), 680-692; Joan W. Scott, "Gender: A Useful Category for Historical Analysis," American Historical Review, 91(1986), 1053-1075; Carroll Smith-Rosenberg, Disorderly Conduct: Visions of Gender in Victorian America (New York: Knopf, 1985); Carroll Smith-Rosenberg, "Writing History: Language, Class, and Gender," in Feminist Studies/Critical Studies, ed., Teresa deLaurentis (Bloomington: Indiana University Press, 1986), pp. 31-54; Hayden White, The Content of Form: Narrative Discourse and Historical Representation (Baltimore: Johns Hopkins University Press, 1987); Dominick LaCapra, History and Criticism (Ithaca: Cornell University Press, 1985); David Harlan, "Intellectual History and the Return of Literature," American Historical Review, 94(1989), 581-609; Judith Newton, " Family Fortunes: 'New History' and 'New Historicism,' " Radical History Review, 43(1989), 5-22.

[2]For a very insightful essay on science and hermeneutics, see Stephen Toulmin, "The Construal of Reality: Criticism in Modern and Postmodern Science," in The Politics of Interpretation, ed. W.J.T. Mitchell (Chicago: University of Chicago Press, 1983), pp. 99-118.

[3]The idea of feminist standpoint has been discussed and debated by several writers. See for example: Nancy Hartsock, "The Feminist Standpoint: Developing the Ground for a Specifically Feminist Historical Materialism," in Discovering Reality: Feminist Perspectives on Epistemology, Metaphysics, Methodology, and Philosophy of Science, Sandra Harding and Merrill B. Hintikka (Boston: D. Reidel, 1983), pp. 283-310; Donna Haraway, "Situated Knowledges: The Science Question in Feminism and the Privilege of Partial Perspective," Feminist Studies, 14(1988), 575-599; Hilary Manette Klein, "Marxism, Psychoanalysis, and Mother Nature," Feminist Studies 15(1989), 255-278; Mary E. Hawkesworth, "Knowers, Knowing, Known: Feminist Theory and Claims of Truth," Signs 14 (1989), 533-557.

[4]Michel Foucault, History of Sexuality, vol.1, trans. Robert Hurley (New York: Vintage Books, 1980.) Other works by Foucault that have influenced my thinking are: Michel Foucault, Power/Knowledge: Selected Interviews and Other Writings, 1972-1977, ed., Colin Gordon (New York: Pantheon Books, 1977); Michel Foucault, Discipline and Punish: The Birth of the Prison, trans. Alan Sheridan (New York: Vintage, 1979); Michel Foucault, Language, Counter-Memory, Practice: Selected Essays and Interviews, ed. Donald F. Bouchard, trans. Donald F. Bouchard and Sherry Simon (Ithaca: Cornell University Press, 1977). For a critical discussion of Foucault, see Hubert L. Dreyfus and Paul Rabinow, Michel Foucault: Beyond Structuralism and Hermeneutics (Chicago: University of Chicago Press, 1982); and Bryan S. Turner, The Body and Society: Explorations in Social Theory (New York: Basil Blackwell, 1984). Other important analyses of poststructuralism include: Johnathan Culler, On Deconstruction: Theory and Criticism after Structuralism (Ithaca: Cornell University Press, 1982); Michael Ryan, Marxism and Deconstruction (Baltimore: Johns Hopkins University Press, 1982).

[5]Chris Weedon, Feminist Practice and Poststructuralist Theory (New York: Basil Blackwell, 1987) argues that poststructuralism is an important perspective for feminist theory because it provides a new way to raise questions about language and subjectivity. Other important essays on feminist theory and poststructuralism are: Linda Alcoff, "Cultural Feminism Versus Poststructuralism: The Identity Crisis in Feminist Theory," Signs, 13 (1988), 405-436; Leslie Wahl Rabine, "A Feminist Politics of Non—

Identity," *Feminist Studies*, 14(1988), 11-31; Joan W. Scott, "Deconstructing Equality-Versus-Difference: Or, The Uses of Poststructuralist Theory for Feminism," *Feminist Studies*, 14(1988), 33-50; Mary Poovey, "Feminism and Deconstruction," *Feminist Studies*, 14(1988), 51-65.

[6]The idea of meaning as an activity is central in Joan W. Scott's work cited above; in other historical scholarship on women such as Nancy M. Theriot, *The Biosocial Construction of Femininity: Mothers and Daughters in Nineteenth-Century America* (Westport, Connecticut: Greenwood Press, 1988); Mary P. Ryan, *Cradle of the Middle Class: The Family in Oneida County, New York, 1790-1865* (New York: Oxford University Press, 1981); Karen Halttunen, *Confidence Men and Painted Women: A Study of Middle-Class Culture in America 1830-1870* (New Haven: Yale University Press, 1982); and in much recent work on women and literature such as Jane Tompkins, *Sensational Designs: The Cultural Work of American Fiction, 1790-1860* (New York: Oxford University Press, 1985); Margaret Homans, *Bearing the Word: Language and Female Experience in Nineteenth-Century Women's Writing* (Chicago: University of Chicago Press, 1986); Mary Poovey, *Uneven Developments: The Ideological Work of Gender in Mid-Victorian England* (Chicago: University of Chicago Press, 1988). American pragmatists, such as William James, also understood meaning as active. See Sandra B. Rosenthal, *Speculative Pragmatism* (Amherst: University of Massachusetts Press, 1986). On ideology as meaning-making activity (as opposed to "false consciousness" or "lies" by the powerful), see V. N. Volosinov, *Marxism and the Philosophy of Language*, trans. Ladislav Matejka and I.R. Titunik (New York: Seminar Press, 1973); Ann Foreman, *Femininity as Alienation: Women and the Family in Marxism and Psychoanalysis* (London: Pluto, 1977).

[7]Theories about the relationship of body and culture that influenced my thinking include: Mary Douglas, *Implicit Meanings: Essays in Anthropology* (London: Routlege & Kegan Paul, 1975); Peter L. Berger and Thomas Luckmann, *The Social Construction of Reality: A Treatise in the Sociology of Knowledge* (London: Allen Lane, 1966); Turner, *The Body and Society*; Jane Gallop, *Thinking Through the Body* (New York: Columbia University Press, 1988); Carroll Smith-Rosenberg, "Domesticating 'Virtue': Coquettes and Revolutionaries in Young America," in *Literature and the Body*, ed. Elaine Scarry (Baltimore: Johns Hopkins University Press, 1988), pp. 160-184; Donna Haraway, "The Biopolitics of Postmodern Bodies: Determinations of Self in Immune System Discourse," *Difference: A Journal of Feminist Cultural Studies* 1(1989), 3-44; Foucault, *The History of Sexuality*; Gisela Bock, "Women's History and Gender History: Aspects of an International Debate," *Gender and History* 1(1989), 7-30; L.J. Jordanova, "Natural Facts: A Historical Perspective on Science and Sexuality," in *Nature, Culture and Gender*, eds. Carol P. MacCormack and M. Strathern (Cambridge: Cambridge University Press, 1980), pp. 42-69.

[8]On abortion in nineteenth century America see: James Mohr, *Abortion in America: The Origins and Evolution of National Policy, 1800-1900* (New York: Oxford University Press, 1978). On the voluntary motherhood movement see: Linda Gordon, *Woman's Body, Woman's Right* (New York: Penguin Books, 1977).

[9]Rosalind Petchesky, *Abortion and Woman's Choice: The State, Sexuality, and Reproductive Freedom* (Boston: Northeastern, 1984) is an excellent discussion of the way the legal framework complicates our ability to form an ethics of abortion.

[10]For a discussion of ideology as meaning-making which stays with a Marxist perspective, see Louis Althusser, "Ideology and Ideological State Apparatuses (Notes Toward an Investigation)," in his *Lenin and Philosophy and Other Essays* (New

14   Sexual Politics and Popular Culture

York: Monthly Review Press, 1971), pp. 127-186; Nicholas Abercrombie, Stephen Hill, and Bryan S. Turner, *The Dominant Ideology Thesis* (London: Allen & Unwin, 1980); Foreman, *Femininity as Alienation*.

[11]For more development of this argument, and for supporting documentation, see Theriot, *The Biosocial Construction of Femininity*.

Hollywood Comedy and Aristotelian Ethics: Reconciling Differences

Cynthia Willett

There is a long established suspicion among critics and philosophers that comic drama may please but at the expense of any veracity. This suspicion turns into outright skepticism in regard to Hollywood films. Northrop Frye writes that, in contrast to tragedy, "the comic ending is generally manipulated by a twist in the plot.... That is, we may know that the convention of comedy will make some kind of happy ending inevitable, but still for each play the dramatist must produce a distinctive 'gimmick' or 'weenie,' to use two disrespectful Hollywood synonyms for *anagnorisis* (recognition)" (Frye 170; see also Schatz 152 and Mark Crispin Miller 67). On the other hand, even those who would applaud Hollywood comedies do so because of their "utopian cast." For example, Stanley Cavell's study of what he calls "Hollywood comedy of remarriage" puts forth the claim that this "genre emphasizes the mystery of marriage...[where] dreams come true" (Cavell 142).

I am defending a certain group of Hollywood comedies, primarily drawn from the screwball comedies of the '30s and '40s and including Cavell's "comedies of remarriage," against both the excessively cynical claim that these films conceal harsh economic realities and the more naive view that celebrates love's magic. My argument is that these comedies serve as a practical moral education to the conditions of happiness. This moral education draws its principles from Aristotle's *Nichomachean Ethics* as well as conjectures from his pupils concerning an Aristotelian notion of comedy. A happy ending, often symbolized by a marriage, results as lovers moderate their excesses around Aristotle's ethical principle of the golden mean.

A strictly classical notion of comedy, however, is limited to a rather static conception of character. Moreover, Aristotle's clear distinction between comic drama, which is said to represent characters who are inferior to the average person, and ethical philosophy, which focuses on perfect virtue, has apparently blocked attempts to understand how comedy might educate imperfect characters to the good life (Cooper 20). For example, Wimsatt and Brooks find that in general "[t]he comically evil character stands still, despite warnings and punishments" (49). And Frye explains that it is the principle of "unincremental repetition, the literary imitation of ritual bondage, [that] is funny" (Frye 168). Comedy ends happily only when the hero overcomes blocking characters, often by exclusion or scapegoating, in order to attain what partakes of a "pragmatically free society" (Frye 169).

While Frye mentions a "pragmatically free society" in order to describe the ending of a comedy, he notes that the means to this ending are usually arbitrary and character development, artificial. Frye pointedly includes Hollywood comedies when he writes that "comedy regularly illustrates the victory of arbitrary plot over consistency of character.... Happy endings do not impress us as true, but as desirable, and they are brought about by manipulation" (Frye 170). In other words, the lucky characters of comedy do not earn their happy endings. These endings are contrived in order to please an uncritical audience.

My argument is that Hollywood comedies of the '30s and '40s, or more generally what I am dubbing "neo-Aristotelian comedies," enact a dynamic process by which eccentric but also frustrated characters develop the ethical education necessary to be happy. The plot progresses not so much from ousting blocking characters as from maturation. Interestingly, however, while this process of maturation does moderate self-destructive vices, it tolerates and even affirms the eccentric, who in more ways than one is "off-center."

In order to explain the character development that occurs in neo-Aristotelian comedies I borrow from Hegel's discussion of tragedy in *Phenomenology of Spirit* (Ch. 6, sec. A) and *Lectures on Aesthetics*. Hegel provides a notion of tragic dialectic as a kind of double education. While Hegel does not develop a parallel notion of comedy, we can extend his remarks on tragedy in order to discern a dialectic in comic films. These films set characters of opposing vices into a dialectical conflict. While character vices, as well as the conditions for a happy life, are better accounted for by the way of Aristotle's and not Hegel's system of ethics, a kind of Hegelian dialectic occurs as each character comes to recognize his/her own limitations as well as virtues.

In general, these films allow us to account for American culture's debt to a moderating ethics borrowed from Aristotle that secures the "pursuit of happiness." Marriage is that unity of two extreme characters (often from upper and lower classes, but also contrasted along lines of artist vs. yuppie, jock vs. intellectual, scientist vs. artist, etc.) where each character moderates some dimension of their personality in order to learn to communicate with a prospective mate. Most typically the comic film juxtaposes the values of practical but rigid to free but irresponsible. For example in *Bringing up Baby* (Cary Grant and Katharine Hepburn; Dir: Howard Hawks, 1938), an uptight scientist learns flexibility from a madcap heiress, who in turn gains a sense of responsibility. This genre of comedy may be the only one to emphasize that both opposed characters learn something. It is such a dual education (a way of "being brought up") that brings forth Frye's "pragmatically free society."

In addition to *Bringing up Baby*, the genre of neo-Aristotelian comedies includes: *The Philadelphia Story* (James Stewart, Katherine Hepburn; Dir: George Cukor, 1940), *The Lady Eve* (Barbara Stanwyck, Henry Fonda; Dir:

Preston Sturges, 1941), *It Happened One Night* (Clark Cable, Claudette Colbert; Dir: Frank Capra, 1934) and more recent films such as *Something Wild* (Jeff Daniels, Melanie Griffith; Dir: Jonathan Demme, 1986), as well as television's *Cheers* and *Moonlighting*. (The television series are neo-Aristotelian comedies without endings).

While a second part of Aristotle's *Poetics* is lost, there is much speculation as to what he might have written on comedy. It is commonly thought that Aristotle must have understood comedy to draw its laughter by ridiculing precisely those types of characters that his *Ethics* finds to be lacking in virtue. This suspicion is supported by Aristotle's student, Theophrastis. Theophrastis lists types of comic characters all of whom are in one way or another excessive or deficient in their demeanor (Jebb). The extant part of the *Poetics* also supports this inference when it qualifies the mode of mimesis proper to comedy. Comedy, like tragedy, Aristotle explains, engages the pleasure of imitating human behavior. Whereas tragedy represents characters who are more noble than the average person, comedy represents humans who are in some way inferior to the average person (*Poetics*, 2.1448a.18; cf. 6.1449b.24-28). Characters who are "bad," i.e., lacking virtue in some respect, but who are not finally dangerous enough to evoke fear nor sympathetic enough to evoke pity, make us laugh (*Poetics*, 5.1449a.31-37).

While this element of the ridiculous seems relatively clear, what Aristotle might have seen as the effect or purpose of the ridiculous in comic drama is less so. Various scholars have attempted to put together an Aristotelian notion of comedy by way of analogy to Aristotle's discussion of tragedy. Just as tragedy effects the catharsis of fear and pity, so comedy is said to effect a catharsis of the unpleasant emotions of envy and anger (Cooper 61). The purpose of comedy, then, would be to set our minds at the ease necessary in order to get on with our lives. Lane Cooper argues that anger and pity are aroused by the feeling that our rewards have not been in proportion with our efforts (Cooper 66-7). Comedy shows us more extreme disproportions in luck than our own, so that we can attain some perspective on the matter and come to accept the element of chance without undue commotion (Cooper 67). Excessive emotions in general are dangerous because they interfere with our capacity to think. Comedy, then, shares with tragedy the effect of purging excessive emotions in order to allow us to resume the highest end of life, philosophical contemplation (Cooper 69).

The cathartic interpretation of comedy explains well how comedy might play a role in securing the life of the philosopher. The problem with this notion of Aristotelian comedy is that it takes into account only one of at least two crucial definitions that Aristotle gives to human nature. Certainly, he defines human nature in terms of the animal with *logos* and describes pure contemplation as our highest activity. But Aristotle also focuses on another equally crucial dimension of human nature. Most of the *Ethics* is devoted to describing the conditions of happiness given that the human being is, by definition, the political animal. Beneath this difference in definition lies an incongruity in Aristotle's system that cannot be developed here. But crucial for us is that the latter determination of what it is to be human suggests an entirely different notion of comic drama.

Before I develop this alternative notion of comedy, however, it is important to note that while the cathartic theory of comedy presents a fair extrapolation of Aristotle's remarks on tragedy, this theory limits comedy to playing at best a negative role in ethical development. In part this is because the cathartic theory holds to a rigid distinction between the *Ethics*, which teaches human perfection, and the *Poetics*, which claims that comedy represents the inferior human vices (Cooper 20). Comic drama, then, directs laughter against the vice and folly of characters with whom we are to have no sympathy. Drama does not show us how to become more noble individuals.

Moreover, the cathartic theory requires that we judge Hollywood film as sentimental and not as true comedy. This is because it is crucial for Hollywood comedies that we identify with eccentrics whom Aristotle would determine to be "bad" characters. Aristotle, at least at times, shows concern with the possible seductiveness of comic characters. For example, in the *Politics* he argues that young people should not attend comic performances until their education will have protected them against the evil influences of such representations (7.17.1336b.19-23). This concern supports the cathartic theory in that it urges us to laugh at, and not imitate, the ridiculous characters of comedy. On the other hand, the audience tends to identify with both the impetuous heiress and the stiff scientist in Hollywood's *Bringing Up Baby*. Moreover, the Hollywood audience demands a happy ending for these eccentric characters and for this alone has itself been subject to ridicule by less sympathetic and, apparently, more sophisticated critics.

My argument, however, is that Hollywood comedies undertake not so much the catharsis of eccentricities as the education of desire to the good life. If I am right, these comedies suggest an alternative notion of Aristotelian comedy, one deriving less from remarks made on tragic catharsis and more from what the *Ethics* tells us is necessary for a happy life.

In his *Ethics*, Aristotle presents the virtuous character as one who adheres to a life of moderation. The right conduct, Aristotle insists, is incompatible with excess or deficiency in feelings and actions. Bad characters are those whose moral bent is away from the mean. For example, Aristotle writes that "the man who indulges in every pleasure and abstains from none becomes self-indulgent, while the man who shuns every pleasure, as boors do, becomes in a way insensible; temperance and courage, then are destroyed by excess and defect, and preserved by the mean." (2.21104a20-25) Because ethics teaches how to live in accordance with human limitations, it is the best guarantee we have of happiness.

I suspect that the shift from screwball comedies of the '30s and '40s to postmodern irony arises in part from the tendency to view screwball comedies as "dreams come true" rather than practical ethics. The purpose, or at least effect, of such comedy would be an immediate pleasure of questionable moral or political value. For example, Woody Allen's *The*

Purple Rose of Cairo (Mia Farrow and Jeff Daniels, 1985) parodies what the director of *Purple Rose* perceives as the vacuity of the Depression "fairy tales."

Interestingly, the Depression films do sometimes allude to their fairy tale leanings but with an important twist. For example, *The Lady Eve* develops a romance between a "working girl" (Barbara Stanwyck) from the underprivileged classes and a high-minded but gullible heir (Henry Fonda). She is a Cinderella who, given the circumstances of the Depression, has had to swindle to make it, and he is her Prince Charming, who will "make an honest woman out of her." The allusion to the Cinderella tale is clearest at the moment when they are in her cabin and she has him kneel down and fit her with the proper slipper. The twist, however, is that she proves to be as much an "Eve" as a Cinderella, in effect, her own fairy grandmother. A happy ending requires that Stanwyck use deception in order to teach Fonda to love a real and imperfect woman, not just a fairy tale illusion of goodness.

Given the education that Stanwyck must set up for Fonda, our sympathy goes out to this trickster who has had to "stoop to conquer." This behavior would never be allowed by a static, and, looking forward to *The Philadelphia Story* overly pure conception of virtuous character. The whole venture is a necessary part of the dialectic required in order to find a way to happiness.

Films such as *The Lady Eve* directly challenge some of Frye's remarks on comedy. On the one hand, Frye argues that the "theme of the comic is the integration of society, which usually takes the form of incorporating a central character into it" (Frye 43). Hollywood films provide no exception to this tendency. On the other hand, however, Frye finds that for the most part comedy "preserves the theme of escape from society to the extent of idealizing a simplified life in the country" (Frye 43). Frye contrasts romantic comedy to more ironic comedy or satire, which plays at human sacrifice in the form of a *pharmakos* (Frye 46). My point is that in early Hollywood something different from either escape or scapegoating is happening. For example, *The Lady Eve* certainly does not scapegoat its eccentric leads. And in Fonda, or at least we who would catch a glimpse of ourselves in Fonda, must learn to become more realistic and less simplifying in his view of love.

The plot of neo-Aristotelian comedies presents, as do romantic comedies in general, some kind of barrier which stands in the way of two lovers. However, while New Comedy, for example, presents this barrier in the form of an external law or third character, e.g. a disagreeable father, Hollywood locates the source of resistance in the relation between the two central characters themselves. These two characters are drawn to each other despite the fact that they seem to be, in some sense, opposites. In other words, "opposites attract." As Hepburn repeats in *Bringing Up Baby*, love manifests itself in conflict, or in what I am calling dialectic. In Hollywood, then, marriage is that unity of two extreme characters where each character undergoes an educative process in order to learn to communicate with a prospective spouse. This moderating process, however, means not so much conforming to a norm, which these characters give no evidence of ever doing, as overcoming exactly that extremity of their behavior that leads to their frustration.

For example, in *Bringing Up Baby*, Grant takes the part of "straight man" and Hepburn takes that of the "buffoon" (the character who will do anything for a laugh). Hepburn appears joyous but also scatterbrained. Grant's character is aptly nicknamed 'Bone.' 'Bone' not only locates the object of his obsessive interest (he is a paleontologist) but also the primary deficiency of his character: he is a responsible but otherwise lifeless and rigid boor. By the end of the film Hepburn retrieves a cruical dinosaur bone, the missing piece of a skeleton that Grant is attempting to reconstruct. Hepburn is returning something to its proper place. Her ususal feminine— if not feminist—habit has been to misplace things. Grant, on the other hand, allows the skeleton to collapse—the "phallic" tall-bone and all—as he realizes that all he really needs is love. Old structures fall and a new and more flexible ethics, one that is not anti-feminist, is affirmed.

Hegel's conception of tragedy as an ethical conflict between two characters, each of whom possesses only a part of the truth, is also useful for understanding neo-Aristotelian comedy. For example, while most readers of Sophocles' *Antigone* empathize with Antigone and find that the tyrant Creon fails to recognize the right of the family to a private sphere of religious practice, Hegel argues that Antigone's claim against the state is one-sided. A community must reserve a place for both political and familial concerns. Similarly, neo-Aristotelian films enact a double education in the conflict between incomplete characters, often one suffering from an excess and the other a deficiency of probity. Hegel did not himself introduce this "speculative" conception of comedy into his system. This failure is in part because he restricts comedy to irony or satire, i.e., a "negative" moment of dialectic.

On the other hand, classical scholars analyze the conflict, or *agon*, of comedy, in terms which are not negative, but one-sided and didactic rather than dialectical. The verbal combat is defined as occurring between two persons, where each supports a thesis opposed to that of the other and exactly one of the two characters is said to uphold the stance of the poet (Cooper 58). Because there is no dialectic between the two positions the resolution is not so much a compromise as either a defeat (and scapegoating) or a conversion of the opponent. The result of the one-sided *agon* fits to Frye's contention that for the most part the happy endings of comedy may be desirable but are not true.

The *agon* of Hollywood comedies is often dialectical, but this dialectic inclines more towards an Aristotelian, or at least a neo-Aristotelian, ethics of community than an Hegelian logic. That is, the result of comic dialectic is happiness and not truth. Moreover, this happiness develops from a kind of "democratic" collapsing of rigid class differences. This leveling out of differences may appear reductive compared to the sublation of opposites that moves through Hegel's *Wissenschaft*. The difference between comedy and Hegelian dialectic occurs because comic dialectic tends more towards the horizontal interrelation of individuals in a community than the vertical subordination of individual and community well-being for the sake of philosophical truth. A typical neo-Aristotelian plot transforms the pure life of the thinker into the less predictable life of the lover. For example, in "Bringing Up Baby," Cary Grant first appears before the camera in the pose of Rodin's "The Thinker" (Cavell, 117) while his final and rather chaotic embrace with Hepburn mimes Rodin's "The Kiss" (Cavell, 121).

The democratic effect of comedy is clearest in *The Philadelphia Story*. At a crucial point Jimmy Stewart (who comes from the lower middle class; his father is a teacher) and Cary Grant (who was born into the wealthy class) meet over a bottle of champagne. Alcohol, which Jimmy Stewart proclaims to be the great leveler, provides the occasion for the first real conversation the two ever have. Stewart loses his lower class toughness and Grant, his upper crust reserve, and together they set each other straight on a number of issues. Hollywood's "great leveler" is laughter.

The comedy of *The Philadelphia Story* teaches us beyond all else to recognize human frailty. All three main characters (Hepburn, Stewart, and Grant) must in various ways come down off their pedestals and admit to a human vulnerability that they have attempted to "blank out." If Hegelian dialectic aims to make gods of us, neo-Aristotelian dialectic, at least in comedy, recalls our ordinariness. This need to own up to limitations is most apparent in Hepburn. Grant accuses Hepburn of playing the "virginal goddess" who preserves her pure self-image by conveniently forgetting her own mishaps. If classical comedies urge us to "forget" in order to be happy, the happy ending of *The Philadelphia Story* requires that Hepburn remember her compromising past. This element of memory rather than forgetting frailties further distinguishes Hollywood comedies as educative without being manipulative.

Cavell points out that the final snapshot view of Cary Grant, Jimmy Stewart, and Katharine Hepburn brings them together before the minister as though in a kind of wedding photo that would marry all three at once (Cavell 133). This raises the question as to why Hepburn turns down Stewart's proposal of marriage and remarries her first husband (Cary Grant). The main dialectic in the film occurs between the aristocratic, even virginal, Hepburn (allusions occur to the Roman goddess Diana) and the prying "I Spy" journalist Stewart, hunting for a good story. Stewart takes the job only because he needs money to support his real vocation as a poet. Hepburn, however, sees his work as dirty. Stewart sees her as part of the barren upper class. As the plot develops, Stewart comes to appreciate her uncommon charm and she comes to recognize the magic of his words.

The development between Hepburn and Stewart allows each to recognize their more noble qualities. This recognition, however, is not the most important lesson that Hepburn is to learn. In fact, Stewart's growing admiration for Hepburn must compensate for a much harder lesson, for he also plays a part in Hepburn's humiliating recognition of her own human frailty. Grant, however, is the primary plot-mover in this second dialectic. Their first marriage had failed because Hepburn could not tolerate Grant's drinking problem. The *agon* places her in the classical role of *alazon*, or of one suffering from excessive vanity, and Grant in the role of *eiron*, that is, a self-deprecating and ironic character.* In the end they may remarry and expect to live happily only because Grant has set things up in such a way that Hepburn has learned to act "naturally." Stewart, who must lose his excessive cynicism, especially as it is directed against everything that Hepburn might personify, cannot take the major credit for getting Hepburn to come down from her throne.

*Aristotle writes, "With regard to truth, then, the intermediate is a truthful sort of person and the mean may be called truthfulness, while the pretense which exaggerates is boastfulness and the person characterized by it a boaster [*alazon*], and that which understates is mock modesty and the person characterized by it mock-modest [*eiron*]" (Ethics 2.7.1108a.20-23).

The Philadelphia Story is also the story of America, or the story of American art, well constituted by the Hollywood film. This film suggests that Hollywood films in general are a healthy blend of upper class theater with low class "pornography." By pornography I mean not the fact that film finds all kinds of excuses to exhibit woman's body. I refer to that part of art that caters to natural curiosity in the private concerns of others and finally to obscene desire. On the other hand, the more than ordinary efforts that Stewart makes to rescue Hepburn's family name from the schemes of "I Spy" 's editor underscores a difference between vicious voyeurism and more moderate forms. Hepburn, the untouchable goddess, too quickly dismisses the tap dancer patronized by her father. The film, however, lets us rest with neither the pretentions of Hepburn nor her father. Instead, the film gestures towards the happy "medium," a genre which would weave together concerns of both father and daughter. That the final still of the film is also a kind of "I Spy" snapshot of the wedding reinforces the notion that the film does not entirely separate itself from pornographic desire.

Many of the films that we include as "neo-Aristotelian comedies" are also cited by Cavell in what he discerns as a genre of Hollywood comedies devoted to remarriage. His *Pursuits of Happiness* raises the question as to why Hollywood comedy centers so many of its plots around the end of remarriage. His response is deliberately vague. Cavell writes that "the spirit of comedy in these films depends on our willingness to entertain the possibility of such a world, one in which dreams come true" (Cavell 142) By "such a world" Cavell refers to the "couple's isolation from the rest of society" (Cavell 142).

Neo-Aristotelian comedies, however, find their happiness not so much in an asocial fairy tale notion of romance as in a dialectical struggle that works through differences in class and values during an era of political and economical tensions. In a way the genre of remarriage may be the first to recognize the resistance of these differences to any easy fairy tale ending. The second courtship admits that differences do not magically disappear but require an education on the part of all parties concerned. Cavell sees the education as one-sided, and directed solely to creation of the "new woman" (Cavell 149). I am suggesting, however, that both characters learn something from their conflict. This education is not so much a "miracle of change" where mystery surrounds the holy bond as a very practical moral education into the conditions of community.

This difference of interpretation appears in a crucial scene of the *Philadelphia Story*. This early scene involves an exchange between Hepburn and yet a third suitor. He is an ex-coal miner who has climbed his way to the top and is engaged to marry Hepburn the next day. In any case, he may be able to work his way out of the mines, but he has difficulty in mounting his horse. Curiously, Hepburn knocks him to the ground and rubs dirt into his stiff jodhpurs. Cavell sees this scene as the shining through of the "low-class grossness of a would-be aristocrat," and her attempt to "cover his failed attempt to cover his grossness" (Cavell 144). The whole scene would tend to support the thesis that old Hollywood comedies celebrate the mystery of the true upper classes and adhere to a rule that classes should not intermingle.

In fact, however, in the context of the film the scene may have the opposite effect. Hepburn appreciates instinctively what she must learn more consciously, that is, the importance of acting "naturally." If her fiancé provokes laughter, it is not because his origins are irremediably lower class. His flaw is that he attempts to forget precisely this. Moreover, Hepburn later indicates that class distinctions and nobility should not be thought to correspond when she praises Mac the doorman over her uncle, the "pincher." At the same time, the film insists on what Hepburn's fiancé wants to deny. He wants to marry a queen. He cannot learn that love is not a form of worship but an appreciation of eccentricies and forgiveness of failures. Her fiancé's moral cleanliness turns out to be the last thing that Hepburn needs. When his moral rigidity proves to be unbending, she must finally reject him. It is those who are uneducable, not the lower class nor the eccentrics, who persist among the scapegoats of Hollywood.

Ethical education and happy endings break down in postmodern film, where heroes are anti-heroes and scapegoats, the norm. Films such as Martin Scorsese's *After Hours* (1985) insert the characters of neo-Aristotelian comedy into a rigid world where oppositions are frozen. In *After Hours* Griffin Dunne plays an unsympathetic character who attempts to escape his sterile world on the upper east side of Manhattan for the exotic lower west side. But if the yuppie seeks a major reversal in his life, the ironies get out of hand. The result is a nightmare of repetitions and reversals without advance until Dunne is by chance returned home to his safe computer terminal.

The new realism suggests that while we are strangers outside of those "networks of power" that constitute our lives, these ossified structures nonetheless leave the feeling that something is missing. While Dunne returns empty-handed to his solitary post, the heroes of *Bringing Up Baby* are able to find that missing something. Crucially, this something turns out not to be the dinosaur bone. Old ossified structures must collapse as a "pragmatically free society" is born. If postmodern film locks us into grids of power that delete both thought and desire, neo-Aristotelian comedy transforms thinker into lover and the desirable into the true.

Acknowledgment

I wish to thank Julie and Warren Olin-Ammentorp for their comments on this paper.

Works Cited

Aristotle. *Nichomachean Ethics*, trans. W.D. Ross.
Cavell, Stanley. *Pursuits of Happiness*. Cambridge: Harvard University Press, 1981.
Cooper, Lane. *An Aristotelian Theory of Comedy*. New York: Harcourt, 1922.
Frye, Northrop. *Anatomy of Criticism*. Princeton: Princeton University Press, 1957.
Jebb, R.C., Jr. *The Characters of Theophrastus*. London: Macmillan, 1909.
Miller, Mark Crispin. "Hollywood: The Ad" in *The Atlantic* vol. 265, no. 4 April 1990 pp 41-68.
Schatz, Thomas. *Hollywood Genres* New York: Random House 1981.
Wimsatt, William K., Jr. and Cleanth Brooks. *Literary Criticism: A Short History*. New York: Random House, 1967.

Women's Voices,
Images, and Silences in Popular Music

Ray Pratt

The silences I speak of here are unnatural; the unnatural thwarting of what struggles to come into being, but cannot. In the old, the obvious parallels: when the seed strikes stone; the soil will not sustain; the spring is false; the time is drought or blight or infestation; the frost comes premature.

—Tillie Olsen, *Silences*, xiii

Ways of thinking about gender and sexuality structure broader conceptions of what is possible and what is not. That seems especially evident in popular music. (Frith and McRobbie) There is a significance that transcends sexuality and sex roles here as one considers the role of music as a "voice"—as a means of expressing *personal* politics—as well as a means of effecting change in society more generally. In the United States since the mid-1960s, the wider political uses of popular music have been limited by the fact the expressive functions of that music have been profoundly skewed toward the needs of men.

Women began the second great wave of feminism at the end of the 1960s. Much of the impetus toward action grew out of their frustrations and indignation at their experience in other progressive movements for social change in the immediately preceding years. Sara Evans has chronicled the personal journey of many politically active women in this way in *Personal Politics*. For many more married women, the transformation grew out of the generalized malaise and feelings of alienation—the "problem that has no name"—described so effectively by Betty Freidan in *The Feminine Mystique* (1963). This eventually involved them in a fundamental critique of inequalities in the then—prevailing model of the institution of marriage. Prior to the '60s era, if there was a usual popular cultural linkage of sexuality to marriage, it was especially seen as a desirable status for women. A clear cultural double standard existed—consider the relative status of images of "old maid" and "bachelor." In popular culture these trends are evident in movies of the '30s through the '50s, though there seems to have a significant Cold War reemphasis on marriage and the family in the '50s as a bulwark against communism as Elaine Tyler May demonstrates in *Homeward Bound*. Marriage rates increased, altering a trend of decreasing marriages through previous decades. Birth rates increased as well. The "baby boom" was the result. The frequency with which "marriage" seems to be mentioned in dialogue in movies in the years before the 1960s is striking for what it demonstrates of the significant changes in consciousness that have subsequently emerged in spite of the concerted Cold War era efforts to contain the aspirations of women beyond the home. (Rosen) In the 1970 census 13.7 percent of women aged 18 to 44 were single and never married. By 1986 this rose to 18.3 percent. Comparable figures for males were 18.9 percent in 1970, rising to 25.3 percent in 1986. Nonetheless, the overwhelming fact that emerges from these data is that nearly all men and women still at some point in their lives *do* marry, in spite of a growing preference for single status. Nearly 81 percent of women who marry have a child (80 percent of white women, 88.5 percent of black women).

In the late '60s and early '70s a critique of conventional family structure and sex roles began to be evident in popular culture, but it was expressed far better in widely-seen films than in the popular music of the era. The content of the music contained a significant amount of one-sided male appeals to women to accede to their (the male's) sexual desires. The film industry, on the other hand, seems to have particularly attentive to changing audience composition and tastes.

The late '60s version of the popular cultural critique of marriage institution began imperfectly in such film caricatures as Paul Mazursky's *Bob and Carol, Ted and Alice* (1969), or the widely seen *Diary of a Mad Housewife* (1970). In *Desperate Characters* (1971) Shirley MacLaine moved as though drugged (psychically numbed?) through a bleak, neorealist nightmare of the terrifying boredom marriage can be. Peter Bogdanovich's acclaimed *The Last Picture Show* (1971) portrayed Cloris Leachman as the neglected coach's wife in the empoverished sort of marriage millions knew, while in the same film Ellen Burstyn's character expressed only cynicism and realism, through pointed dialogue explicitly making the way of the world clear to her daughter played by then—"cover girl" Cybill Shepard. The same year saw Glenda Jackson's strong performance as the New Woman in John Schlesinger's *Sunday Bloody Sunday*. Marjorie Rosen in *Popcorn Venus* saw it as "the most gloriously intelligent" film on issues of gender and sexuality of the era. (361) Here one sees Jackson involved in another, rather less appealing strategy of survival, differing from that of socially marginal blacks who did so much with music from the blues to rap. As Rosen put it, "even if it means more loneliness, perhaps permanent loneliness, Jackson is embodying not a mythic vision of courage, but the kind of small but hurting bravery today's divorced, widowed, or single women must face in day-to-day living." (Ibid.) By the 1980s, however, fewer younger, educated single women would put up with such a design for living, which held neither promise of fun nor real happiness. Their impatience would be evident in the popular music of the time in such figures as Madonna and Cyndi Lauper.

The early '70s were filled with conflicting images. The period also saw a number of highly popular and critically—acclaimed films depicting brutalizations and rapes of women. *A Clockwork Orange* (1971), *Straw Dogs*

(1971), and *Klute* (1971) all involve extended brutal treatment of women, often coupled with the suggestion women could not solve problems without the aid of a man. *Strawdogs* and (a bit later) *Last Tango in Paris* involve forcible rape, but with a twist—eventually the woman is portrayed as becoming sexually aroused and enjoying it. Yet all these films still might be seen as both reflecting (viewing positively, or, alternatively, expressing a backlash against, women's liberation) and facilitating the social identifications of those on various sides of the extracinematic social conflicts and transformations underway in sex role expectations. The reaction against liberation of women from traditional gender roles and family structures would crest in the 1980s, becoming part of the massive reaffirmation of traditional family values in the Reagan era evident in *Ordinary People, Kramer vs. Kramer, On Golden Pond,* and *Terms of Endearment* (see, e.g., Ryan and Kellner 157-165) and culminating in the box-office and home-video smash success of *Fatal Attraction* in 1987-88.

Undermining of the old ideology of unequal marriages and male dominance proceeded in the early '70s to the point that, in succeeding years, at least for a stratum of feminist radicals, such words as "home" and "family" could (from this writer's experience) be hurled by women as epithets, redolent with the most biting sarcasm and negativity, as these institutions came to be understood in a generational subculture (for those familiar with a growing body of powerful feminist theoretical analyses) as the sites of unspoken terror, psychological and physical violence, or (for a minority of greater numbers) a longer-term slow, numbing psychic death. But this particular perspective would not emerge in *mass* popular culture until the middle of the '80s with such TV productions as *The Burning Bed* (1984)— itself a popular culture phenomenon. It gained in two showings one of the largest audiences captured by a TV movie production and featured a stunning and committed performance by former pin-up and star of *Charlie's Angels* TV series, Farrah Fawcett. Popular music lagged far behind with the first major popular song on violence against women not emerging until Tracy Chapman's "Behind the Wall" in 1988.

In popular music, aside from the initial emergence of several non-feminist folk singers in the early '60s (Joan Baez's first album reached #3 on the album charts), and such early proto-feminist works as Lesley Gore's striking early '60s "You Don't Own Me," and the uniquely revelatory reworkings of male material by Aretha Franklin (her brilliant 1967 transformation of "Respect", a striking example of a functionally feminist deconstruction and revisioning of the macho Otis Redding original, and her succeeding similar work such as "Think"), critical themes would infrequently appear. But when they did, they often sold very well. The early '70s period produced some searing dissections of relationships in recorded songs by Dory Previn and Joni Mitchell. Carol King's #1-ranked "It's Too Late" from the 1971 mega-platinum *Tapestry* album of her own compositions (the album sold some 13 million units over the next few years), with its open recognition of a relationship that couldn't be saved, or "Will You

Still Love Me Tomorrow" (though it first appeared as a #1 hit in 1961 by the Shirelles) which illuminated once again the way women's expressive sexuality was used by men, this time in the alleged openness of the late '60s and early '70s counterculture, are intelligent examples in the era's mass popular music. Similarly, Helen Reddy's "I am Woman" reached #1 status in 1972-73 and she was nominated for a Grammy. King's and Reddy's tremendous market appeal functioned as positive role models for women in music generally, but in spite of sales success, remained overall rarities in a culture governed at the personal level by the search for what Christopher Lasch termed the *Haven In a Heartless World*—the ideal marriage or relationship.

Critical comments on the institution or the frustrations and duplicities in sexual relations it generated, appeared in productions not in the pop mainstream, or in so-called "women's music" in the '70s and '80s, there, too, visions of the good or "equal" relationship—whether conventionally heterosexual or homosexual/lesbian—seemed to lie as a utopian hope beneath the surface. Overt critiques of inequality and violence in relations between the sexes never appeared in mainstream musical "product," even at the end of the '80s, until Chapman's "Behind the Wall," the first song on any popular album (let alone a number one album) which deals with violence against women. Similarly, songs exulting in women's independence or the joys of freely—chosen sexuality (aside from the blues and rhythm and blues idioms) were, aside from Janis Joplin's statements, quite rare until the mid-80s.

Limits of the '60s Counterculture

If, in the late '60s, figures such as Janis Joplin and Grace Slick provided the appearance of strong role models for women, they were highly problematical images given the realities of the time. Slick, of the San Francisco-based Jefferson Airplane, provided searing vocal lines and an almost menacing image of beauty and controlling strength, but provided little lyrical or ideological critique of male-female relationships beyond a persona that seemed to convey that she would always be in charge of herself and perhaps her partner, too. Slick's potent image was softened somewhat when integrated with the overall "counter-culture" posture of the Airplane (later, Jefferson Starship, or just Starship).

In retrospect the counter-culture was exceptionally one-sided in the sexual liberation promised and promoted. Ellen Willis (one of the few women who have had status among the large male fraternity of rock intellectuals) put it in her essay on the tragic figure of Janis Joplin, "the male-dominated counterculture defined freedom for women almost exclusively in sexual terms. As a result, women endowed the ideal of sexual liberation with immense symbolic importance; it became charged with all the secret energy of as yet suppressed larger rebellion. Yet to express one's rebellion in that limited way was a painfully literal form of submission." (276) There was, from all appearances, a lot of submission. The dimensions of the inequality are striking.

In the *Rolling Stone Illustrated History of Rock & Roll* (1980), which focuses largely on the period from 1950 through 1980 there are 82 articles, of these just three are exclusively on women (the "Girl Groups," Janis Joplin, Aretha Franklin) and perhaps five others include a substantial amount of material on women. This ten percent is a fair representation of the significance of women in this variety of music so overwhelmingly present in recent cultural history. Numerous other studies document the relative absence or minority percentage of women performers in recorded music for half a century until the emergence of a number of strong female performers in the 1980s.

Peter Hesbacher and associates studied artists who had reach the #1 position on *Billboard* magazine single charts. They found that between 1940 and 1974 only 12 percent of those reaching the top position were solo female artist, five percent were female groups, and seven percent mixed male/female groups. (pp. 1-16) In a 1980 study of careers of male and female artists Hesbacher and Anderson developed three "epochs" from 1940 to 1978. Women's careers showed slightly less longevity than men in each of the three periods (measured by period between first and last #1 chart appearance).

While such chart success is not the only indicator of success or influence in popular music, it is easier to measure and a sure indicator of visibility. Though a useful indicator in a capitalist music market, it certainly provides no measure of quality nor enduring cultural influence. Annual singles' ranking based on the top 50 annual songs provides a more comprehensive view of the industry than the #1 rankings noted above, but by the end of the '80s, the singles category became less and less relevant as an indicator. In a study of women in popular music from 1955 to 1984 based on the top 50 ranking, Alan Wells found women often exceeded the "12 percent" figures in the previous studies, registering an even 18 percent in the '80s. A weighted score by position on charts put women with 20 percent or more of total points in 1955, 1962-66, 1973, 1977, 1979, and 1981. But, in spite of the intervening wave of feminism at the end of the '60s and into the early 1970s, no consistent pattern of greater representation over time was evident. Women held a similar approximate 20 percent of the top 100 albums in the *Rolling Stone* annual charts from 1979-84. A glance at the charts in any recent issue of *Billboard* or *Rolling Stone* demonstrates the situation continues—usually something less than 20 percent of the entries are by women.

In the 1980s, studies of videos on music television reveal a similar bias. Jane D. Brown and Kenneth C. Campbell found videos with white males taking up 83 percent of MTV time. Those with women as central figures made up 11 percent of a 24 hour period, with blacks in even smaller percentages. Even in the limited opportunities for representations of women to be shown, there was considerable bias toward male definition of roles. In their characterization, "white women are often shown in passive and solitary activity or are shown trying to gain the attention of a man who ignores them." While other interpretations which will presently be considered suggest alternative feminist readings of the minority of female images in popular music, the sheer weight of numbers raises important questions.

Whose Music Is It?

To whom has this sexually expressive popular music spoken over the nearly four decades of its existence? Much popular music analysis has emphasized the manner in which black forms have been appropriated or "ripped-off" in a society dominated by whites (as have the preceding chapters). It is ironic the liberatory theoretical perspectives that have been applied, usually by male observers, to analysis of the role of blacks in American music have rarely been directed to the way the music business has dealt with women.[1]

Where were the women? What were they doing? Why were they silent (or underrepresented) musically? Chapple and Garofalo in *Rock 'n' Roll is Here to Pay* (perhaps the best discussion to date on the problem) place the blame on the overwhelmingly male character of the industry (as do other writers). (see pp. 289-296) But the problem is probably even more profound and basic. There are interrelated explanations: Women, of course, simply weren't involved in music or any area of the work force outside the home in the same numbers as men (though their representation in popular music has not appreciably changed with their increased presence in the work force over the past two decades). In addition, within popular music, they might have been less "popular," even if involved, though that may reflect less aggressive company signing and development of female artists as well as underemphasized promotion and marketing of them. The latter pattern is evident from a survey of recording artists based on biographies distributed by companies undertaken by Denisoff and Bridges. It had a sample of 522 males to 58 females, and a rock music sub-sample of 266 males to ten females. Clearly a more fundamental yet very complex process of bias and exclusion was at work.

The Sexual Line of Fault

There is a profound disjuncture between the ways popular music has been thought about and discussed—as sociologist Dorothy Smith put it in another context, in the "symbols, images, vocabularies, concepts, frames of reference, institutionalized structures of relevance..."[2]—and the way life is actually lived for over half of the population—for women. What does it *mean* that virtually the entire popular music business—especially rock—from its inception is and has been run by, controlled, commented on, written about almost exclusively by men?

In one of the few significant early essays in the sparse literature on rock music, gender and sexuality Simon Frith and Angela McRobbie suggested rock operates simultaneously as a form of "sexual expression" and a "form of sexual control." (p. 5) If the initial flowering of rock 'n' roll to a white audience in the 1950s was to significant degrees based on release of repressed sexuality, it was one importantly biased as far as *performance* toward a particular kind of male expression. The alleged liberatory quality of the '60s rock that followed did little for women. Though there were significant and powerful female figures through the period since the '60s, that has not been produced a position for women as performers in popular music in any way approaching their representation in the population at large. Women's participation in popular music since the '50s has been much more in the area of *consumption*—buying pop-cultural musical "product" responsive to their psychological needs and fantasies.[3] The affects of the so-called "rock revolution" on social roles was not very great. As Frith put it in another context, rock "works with conventions of masculinity and feminity that situate both performers and audiences along clear gender lines—males as active participants, females as passive consumers." (1985, 22)

The last quarter century has not, however, been without some positive roles for women, nor of movements which critiqued and sought fundamentally to alter or broaden roles of men and women in popular music. Two of them were punk rock in Britain and the U.S., and the "Women's Music" movement in the U.S.

Certainly the often savage critiques of the punk movement in Britain and the U.S. during the late 1970s, persisting in "hard core" punk through the '80s and in more subtle and elegant statements from the numerous post-punk "new wave" bands such as Blondie and The Talking Heads (the latter the most thematically searching, culturally critical, and artistically creative group to arise in the period), all opened-up possibilities for a greater and more egalitarian status for women in bands, and a somewhat wider range of sexual orientation and "gender bending" in the 1980s. At first, this occurred through sheer obliteration of previous "cock-rock" styles and a frontal assault on all social conventions. Part of the significance of punk for girls and women is based on its outright rejections of "conventions of traditional sexuality" (Steward and Garratt 157-158). Both the "hippy ideal of free 'permissive' love *and* the straighter conventions of love, romance and engagement rings were attacked, undermined and repudiated outright. In every way punk sexuality was angry and aggressive, implicitly feminist." With British punk rocker Tom Robinson opening the way with "Glad to Be Gay" in 1978, which received significant air play in U.S. cities, over the succeeding decade there were several explicitly homosexual male rock groups in Britain, though their images were softened or blurred beyond recognition by American promoters.

But these developments did not significantly improve the career opportunities of women in spite of the emergence in the 1970s of such radically contrasting models as Patti Smith or Debbie Harry out of the New York punk/new wave scene. After attaining significant attention they both practically vanished from the popular music scene. Smith reappeared in 1988 (after having children) with the powerful and critically acclaimed *Dream of Life*. Harry simply did not make it in a major way as an independent artist after achieving widespread "pin-up" status at the end of the '70s. There

are problematical examples. Perhaps part of the problem is generational—
there is a process of ageing which is separate from the phenomenon of
"ageism" (though the two are intertwined). It is simply easier for record
consuming youth to relate to singers closer to their age. Thus Madonna
and Cyndi Lauper supplanted Debbie Harry.

There is, overall, another important (and deeper) pattern. Since the 1950s,
the development of popular music in the United States, especially the most
commercially successful product-rock, reveals the continued operation of
a sexual "mobilization of bias"—a set of "predominant values, beliefs, rituals
and institutional procedures that operate systematically and consistently to
the benefit of certain persons and groups at the expense of others."[4] In the
music business, it mirrors and reinforces sex bias in the larger economy
and society, often presenting the most extreme caricatures of sex role models,
as a few hours of watching MTV or other television music video programs
demonstrates.

Because of the prevalence of male performers, existing popular music
might better be labelled the "male-stress" of music. But no equivalent channel
has existed for women, who have had to fight for representation as performers
and to assert any authorship of their commercial products. As consumers,
women and especially feminists, must search long and diligently for positive
models. They must often engage in "against the grain" reinterpretations
of images presented to them. As Frith and McRobbie argue, "any analysis
of the sexuality of rock must begin with the brute social fact that in terms
of control and production, rock is a male form." (p 5) The dimensions
of male domination are overwhelming. Most popular musicians, and even
more writers, creators, technicians, engineers and producers are men. The
roles of women in creative roles are limited and "mediated through male
notions of female ability." Among the women musicians who "make it"
nearly all are singers. Usually it is areas of publicity in which women in
the business are found, pushing a largely male-defined product. The female
image is made by males. Indeed, *in general*, the "images, values, and
sentiments" of popular music are male products. The situation is so
profoundly biased that male images as well as female are constructed, though
a great variety of "male sexual poses" are presented, but "most often expressed
in terms of stereotypes" (Ibid).

Yet the relationship is not as unidirectional as once it appeared. There
is always a dialogic aspect to the popular music process. At the basic level
of consumption women are aggressively attentive actors as fans. As Steward
and Garratt argue in *Signed, Sealed and Delivered*, the whole structure of
popular music "rests on the backs of those 'silly screaming girls.' They
bought the records in millions and made a massive contribution to the early
success of Elvis, the Beatles, the Stones,...Michael Jackson and many of
the others who have since been accepted by the grown—ups and become
monuments, reference points in the rock hierarchy." (142) Importantly, for
both males and females, the music either in performance or consumption,
meets or responds to needs, providing a way for making some sort of "sense"

of one's own gender role and sexuality. While this orienting of roles takes place often in structures, illusory, stereotypical and highly alienated ways, nonetheless, people still utilize popular music and its imagery "to understand what it means to have desires, to be desirable" (Frith 1985, p 23).

There remains the profound disjuncture between women's experience and the availability of forms through which that experience can be socially expressed. No where is that more evident than in rock, the most widely heart musical form. In some other genres of music, notably country, and some black gospel, and among the limited number of women active in the blues, and among jazz vocalists, that is much less the case. As a general rule, however, women in popular music, until very recently, have found themselves (though only a minority are conscious of it) speaking in voices created by others, in a musical vocabulary and tradition of discourse established by men. What are the consequences?

At one level the very fact of *any* kind of participation for women may have certain liberating consequences and provide role models that might further stimulate other women to consider doing more than clutching at the ankles of posturing males on the stage or buying their records. Whatever the sexism in the predominant content of popular music product in recent decades, the creative free space provided by the music does open powerfully expressive possibilities. There is some emancipatory potential in the "free spaces" provided by the liberating structure—the opportunities for individual improvisation and development of a unique style, voice, and persona, in spite of the prevailing sexist content. But to examine the overwhelming body of popular musical product is to discover crucial biases in the materials that have been produced through the 1980s.

If popular music is correctly seen as a medium of mass communication, unique aspects of most women's life experiences have *not* been effectively communicated. There are important differences in the way women and men live their lives, in the degree of autonomy permitted each by the realities of social life. Both physiologically, and culturally, through myriad forms of social determination of gender, the kinds of experiences which they undergo, and the socially structured pattern of sex role expectations, the lives of women and the ways they see the world are profoundly different from men. If functional biological differences between the sexes are no longer credible bases for role determination, gender remains one of the most significant deciding differences in determination of work roles in the society. This division of labor is a product of cultural role expectations that significantly influence conscious choice by the majority of employed women who find jobs within 20 of 420 classifications developed by the U.S. Department of Labor.

There are real differences between the sexes in cultural meanings given to physical differences, and in the reality of life experiences. Women discover early that they menstruate, men do not. Women get pregnant and 80 of the eighty-two percent who marry, bear children; men experience this, only indirectly through their partners if they are close enough to notice, and, of course, through the legal expectation they will pay their share of child support (an expectation often not fulfilled on their part or frequently rejected by the mothers who, for a variety of reasons, don't seek any further contact with the child's father). Even among single women never married (18.3 percent of the total population in 1986) increasing percentages of women 18 to 44 report having a child (14.3 percent in 1970, 6.5 percent of whites, 47.8 percent of blacks; by 1986, 18.1 percent of all single, never married women, 8.5 percent of whites, 44.7 percent of black single, never married women had given birth to one or more children).

Women, far more frequently than men, are subjected to personal and sexual abuse, incest, rape, battering, unwanted pregnancy, and the financial and psychological costs of raising children alone that they did not plan nor want and for which they are inadequately compensated through lack of effective enforcement of child-support laws. Women are more frequently impoverished and fall into poverty at such increasing rates relative to males, that the phenomenon of "feminization of poverty" became a significant object of social analysis in the mid-1980s. Women in the mid-1980s earned about 65 cents to every dollar earned by men. They are less likely to be covered by medical insurance. Women are victimized moreover, by (diminishing) double-standards concerning sexual behavior and appearance. Ageism is rampant in popular culture, but women suffer more. Many male film stars, for example, have endured across generations to play opposite an ever-revolving cast of younger women. Women are much more likely to be used and "used up," and when discarded in divorce, their economic status almost always is substantially lower than it was prior to divorce. Profound inequalities in pay scales and salaries between women and men persist and in spite of token integration of most job classifications, most working women still remain in such "women's" jobs as secretary, waitress, nurse, domestic or as elementary educator. But how many of these phenomena, which are social issues involving the situations of tens of millions of women and their children, or the greater numbers of single women who do not have children and seek fulfillment through a career, all widely studied and written about, ever make it into popular music?

These life experiences have produced distinctive ways of thinking and looking at the world the male-dominated social science disciplines only began to discover when feminist critiques pointed out the appalling phenomenon that most social science models were based *almost wholly* on studies of men! Carol Gilligan's *In a Different Voice* (1982) and the multi-authored *Women's Ways of Knowing* (1988) signalled the emergence among a new wave of feminist social scientists of recognition of women as beings distinctively different from men in their modes of thinking, moral reasoning and orientation toward the world.

Musically, these differences exist masked within modes of critical and theoretical discourse, largely practiced by men, and constructed, as political theorist Carole Pateman put if, "from within a division between the public (the social, the political, history) and the private (the personal, the domestic, the familial), which is also a division between the sexes." (1986, 6) Pateman (and a broad range of feminist thinkers) have argued that theorizing about social phenomena generally (as well as the standards that evaluate it) proceeds within a largely masculine, public world, a "universal" sort of world in which "the private world of particularity, natural subjection, inequality, emotion, love, partiality—and women and feminity" (Ibid) is repressed. Generally the sociological fact of the patriarchical separation of the two spheres and its influence on the ways virtually anything in popular culture, and certainly popular music, is discussed has until the last decade rarely been considered. While rock and other popular music critics might be generally politically "liberal" or "progressive," they are almost always men. What does this mean? What are its implications?

Much of popular music has been the domain of musical discourses of heroic *male* individuals seeking an authenticity of expression and existence that take for granted a conception of individuality based on a sexually particular character of the individual. This "individual" is distinctly masculine, but he appears (or is made to appear) somehow as universal. If there has been bias in the nature of the system of popular music, then, the counter-view might be expressed by a well-intentioned (and usually male) consciousness, the remedy should be simply to incorporate the excluded individuals. This would, however, leave intact "the sexually particular characterization of the public world, the individual and *his* capacities." (Ibid, emphasis added) This public world as presently known has largely been a male world.

According women a position of genuine equality in popular music becomes inevitably a demand for the social *autonomy* of women generally. And that will require significant changes in the overall structure of priorities in the larger society. If it is no longer credible that the capacities of women as performers/creators necessitates their exclusion, it does not suffice simply to assert that there are no differences between the situations of women and men, nor that existing differences are irrelevant.

The history of art and popular culture is full of "silences." Those of women relate significantly to powerful cultural gender role stereotypes concerning "appropriate" public postures and role models, prescribing demeanor in relating to men in relationships and in the work place, but also to the private world of marriage, maternity, family and childcare, and general cultural expectations that, because women must bear children, they must assume primary responsibility for caring for and raising them. This does not deny the fact that increasing numbers of women consciously choose to forego having children and choose to live alone (18.3 percent of the total population), but these remain the minority of women.

Whatever their status, and whatever the proliferation of role models, there remains the persisting social effects of the fact of a long standing and continuing overwhelming social bias, no longer, if ever credible, toward women not only giving birth to children, but also assuming virtually total responsibility for child rearing and care (in spite of '70s and '80s yuppie images of the child-toting "new father"). This factor alone may be the singly most significant in accounting for extended gaps in the careers of women in any creative area. It still has not been adequately considered in the public consciousness, being dealt with only occasionally on film and television, and rarely if ever in mainstream popular music.

It is difficult to find a male equivalence to the enforced absence from career imposed upon women by childbearing. Perhaps Elvis's stint in the Army. Perhaps the somewhat inaccurate perceptions of John Lennon's alleged period of preoccupation with caring for his child and his relative absence from public musical life for several years are ones in which the equivalent effects of this bias have been dramatized to men (Weiner 283-306). Other examples might well be jail terms that cut short the careers of many male artists, whether for drug possession or other crimes. What are the implications for women in imposed child-caring roles of such imposed male silences? Why is not such experience unique to women reflected in popular music in proportion to their position in the general population? These women are not a "minority." Women constitute well over 50 percent of the adult population of the United States. But, significantly, their existence at all social class levels and as part of all ethnic and racial groups has inhibited, or at least segmented, the development on a *mass* basis of a particularly feminist kind of *musical* "culture of resistance" that developed historically in the black musical tradition. Nonetheless feminist or distinctive women's perspective have entered ordinary discourse over the past two decades (at least in terms of rhetorical invocations of women's equality by male politicians, and adoption of "his/hers" or use of impersonal pronouns and similar efforts to reduce sexism in language). A distinctive feminist culture is evident in art, poetry, literature, and film. If this may be said to exist in music, it is in a particularly underrepresented, distorted, and attenuated form.

A Women's Musical Discourse?

When Kate Millett in *Sexual Politics* and, earlier, Betty Friedan in *The Feminine Mystique* began to unveil the essentially ideological nature of all that had previously been taken for granted as the reality of the role of women, the relations between the sexes, and especially the lived experience of the daily life of women, they opened up the possibility of thinking about that experience and expressing it in musical discourse in ways different from those in which it had been previously expressed. But what forms could it take up? Which would be open enough to permit the investment of energy and content in ways that would be affectively empowering and satisfying to listeners?

Sociologist Dorothy E. Smith has described her early experience as a student of literature and her personal conflicts growing out of her reaction to aspects of the work of D.H. Lawrence (who was presented to her as a "genius") after her recognition that his "ultimate idealization of sexual relations between women and men was one where women's consciousness, her sensation, was so totally annulled before the man's that she should forego even orgasm and accept essentially the annihilation of her own consciousness in the sexual act" (1987, 51; 1979, 136-37). Smith *felt* this, but, at that time, saw she had no vocabulary, no effective tradition of discourse in which to express her critique without being typed (among several possible deprecating characterizations) as "unwilling to accept her femininity"—model of feminity defined by others. There was a gap between her experience and the established, sanctioned, social forms of expression which were located in the middle of a male-dominated system of relations of power between men and women.

In music, a similar situation has prevailed in critical work and in virtually every aspect of popular music creation, production and distribution. Only in the late 1980s does there seem to be significant movement away from this situation, and that may be significantly a matter of market demographics (those "baby-boom" generation, socially liberal, but economically conservative, upscale "yuppie" consumers, who have moved rapidly into compact discs, for example, also seems to value women's equality and women artists). That does not obviate the fact the particular musical forms and modes of expression which have, until the '80s, been available as women's blues, gospel, and jazz vocalizing, all have been made and are controlled and evaluated by men. There are important exceptions to this pattern in the work of Tina Turner, Aretha Franklin, Cyndi Lauper, and Madonna and in the enduring models provided by classic women blues and rhythm and blues singers, but the pattern of bias remains.

In whatever area of popular music one can conceive of over the past century, women simply do not appear to men as men do to each other as persons involved in the common construction of a particular kind of social reality, a cultural product that is itself a kind of ideological construction, a way of understanding the world. As Smith has described sociological discourse, musical discourse, too, has been characterized by "a circle effect—men attend and treat as significant what men say and have said.... What men were doing has been relevant to men, was written by men about men for men. Men listened and listen to what one another say. A tradition is formed, traditions form, in a discourse with the past within the present. The themes, problematics, assumptions, metaphors, and images forms as the circle of those present draws upon the work of those speaking from the past and builds it up to project into the future" (1979, 137).

Sheila Rowbotham related a number of years ago a graphic illustration of the way women have, historically, been conditioned to treat themselves as they are looked at by men in mass popular culture. She describes how a portion of the Beatles *Magical Mystery Tour* seen on television demonstrated to her "the extent to which I identified with men, used their eyes.... Half of me was like a man surveying the passive half of me as a woman—thing" (40). The crucial events involve a group of people including the Beatles who go on a bus trip:

There is the atmosphere of excitement, of all being on the bus together and enjoying a treat.... Then at one point all the boys in the film are segregated from the girls. You follow the boys in the film, wriggling in your seat in front of the telly, in mounting excitement. It's like going in the Noah's Ark at Blackpool when you're six or listening to a very loud rock music when you're thirteen. I got the same tightening down at the bottom of my spine. Well there I was clenching my cunt and where should they go but into a strip-tease. I had caught myself going to watch another woman as if I were a man. I was experiencing the situation of another woman stripping through men's eyes. I was being asked to desire myself by a film made by men. Catching myself observing myself desiring one of my selves I remained poised for an instant in two halves (pp 40-41).

In the intervening years women's images in popular music have remained in two halves; one constructed by a male-dominated industry and dominant cultural images of desirable female qualities, and another more ambiguous sort of model that has had to be fought for by artists such as Tina Turner, Cyndi Lauper, and Madonna.

One ultimate effect of contemporary representations of women seems to be reinforcement of a competitive ethic of sexual objectification. Only rarely in mass popular culture, for example in such a film as *9 to 5* (1980) (in some ways itself an absurd caricature), is there the assertion of an alternative, non-competitive "women's" ethic and way of adapting to or solving life's problems.

If stronger images of women have appeared in greater numbers (though measurement of position in album and singles charts over three decades does not seem to indicate any consistent upward pattern of progress in capturing a greater market share for women artists) it does not mean a change in predominant content of the product. But at least the presence of the images provides new possibilities for generation of alternatives. The format of music television provides a few free spaces—"windows" in which some exceptionally creative videos portraying women have been presented. While these are a small minority of the women shown in 11 percent of music videos, they are possibly much more memorable shown against the background of Whitesnake, Billy Idol, Sammy Hagar, Robert Palmer, George Michael, Guns 'n' Roses, et.al.

Is the struggle to overcome gender stereotypes being won by women? Widespread lip service to formal equality of the sexes does not suggest understanding of the more complex realities of women's lives and their essential inequality and lack of real social autonomy imposed, in one area of life, by underdevelopment of the most elementary and basic public programs of medical, pre-natal and child care; and, at another symbolic level, with their functions as objects and fantasized images of male longings for "shelter from the storm." At the level of social power and influence in the controlling bureaucracies of society, only the most modest progress has been evident. If the music business remains a patriarchal structure run almost exclusively by white males, so does the whole society.

Musically, the situation could be characterized as attainment of a partial kind of affirmative action for sexual commodification. Popular music, at its worst (the image content of most music videos) usually functions to perpetuate all the old gender stereotypes, with a few spaces for ambiguous (not feminist) alternatives. In some of its better examples, R.E.M.'s "For the One I Love," several of Tracy Chapman's songs, including the popular "Fast Car," it would seem to seek to go beyond mere equality of sexual objectification and, as with the best popular cultural artifacts, to embody enough ambiguity to permit freely negotiated interpretation and response, "letting us be both subject and object of the singers' needs (regardless of our or their gender)" (Frith 1985, 23). Beyond that, to demand the revisioning of women's place in popular music is to demand the kinds of fundamental changes in culture and consciousness, as well as progammatic transformations of social life that will permit real social autonomy for all classes and ages of women. Perhaps only then will the construction of more realistic representations of women and men be evident, though that can never be the only function of a people's popular culture which, in its central qualities, must also embody frequently conservative, but often futurist elements of unspoken and utopian longings.

Notes

[1]In addition to the work of Simon Frith previously mentioned, Steve Chapple and Reebee Garofalo, *Rock 'n' Roll is Here to Pay: The History and Politics of the Music Industry* (Chicago: Nelson Hall, 1977), especially chapter 8, "Long Hard Climb: Women in Rock"; and, Christine Ferreira, "Like A Virgin: The Men Don't Know, But the Little Girls Understand," *Popular Music and Society*, 11:2, 1987, p 5-16, are distinguished exceptions.

[2]The phrase comes from Dorothy E. Smith's revelatory essay, "A Sociology For Women," in Julia A. Sherman and Evelyn Torton Beck, eds., *The Prism of Sex: Essays in the Sociology of Knowledge* (Madison: University of Wisconsin Press, 1979), p 135-188. Her work is collected in *The Everyday World as Problematic* (Boston: Northeastern University Press, 1987).

[3]Simon Frith, in a significant reworking of some of the ideas expressed in the 1978 essay with Angela McRobbie, has pointed to the one-sidedness of the earlier views, rejecting the notion that "sexuality has some sort of autonomous form which is expressed or controlled by cultural practice." See "Confessions of a Rock Critic," *New Statesman*, 23, August 1985, p. 23.

[4]The term "mobilization of bias" derives from political science discourse. It was originated by E.E. Schattsneider, see his *Semi-Sovereign People* (New York, 1960), p. 71. As elaborated by Peter Bachrach and Morton Baratz, the concept represents the tendency of political systems and sub-systems to develop "a set of predominant values, beliefs, rituals, and institutional procedures ("rules of the game") that operate systematically and consistently to the benefit of certain persons and groups at the expense of others. Those who benefit are placed in a preferred position to defend and promote their vested interests." Peter Bachrach and Morton Baratz, *Power & Poverty: Theory & Practice* (New York: Oxford University Press, 1970), p. 43.

Works Cited

Belenky, Mary F. *et al. Women's Ways of Knowing: The Development of Self, Voice and Mind.* New York: Basic Books, 1988.

Brown, Jane D. and Kenneth C. Campbell. "Race and gender in music videos: the same beat but a different drummer," *Journal of Communication* 36.1 (Winter 1986): 94-106.

Chapple, Steven and Reebee Garofalo. *Rock and Roll is Here to Pay.* Chicago: Nelson-Hall, 1977.

Denisoff, R. Serge and John Bridges. "Popular Music: Who Are the Recording Artists?" *Journal of Communication,* 32.1 (Winter 1982): 132-142.

Evans, Sara. *Personal Politics: The Roots of Women's Liberation in the Civil Rights Movement and the New Left.* (New York: Vintage Books, 1982).

Ferreira, Christine. "Like a Virgin: The Men Don't Know, But the Little Girls Understand," *Popular Music and Society,* 11.2 (1987):5-16.

Frith, Simon and Angela McRobbie. "Rock and Sexuality," *Screen Education,* 29(Winter 1978-79):3-19.

———— "Confessions of a Rock Critic," *New Statesman,* 23 (August 1985), reprinted in *Music for Pleasure.* (New York: Routledge, 1988).

———— *Music for Pleasure: Essays in the Sociology of Pop.* New York: Routledge, 1988.

Gilligan, Carol. *In a Different Voice: Psychological Theory and Women's Development.* Cambridge, MA.: Harvard University Press, 1982.

Hesbacher, Peter, et. al. "Solo Female Vocalists: Some Shifts in Stature and Alterations in Song." *Popular Music and Society,* V (1977):1-16.

Hesbacher, Peter and Bruce Anderson, "Hit Singers Since 1940: Have Women Advanced?". *Popular Music and Society.* VII.3 (1980). 132-139.

Jameson, Fredric. "Reification and Utopia in Mass Culture." *Social Text,* I (1979):130-148.

Kaplan, E. Ann. *Rocking Around the Clock: Music Television, Postmodernism, & Consumer Culture.* New York: Methuen, 1987.

Lasch, Christopher. *Haven in a Heartless World.* New York: Basic Books, 1977.

May, Elaine Tyler. *Homeward Bound: American Families in the Cold War Era.* New York: Basic Books 1988.

Olsen, Tillie. *Silences,* New York: Delta Books, 1982.

Pateman, Carole. "Feminist Critiques of the Public/Private Dichotomy." S. Benn and G. Gaus, eds., *Public and Private in Social Life.* New York: St. Martin's Press, 1983.

Pateman, Carole. "The Theoretical Subversiveness of Feminism." Carole Pateman and Elizabeth Gross, eds., *Feminist Challenges: Social and Political Theory,* Boston: Northeastern University Press, 1986.

Rosen, Marjorie. *Popcorn Venus: Women, Movies, and the American Dream.* New York: Coward, McCann & Geoghegan, 1973.

Rowbotham, Sheila. *Woman's Consciousness, Man's World.* New York: Penguin Books, 1973.

Ryan, Michael and Douglas Kellner, *Camera Politica.* Bloomington: University of Indiana Press, 1988.

Smith, Dorothy E. "A Sociology for Women" Julia A. Sherman and Evelyn Torton Beck, eds. *The Prism of Sex: Essays in the Sociology of Knowledge.* Madison: University of Wisconsin Press, 1979, 135-188.

Steward, Sue and Cheryl Garratt. *Signed, Sealed, and Delivered.* Boston: South End Press, 1984.

Weiner, Jon. *Come Together: John Lennon in his Time.* New York: Random House, 1984.

Wells, Alan. "Women in Popular Music: Changing Fortunes from 1955 to 1984." *Popular Music and Society,* 10.4 (1986):73-85.

Willis, Ellen. "Janis Joplin," Jim Miller, ed., *The Rolling Stone Illustrated History of Rock & Roll,* New York: Random House, 1980.

Kate Clinton:
The Production and Reception of Feminist Humor

Cheryl Kader

Q: Do you think your kind of stand-up comedy is very different from male stand-up?

A: I don't know many men who stand up and say, I'm a lesbian.

Claire Dowie, stand-up comedian.

With the revival of feminism in the late 1960s, debates on the relationship between politics and culture took on new dimensions. The advent of diverse feminist art forms, including film, theater, music and painting, which claimed "political engagement" as their point of articulation, yet which appeared to share few if any ideological or formal characteristics, precipitated an "aesthetic and politics" debate every bit as partisan as that which had preoccupied Marxist theorists and critics earlier in the century. However, since both the subject and object of debate were now female, feminist approaches to culture could not simply be imposed upon older methodologies, as if earlier debates and critical paradigms could be modified to accommodate feminist practices. Clearly the very terms of the debate would have to be renegotiated.

The body of critical writing on feminist aesthetics developed over the past twenty years testifies to the continued fascination of such investigations. Questions such as the status of consciousness—raising in political art; the relation of form to prevailing notions of "truth" and "subjectivity" and of feminist culture to forms of dominant culture; studies of address and audiences; and the contested ideological and political significance of feminist culture continue to challenge feminist critics who study signifying practices and their complex relation to the institutions which animate them. It is crucial to distinguish among the many forms of feminist culture—to maintain their differences while keeping in mind the ways in which cultural practices often cross over and confound generic and formal boundaries. And since we have learned that feminism, as theory or practice, can no longer be schematized as a monolith, I believe that the most productive work in feminist cultural studies is accomplished through an analysis of specific practices. So, with all these preliminaries in mind, I propose to look at the work of one performer, comedian Kate Clinton, and at the production of conventions and modes of communication specific to her performance.

The Production of Performative Space

The anthropologist Victor Turner, contending that experience always seeks its most aesthetic expression in performance, held that cultures could better be interpreted through their rituals than through their habits (see Bruner 13). Rituals such as theater, story-telling, and dance can be understood as ways in which people—especially those underrepresented within dominant discourse—articulate the meanings they assign to their everyday realities. Neither wholly "inside" nor "outside"; neither totally contained by nor free from what Theodor Adorno called "the administered universe," these public performances constitute, in Turner's words, episodes of "plural reflexivity— ways in which a group or community seeks to portray, understand, and then act on itself" (33). Such productions occupy a *liminal space,* a borderline area between daily social practices and those of experiment and play. I speculate that these public moments, historically contextualized, can be approached as cultural rehearsals for/of political engagement. As such, they are worth studying for the ways in which they resist complete integration into the social order.

Kate Clinton is a lesbian feminist comedian who has been performing before mixed and women—only audiences for the past 10-12 years. Meditations on women's experiences and the "every day realities" of lesbian existence, her performances constitute sites of "public liminality" (Turner), occasions wherein a group communicates itself to itself. How Clinton represents herself on stage, and the manner in which she positions herself in relation to her audience, indicate that what is significant is the performative space itself, and that the context in which her humor is received is both an extension of its productive relations as well as the creation of a space "elsewhere": in the interstices of hegemonic culture.

Unquestionably, the audience at a Clinton performance is composed largely of the already "converted." Because Clinton is well-known on the women's concert circuit, both as a comedian and a political activist, she has established a following. The women in the audience have usually seen or heard her before, either at a local club or theater, on stage at one of the annual women's music festivals, or on record or tape. The few men in the audience are either gay or in attendance with their female partners who may have "prepared" them in advance! Occasionally someone walks out; however, the focus of Clinton's humor is not anti-male.

For one recent engagement in a large mid-west city, individual women and women's groups transformed a (straight) downtown club—disco into gendered social space. Through the efforts of local women's media groups; a female M.C. who, from the stage, announced up-coming events of interest to women; and of Clinton herself, who began her routine by referring to the 1987 March on Washington for Gay and Lesbian Rights, the evening was orchestrated by women. This is not insignificant, for, to borrow a phrase from Derrida, such a reinterpretation of space challenges "the monological arrogance of 'official' systems of signification"; systems of signification which are, themselves, indices of social relations—producing and produced by the deployment of power within social and conceptual systems.

While the nature of stand-up comedy is that the performer is center stage, the sole protagonist, Clinton's act is prefigured and thematized by an evolving dynamic between performer and audience. I have briefly demonstrated how this space is activated and carved out of the social structure. In Victor Turner terms, such a space is "antistructural"; it indicates the separation from ordinary structural and structuring institutions and social positions and the formation of bonds—most often transitory—which "ignore, reverse, cut across, or occur outside of structural relationships" (*Dramas, Fields, and Metaphors*). At odds with heterosexuality, the performative space created by Clinton and her audience is intrinsically "decentered," and, like those anti-structural moments elaborated by Turner, both positive and generative. A crucial site for the contestation of meanings made available by hegemonic discourse, the clandestine and liminal space occupied by the lesbian critical perspective is "that which has never been," to borrow from the title of Bonnie Zimmerman's essay on lesbian feminist criticism. In so far as Clinton's humor has the power to destabilize the normative constraints of socio-cultural signifying systems, dislocating established frontiers as it yields new meanings, its enactment is, in Turner's words, "an instant of pure potentiality."

Clinton's humor often draws upon current mainstream concerns: therapy, politics, T.V., religion, for example. Clinton, herself, is a "recovering Catholic," who attended school at "Our Lady of Psychological Warfare"; another major lesbian feminist comedian, Robin Tyler, is Jewish. Both relentlessly pursue the cultural contradictions of sexuality-religion-politics in their acts. However, these everyday contexts are given a "lesbian slant." For example, Clinton reflects upon the consequences of appearing at a rally for the Republican Party carrying "lesbians love Bush signs (this, just prior to the elections), or to the practice of "de—dykeing" the apartment when preparing for visits from the family—commonly referred to among friends as "straightening up"! Expressions in different domains of culture are thus revealed as decentered and radically plural.

In her retelling and re-shaping of everyday events, Kate Clinton occupies the role of *storyteller*. As Walter Benjamin observed: "The storyteller takes what he tells from experience—his own and that reported by others. And he, in turn, makes it the experience of those who are listening to his tale" (87). I don't mean to suggest that Clinton's performance captures reality, albeit a radically different and unassimable one, or that it pretends to an unmediated knowledge of the world from the position of the "other." However, I do believe that her experiments with symbolic and social conventions involve more than the post-modern recognition that language always works at a loss. "Will there be fried foods after the revolution?" she enquires, referencing lesbians' preoccupation with tofu and sprouts. "Clearly, we need to talk about this." These dissonant moments point to the ways in which words and categories articulate the production of society as a whole, while for Clinton, they simultaneously embody modes of signification and representation which *reorganize* and thus *reenvision* ways of being in the world.

When writing about lesbianism, it is customary to begin with a definition. For example, both Adrienne Rich in her essay, "Compulsory Heterosexuality and Lesbian Existence," and Lillian Faderman in her book, *Surpassing the Love of Men*, situate their work by defining the term, although they differ as to what characterizes lesbian experience. These two studies have, deservedly, proven highly influential in the newly emerging field of lesbian scholarship, affording us, in Rich's own words, the opportunity of "asking women's questions, of seeing with fresh eyes, and of entering an old text from a new critical direction"; recently, however, the unstable or provisional nature of "identity" has become the focus not only of post-structuralists but of women of color, Jewish women, lesbians and others concerned with radical articulations of difference. Since what is at stake for me is a notion of a gendered subjectivity which can account for the heterogenaiety of lesbianism and its effects, the only claim I will make about lesbianism is that all lesbians participate, to greater or lesser degrees, in a structuration of social life determined by a sexual orientation sustained in a disjuncture with the "norm" of heterosexuality. In this way, I recognize those different subject positions and non-reducible identities which are taken up in individual histories and practices. Eve Kosofsky Sedgwick makes a similar point in a recent article entitled "Epistemology of the Closet," when she states that gay identity is problematized by the fact that "no one person can take control over all the multiple, often contradictory, codes by which information about sexual identity can seem to be conveyed" (50). She posits a drama of homosexuality played out between "the epistemologically charged figures of 'the closet' and 'coming out' " (40). Sedgwick's mapping of gay identity captures the tensions generated by our negotiation of a space which is at once so indeterminate and so overdetermined.

Michel Foucault uses the term "technologies of power" to designate the whole range of techniques and practices, social and cultural, for the disciplining, administration and formation of populations of individuals. Heterosexuality, too, is both medium and outcome of a "complex political technology." The implementation and introjection of heterosexist modes of thought are constitutive of particular subjectivities, which, in their turn, sustain the production and consolidation of reference and meaning. Thus, the lesbian perspective is dramatized by a critical consciousness about heterosexist assumptions and is engaged in "unlearning" the norm of universal heterosexuality. In creating our own cultural practices we cannot ignore the variety of ways, the overt and not so overt mechanisms of suppression and control, which have governed and continue to guarantee the silencing and exclusion of lesbians as subjects of history and as authors of our own experience.

What is transmitted through heterosexual narratives is a set of rules that constitutes the social bond; consequently, the experience of lesbianism in the rupture with heterosexuality referred to previously, whether as an act of resistance (Rich), a romantic friendship (Faderman), or "the rage of all women condensed to the point of explosion" ("Radicalesbians' Manifesto"), remains to be accounted for. Yet, this account is precisely what existing power relations and the knowledge structures they generate disqualify or render unspeakable. Even a project to demystify the workings of the linguistic and cultural establishment—the interrogation of difference—has too often come to reside, uncontested, in the service of ideological cohesion and uniformity. In the words of historian Linda Gordon, "Different but equal may be the gender version of separate but equal. The very notion of difference can function to obscure domination, to imply a neutral asymmetry" (26). Experience, however differently encoded, would appear to be indissoluble from the construction and transformation of meaning; it is that which is behind a particular system of thought, that which is involved in deciding *what counts* as meaning. Since heterosexuality functions as a rational and legitimating discourse, enabling and producing knowledge, oppositional or non-dominant meanings are generated at the interfaces between established cultural systems, in the spaces rather than in the margins, in the movement between hegemonic discourse and institutions.

Reception

The assumption of a lesbian audience, for Clinton's humor implies a spectator who is neither male nor heterosexual, means that the performer directs herself to subjects positioned, like herself, both inside and outside ideology. Consequently, Clinton is able to reference lesbian life-styles, for example, the etiquette of messing up the second bed at a motel when travelling with one's same sex lover, and, together, performer and audience construct a space of self-referentiality based upon a shared symbolic repertoire. What interests me is the manner in which Kate Clinton's humor helps to create a record of lesbian social organizations and relations.

In an essay entitled, "The Violence of Rhetoric: Considerations on Representation and Gender," Teresa de Lauretis argues for a theory of gendered subjectivity grounded in "history, practices, and the imbrication of meaning with experience" (42). A subjectivity determined as much by the outer world of social reality as by discursive practices will depend upon a "different production of reference and meaning" than the term (subjectivity) is currently accorded within non-feminist theoretical accounts. De Lauretis' insistence upon the complex relation between expression and experience— the meanings that get assigned to women's daily lives—serves as a useful point of departure for my own investigations into the conditions of possibility for a lesbian-centered perspective.

Our understanding of the world is shaped by our location within social practices and relations—a fluid and at times contradictory location—and by those institutions of which we feel ourselves a part. Thus, the dialectic of inclusion-exclusion which forms the generative matrix for lesbian subjectivity has consequences for the ways in which lesbians produce and organize meaning. The lesbian's position within the social formations guaranteed by heterosexuality is crystallized by those structures of knowing/ unknowing which inform her relations with others. At the same time as she is excluded from the dominant symbolic economy, her difference (whether figured as deviance, otherness, or opposition) grounds a set of experiences and perceptions which, at the very least, undermine the normative and, therefore, normalizing practices and discursive strategies of heterosexuality. Nevertheless, the movement out of a heterosexually oriented frame of reference can only be accomplished provisionally, for lesbians share a position within the dominant ideology at the same time as they inhabit—voluntarily or not, but ineluctably—the place of the outcast or exile. And this ambiguity is as true, although lived differently, for the most radical lesbian separatist or gay activist as it is for the closeted individual unable or unwilling to sustain the consequences of self-disclosure. Our knowledge structures, the heterogeneous network of associations, references, and representations which provide the framework for and determine the nature of understanding, are the effect of those conventions implicitly or explicitly operating in different and often contradictory cultural and political modalities.

In *A Room of One's Own*, Virginia Woolf writes, "Again if one is a woman one is often surprised by a sudden splitting off of consciousness, say in walking down Whitehall, when from being the natural inheritor of that civilisation, she becomes, on the contrary, outside of it, alien and critical" (101). As a result of our socially constructed positions under patriarchy, women, Woolf suggests, have learned to respond to the world with a "double consciousness."* Our critical perspective is informed by and emerges for our lived experience of contradiction—the complex negotiations demanded of women within an "alien culture." Thus, while gender shapes interpretation, gender, in turn, is, itself, organized through other categories of difference—class, race, sexuality, etc.

Foregrounding lesbian subjectivity—one's experience of self as other within the heterosexual social order—as the "ground" for the production and transmission of meaning enables us to see how the lesbian imagination partakes of Woolf's "double consciousness": the shifting perspective of one caught between the lived contradictions of dominant orders and those oppositional experiences, practices and meanings which emerge out of an awareness or consciousness of oppression. This formulation situates the practice of *reception* socially and symbolically, ascribing subjective agency to the *spectator* as an inventor or architect of meaning. Performer and spectator alike engage in fashioning a "different production of reference

---

*The condition of the "double consciousness" is taken from the writings of W.E.B. Dubois, *The Souls of Black Folk: Essays and Sketches*, New York: Fawcett Premier, 1961.

and meaning"; it is a shared lesbian critical perspective that inaugurates desire and is involved in dismantling the specific configurations of language, meaning and power constitutive of heterosexuality.

"I thank you all for coming out" quips Clinton, at once referencing the "multiple spaces" or "shifting identities" inhabited by her audience, and at the same time, *creating* that audience through her utilization of previously assimilated, shared conventions. When she notes that the "pink triangles" attached to the rear of certain vehicles indicates that "slow moving gay people are on board," Clinton is employing two frames of reference or levels of interpretation. The one defamiliarizes the codes of the dominant culture, including those organizing principles by means of which we learn to read texts and make sense of our experiences; the other reorders or restructures the object world, interpelating its subjects according to a specific set of shared assumptions. Clinton uses the "everyday spaces" of discourse and social relations as her stage yet demarcates and contextualizes them by means of an address which implies a lesbian audience. She draws upon "a collective experience," by which I do not mean to posit an essentialist or universal subject. Rather, I wish to emphasize a "community of spectators" which does not merge identities or wipe out differences, but which liberates its occupants from uniformity to general norms, however temporarily.

"Coming on to her audience," flirting, positioning herself as an "ex-femme," referencing the lesbian community: "Can you fake heterosexual-ity?"—Clinton's selfrepresentation is as a subject defined in terms of sexual similarity to her audience. Her performance is an act of love(making), a "we're O.K." that speaks to lesbian desire and to a lesbian discourse generated at the nexus of traditional (normative) meanings, performing self, and communal response.

Meaning and the Transmission of Lesbian Narratives

I have demonstrated how the construction of lesbian narrative space takes place in the oscillation between referent [object, experience] and the body of the lesbian critical subject. One other artist who has addressed herself to the problematical interaction between lesbian subject and text and whose writing consistently takes up the difficult relation between the lesbian body and discourse is Monique Wittig. Although of a radically different nature than Clinton's, Wittig's nuanced texts can help illuminate the humorist's own positioning of the lesbian subject as/at the center of discourse and the production of meaning. As Teresa de Lauretis notes about Wittig: "The project, the conceptual originality and radical import of Wittig's lesbian as subject of a 'cognitive practice' that enables the reconceptualizations of the social and of knowledge itself from a position eccentric to the heterosexual institution, are all there in the first page of *Le Corps Lesbien*" ("Sexual Indifference" 167).

Wittig's elaborate language games are graphic attempts to expose the ways in which meaning is mediated by convention and the relations of ruling (of gender), and how it is that the relations of words to each other, rather than to their *contexts*, provides the conditions for the realignment of meaning with heterosexual "reality." Wittig writes: "The discourses of heterosexuality oppress us in the sense that they prevent us from speaking unless we speak in their terms. Everything which puts them into question is at once disregarded as elementary. Together with the unrelenting tyranny they impose upon our physical and mental selves, these discourses deny us the very possibility of creating our own categories" ("The Straight Mind" 105). Since compulsory heterosexuality is composed of forces which disable lesbians, while conferring a "status" (of sorts) upon the woman attached to a man, it follows that for Wittig, a gender based economy is a phallic economy, and within such an economy lesbian representation is incomprehensible. For Wittig, therefore, the production of lesbian meaning, like the construction of the lesbian body, is possible only in the break with heterosexuality which is prefigured in the destruction of gender. Wittig insists upon lesbian difference as the "instrument" by means of which "the categories of sex [will be made] obsolete in language" ("The Mark of Gender" 70).

Wittig's struggle to transcend gender (not to be confused with the blurring of boundaries between genders or the claim to a "feminine writing") is, I think, similar to my own contention that the lesbian perspective deterritorializes; as such, both interventions cannot be reabsorbed into the male symbolic order since, by calling the male enterprise into question, they are inherently destabilizing, "[The lesbian] poet generally has a hard battle to wage, for, step by step, word by word, she must create her own context in a world which, as soon as she appears, bends every effort to make her disappear. The battle is hard because she must wage it on two fronts: on the formal level with the questions being debated at the moment in literary history, and on the conceptual level against the that-goes-without-saying of the straight mind" ("The Point of View: Universal or Particular?" 67).

In Wittig's prose, the insertion of the lesbian body into the text "lesbianizes" the world; having dismantled the male subject and witnessed it "truncated out of language," the lesbian body is established as the bearer of meaning. Wittig's texts constitute an assault on the heterosexual order and the reconstitution of the lesbian subject from within a "perspective given in homosexuality" ("The Mark of Gender" 72). They yield a body created otherwise and elsewhere—in the interfaces between established cultural systems, a rewriting of the lesbian body beyond its precoded, conventionalized representations.

A story is born on the boundaries of the real, in a space that is at once present and potential. Walter Benjamin writes: "All great story tellers have in common the freedom with which they move up and down the rungs of their experience as on a ladder. A ladder extending downward to the interior of the earth and disappearing into the clouds is the image for a collective experience to which even the deepest shocks of...individual experience...constitute no impediment or barrier" (102). Juxtapositions of a remembered past and an imagined future, stories are hybrids whose origins are located in an experience which is either one's own or one reported by others. "Thus the tracks of the storyteller," Benjamin notes, "are frequently evident in his narratives, if not as those of the one who experienced it then as those of the one who reports it" (92). In turn, the storyteller makes that experience the listener's, fashioning the raw material of experience in a "solid, useful, and unique way" for listeners whose own subject positions are in part fashioned through the unfolding of the narrative.

Clinton's stories are humorous records of the struggles for survival in a world not of one's making, a cultural order of which women, especially lesbians, are neither the architects nor the inheritors. In addition, in its mobilization and transformation of the everyday through specific signifying practices, Clinton's humor represents the longing for "something else"— the hope that things can be different. In her narrativization of lesbianism, Clinton presents us with the everyday: relationships; family; work; politics and the "promise" of an emancipatory future.

[Clinton wonders how the film, *Tootsie*, might have been different if Dustin Hoffman, who makes a better woman as a man than a woman would, could have felt just once what it's like to sneeze and blow out a tampon!]

In this conjunction of the present with an imaginary and imagined future, what is being invoked, paradoxically, is a communal *past*. In the course of Clinton's act, the audience discovers itself and recovers a history as it exists in the organizing and articulating of experience, and as it has been lived on the margins, in the silences, and in the deliberate erasures and "forgettings" of patriarchal and heterosexist cultural traditions.

It is precisely this dialectic of the known and the new that is at stake in Clinton's performance. The everyday realities of dealing with an alien social order are given a new focus and a new perspective; gender and sexuality become self-conscious and reflexive, as one part of the social system employs shared cultural symbols to provide a critique and a reframing and remodelling of (conventional) reality. It is a lesbian sensibility that governs, so that what has conventionally been seen as "meaningful" in one framework becomes seen by its participants as something else. Plural or public reflexivity is, in Turner's opinion, a metacommentary on the history of the group. The political edge of Clinton's performance is determined by this dimension of *reflexivity* which is sustained in the suspension of the boundaries between performer and audience and between pleasure and serious consideration.

In her book, *Feminist Spectator As Critic*, Jill Dolan credits "the lesbian subject position [with being] the unarticulated but inferred 'elsewhere' in [Teresa] de Lauretis' discourse" (116). In her chapter on sexuality in performance, Dolan theorizes—as I do—the relation between lesbian performer and lesbian spectator, speculating that lesbian performance, in its foregrounding of same sex desire and its transgression of gendered sexual roles, frustrates the male gaze—customarily the fulcrum of representation. "The female body may no longer be a hysterical spectacle, but a term in the new representational debate" (115). What Dolan suggests, and my brief sketch hardly does justice to the complexity of her thought, is that, by signifying active female desire and by playing with gender roles, the lesbian subject confounds heterosexual culture and "subverts" the structures of power organized around gender. By its presence, the lesbian body demystifies the dominant signifying system, acceding to its place in (gendered) representation through "playful" experimentation with roles and behaviors.

In my view, the gendered social space delineated by and in Kate Clinton's performance, "posed" as de Lauretis states it, "from outside the heterosexual contract" in a movement between "the discursive space of the positions made available by hegemonic discourses and the space-off, the elsewhere, of those discourses" (*Technologies of Gender* 26), constitutes more than simply a *playful* reimagining of the world, since it grounds its temporary reconstruction of social relations in both "history" and "the everyday." It is a space where the social relations of heteropatriarchy—and, therefore, the production of specific knowledge—power positions—are deconstructed and contested. Clinton's humor obeys the impulse to entertain and to be serious; to pass the time and to collect meanings. In bringing together the ordinary and the extraordinary, her humor questions the meanings assigned to "reality," helping its audience make sense of their daily lives. In acknowledging how the experiences and perspectives of lesbians have been systematically assimilated into the heterosexual norm, the lesbian intervention into discourse or culture (never unmediated) like the lesbian option it indexes is generated out of contradiction and tension.

Michel Foucault employs the term, "subjugated knowledge," to refer to a thematic which is both historical, i.e. "disguised within the body of systematising theory" whose aim is coherence and unanimity, and particular: a kind of guerilla tactic which depends upon "the harshness with which it is opposed by everything surrounding it" (82). This oscillation between a continuous, yet buried and disenfranchised, knowledge and a discontinuous or illegitimate knowledge asserts the fugitive, *non-conciliatory* nature of any discourse fashioned to challenge or contest the totalizing effects of majority theory, whose very definition lies in its power to de-authorize and isolate minority theories and the forms of knowledge which circulate about them. I am suggesting that the lesbian critical perspective takes place in just this interspatial and insurgent realm.

The growth of a visible gay rights movement and of feminism, notwithstanding, lesbian existence continues to be precarious: the site of palpable dis/ease both for those of us who choose to define ourselves by the term "lesbian" and for those who define themselves against it. And in the light of protracted attempts at anti-gay legislation and the homophobia aroused by the spread of AIDS and by the institutional efforts to combat it, it is clear that homosexuality remains *unrepresentable* within established knowledge systems and discourses. Consequently, efforts by lesbians to take hold of our experiences are prefigured not only in a critique of heterosexism and homophobia but in new ways of thinking eventuating in the construction of new meanings. The emergence of such a subjugated knowledge—which can provide new ways to talk about experience, yet is, simultaneously, the outcome/product of those experiences—is founded in that rupture, or break, with heterosexuality articulated in lesbian subjectivity.

Humor functions on recognizable characteristics and behavior patterns: the comic reveals something about herself, members of the audience recognize that they have the same characteristics and the joke is made. In this interchange the audience forms a group, they are the 'type' of person to laugh at the 'type' of observation made.

Banks and Swift, *The Joke's On Us*

Clinton's humor is not particularly anti-male; she rarely reverts to "penis jokes" in the manner in which women have always had jokes publicly made against us. She is not interested in merely redressing the balance and making men the brunt of her comedy. Her performance, while it calls into question the objectification of everyday social relations, is also constructive and affirmative, creating something else to be out of the everyday. Self-mocking, it is yet a humor of understanding; women laughing together, sharing a common language about experiences and memories in the absence of men.

In her essay, "Situation Comedy, Feminism, and Freud: Discourses of Gracie and Lucy," Patricia Mellencamp reflects on Freud's distinction between "the joke" and "the comic." It seems that what marks the comic is its attention to social factors—" 'the comic' derives from the relations of human beings 'to the often over—powerful external world' "(91). According to Freud, the outcome of a comic episode lies in the triumph of the social and the "degradation" of the individual. I contend that Clinton's comedy is an *inversion* of the degradation or helplessness experienced by many in its audience (P.T.L. is transformed into Praise the Lesbians!) as well as by the performer herself, perhaps, as lesbian comedian. Clinton is a "sexual outlaw" who, by foregrounding difference, exposes society's fascination with women's objectification: bodies, fashion, diets, sex, menstruation are narrativized from the perspective of society's "others." For example, Clinton reflects upon the lesbian who has had a child through artificial insemination. She has taken the baby with her to a faculty meeting (!), and the baby is babbling, da-da-da. A colleague who is acquainted with the situation leans over and exclaims, "listen, she's trying to say, 'doner'!" However, what occurs is nothing as simple as the reversal of subject-object positions, for spectators and performer are always in two contexts simultaneously—as both insiders and outsiders, their positions are at once multiple and shifting.

Given the unique combination of Clinton's audience, the effect of her comedy is not accompanied by the same constellation of emotions Mellencamp posits for the female viewer of, say, "I Love Lucy," where she argues that comedy serves to displace unmanageable feelings of distress or anger on the part of Lucy's similarly "domesticated" female spectator. While the release of women's anger is clearly an issue, I suggested earlier that performances like Clinton's might be conceptualized as cultural rehearsals for political action. As such, they aspire to mobilize feelings in the service of social change rather than displace or contain them.

Nevertheless, the question of whether lesbian feminist humor as, at most, a marginal phenomenon, can be invoked as a *political* tool demands further elaboration. Clearly, Clinton's techniques of storytelling, ritual, and audience identification provide possibilities for reflection on the place of the lesbian subject within social relations (lesbian and otherwise); however, can we assume that her comedy represents a catalyst for social transformation rather than, simply, a gathering place for the already converted?

"Post—feminism? — Had I died and didn't know it?" Kate Clinton

While the content of Clinton's performance is undeniably political and her self-representation is that of a politically committed artist, I suggest that neither element by itself is sufficient to justify calling her work "politically engaged." Rather, it is the combination of content, self-representation, and audience subject positions which, together, produce a realignment in traditional performance aesthetics and a reimagined social reality. And it is partially on account of these symbolic reorganizations that the possibility/potential for radical social change is kept alive and can be mobilized. In the performative space created by Kate Clinton and her audience, the heteropatriarchal order is appraised and rearranged from the perspective of the "other"; while the experience of "otherness" is put into circulation in defiance of the "natural order." When the historical and cultural particularity of the sign "lesbian" is upheld and the lesbian body is celebrated, then lesbian difference—no longer the site upon which the semi-arbitrary play of masculine knowledge and heterosexual desire are enacted—becomes, itself, the locus of meaning. More than simply reflecting the heterosexual image back upon itself, discourse takes on a new meaning—it becomes a reverse discourse, a counter knowledge, the product of lesbianism speaking on its own behalf. However, this activity is not limited to a movement between homosexuality and hegemonic discourse; like the lesbian's own subject position that it rehearses, lesbian counter meaning is traversed by the complex positionalities and multiple identities that adhere in a society divided by race, class, and ethnicity.* This discord within "historical reality" Fredric Jameson calls "an enigma for thought, an aporia" (213). He insists that we hold onto this aporia, for it "contains within its structure the crux of a history beyond which we have not yet passed" (213).

This, then, may turn out to be the most significant aspect of Clinton's performance, in that her attitude toward everyday reality succeeds in revealing the contradictions and discontinuities within cultural systems and social relations, with the result that the struggle over meaning in everyday life

---

*For a provocative "reading" of the contextualized body, see Minnie Bruce Pratt, "Identity: Skin Blood Heart" in *Yours In Struggle*. New York: Long Haul Press, 1984.

becomes a political activity. Her experimental stance toward social structures, the material world, and experience succeeds in producing a *separation* from the dominant culture, opening up a space for a restructured history and a reconceptualized subject. In such a context, in the interface between multiple frames of reference, the lesbian subject is engaged in the negotiation of dominant cultural space and the production of self and community.

Acknowledgments

For their formative roles in the production of this essay, I would like to thank Tania Modleski who introduced me to new ways of seeing; my colleagues in feminist studies at the University of Wisconsin-Milwaukee and at the Center for Advanced Feminist Studies, University of Minnesota-Twin Cities; and my partner Julie, whose support and encouragement are the corner-stones of all my work.

Works Cited

Banks, Morwenna and Amanda Swift. *The Joke's On Us*. London: Pandora, 1987.
Benjamin, Walter. "The Storyteller" *Illuminations*. New York: Schocken Books, 1969.
Bruner, Edward M. "Experience and Its Expressions" *The Anthropology of Experience*. Victor W. Turner and Edward M. Bruner, eds. Chicago: University of Illinois Press, 1986.
de Lauretis, Teresa. "Sexual Indifference and Lesbian Representation" *Theatre Journal*. Spring 1988.
———. *Technologies of Gender*. Bloomington: Indiana University Press, 1987.
Dolan, Jill. *Feminist Spectator as Critic*. Ann Arbor: U.M.I. Research Press, 1988.
Faderman, Lillian. *Surpassing the Love of Men*. New York: William Morrow & Co., 1981.
Foucault, Michel. *Power/Knowledge*. New York: Pantheon Books, 1980.
Gordon, Linda. "What's New in Women's History" *Feminist Studies, Critical Studies*. Teresa de Lauretis, ed. Bloomington: Indiana University Press, 1986.
Jameson, Fredric. *Aesthetics and Politics* London: Verso Press, 1977.
Mellencamp, Patricia. "Situation Comedy, Feminism, and Freud: Discourses of Gracie and Lucy" *Studies in Entertainment: Critical Approaches to Mass Culture*. Tania Modleski, ed. Bloomington: Indiana University Press, 1986.
Pratt, Minnie Bruce. "Identity: Skin Blood Heart" *Yours In Struggle*. Elly Bulkin, Minnie Bruce Pratt, and Barbara Smith, New York: Long Haul Press, 1984.
Radicalesbians. "The Woman Identified Woman" *Notes from the First Year*.
Rich, Adrienne. "Compulsory Heterosexuality and Lesbian Existence" *Blood, Bread, and Poetry*. New York: W.W. Norton & Co., 1986.
———. "When We Dead Awaken: Writing as Re-Vision" *On Lies, Secrets, and Silence*. New York: W.W. Norton & Co., 1979.
Sedgwick, Eve Kosofsky. "Epistemology of the Closet" *Raritan* VII:4, Spring, 1988.
Turner, Victor. *Dramas, Fields, and Metaphors*. Ithaca: Cornell University Press, 1974.

_____ "Frame, Flow and Reflection: Ritual and Drama as Public Liminality" *Performance in Postmodern Culture*. Michel Benamou and Charles Caramello, eds. Wisconsin: Coda Press, 1977.

Walker, Nancy A. *A Very Serious Thing*. Minneapolis: University of Minnesota Press, 1988.

Wittig, Monique. "The Mark of Gender" *The Poetics of Gender*. Nancy K. Miller, ed. New York: Columbia University Press, 1986.

_____ "The Point of View: Universal or Particular?" *Feminist Issues*. Fall 1983.

_____ "The Straight Mind" *Feminist Issues*. Summer 1980.

Woolf, Virginia. *A Room of One's Own*. New York: Harcourt, Brace, Jovanovich, 1957.

Zimmerman, Bonnie. "What Has Never Been: An Overview of Lesbian Feminist Criticism" *The New Feminist Criticism*. Elaine Showalter, ed. New York: Pantheon Books, 1985.

Desire and Sexuality

Party Lights:
Utopic Desire and the Girl Group Sound

Paul Gripp

The Girl Group sound only existed from 1958 to 1965 and only flourished for a briefer period within those signposts. Like its most immediate predecessor, doo-wop, the music emphasized voice over instrumentation (at least until the advent of the baroque productions of Phil Spector and George "Shadow" Morton and arguably even then), and the lyrics were sweet (sometimes syrupy) and innocent (sometimes naive). And, like pop music in general, the central theme of Girl Group music was love—what distinguishes the Girl Groups is their special emblem of that love, "The Boy," as the critic Greil Marcus has christened him:

The Boy is the central figure in the lyrics of girl group rock. He is shadowy: the boy who'll love walking in the rain, the fine, fine boy, the leader of the pack, the angel baby. He is irresistible—and almost never macho. He is sensitive. He must be pursued. How to reach him? (160).

The Girl Groups hunted this creature with the single-minded intensity of a fatally poisoned victim seeking a hidden antidote. Usually, their search was doomed; in most Girl Group rock, the utopia of actual union with The Boy is either infinitely deferred or spoken of in the past tense. Above all, this is a genre delineating the joy and pain of desire.

Like much of the rest of the music on the radio in this period, the Girl Group sound originated from the pens of songwriters working in the "New Tin Pan Alley" in New York City. The productions of these songwriting "mills," as they were called, are often referred to as "Brill Building Pop," because so many of the mills resided in or around the Brill Building at 1619 Broadway. While these companies were often fly-by-night and certainly more interested in money than craftmanship, some fine songwriters were produced by this system, most notably the teams of Jeff Barry and Ellie Greenwich, Cynthia Weil and Barry Mann, and Carole King and Gerry Goffin. These man and woman teams authored numerous hits, accounting for most of the Girl Group sound's finest moments between them. All were white and from middle-class homes in and around New York City and all were close to teenage in years themselves. They worked in virtual sweatshop conditions, under pressure to churn out three or four songs a day. Barry Mann recalled:

'It was insane. Cynthia and I would be in this tiny cubicle, about the size of a closet, with just a piano and a chair; no window or anything. We'd go in every morning and write songs all day. In the next room, Carole and Gerry would be doing the same thing...'. (Shaw 124)

While these songwriters were positioned above the actual performers of the music, status and salary—wise, one can see that they were still "workers." Perhaps as a result, they penned the most socially-conscious popular songs of the day. As Barry Mann said, " 'When we were writing back then, we really did think we could change the world' " (Ward 236). However, it would be dangerous to take this statement as a radical manifesto, for the "protests" of these writers were conventional expressions of a New Deal to New Frontier liberalism; even working class vignettes like "Uptown" and "He's Sure the Boy I Love" offer the palliative of romantic bliss—as in the latter's chorus, "When he holds me tight, everything's right, crazy as it seems"—to resolve the social contradictions they introduce.

Element two in the Girl Group equation were the producers. These producers usually exerted dictatorial control over all aspects of the recording process once the songs left the writing mills. They were all white and male and typically paternalistic and exploitive when it came to the treatment of their performers, who were very young black or white women, usually from the working class. The still primitive—by today's standards— environment of the recording studio ensured the large degree of freedom the producers were granted even when under contract to a major company; record company executives, out of touch with American teenagers and thus unable to predict what would sell, were more than happy to allow the autonomy of lots of relatively cheap studio time when a big hit could result that would pay for tens of failures.

Girl Group performers—that is, the vocalists—(the musicians were hired on a per song basis by either the record company or the producer) were unknowns who were often discovered more-or-less randomly by their producers. The public usually knew the performers, if they were a group, only by the group name; even the most ardent fan would have been hard— pressed to come up with the names of individual members. The record companies encouraged this anonymity on the theory (proven time and time again in practice) that it made it easier to replace group members if they dropped out or proved too intractable. The most famous example of the demonstrated interchangeability of Girl Group performers is the producer Phil Spector's appropriation of Los Angeles based singer Darlene Love to do the lead vocal for "He's a Rebel" because the Crystals, who had been slated to record the song, were in New York. Spector was in a hurry to release the song before a rival version appeared, so, since he was in Los Angeles, he used Love and a group called the Blossoms to cut the record.

The record, which became a huge hit, was released under the Crystals appellation (Ward 237). This contemptuous treatment of the artists as if they were spare parts was the norm, not the exception. The women in these groups were often warned, as music historian Alan Betrock paraphrases, " 'Hey, kid, there's plenty more out there waiting to take your place. If you don't like it, why don't you leave?' " (80). The swan song group of the Girl Group era, the Shangri-Las, told a harrowing tale of exploitation. According to Betrock, "no one...can recall getting any royalties. The miniscule three or four percent royalty the group was owed amounted to three or four cents a record, but even at that rate a million selling record should have earned the group thirty or forty thousand dollars" (106). But apparently, the Shangri-Las only received living expenses: " 'It was like being drafted,' " one of the musicians who backed the Shangri-Las on tour later recalled, " 'We were altogether in the same boat, so we made the best of it. We never really thought about money—we did it for the fun and innocence and love of art' " (108).

The good-natured, fervently emotional camaraderie of the records of these groups stands out when contrasted with the calculated dreck that dominated the airwaves in the early 1960s. While it may be a cliche to claim that rock 'n' roll "died" in the period after Elvis got drafted, Buddy Holly died, Chuck Berry went to jail, Little Richard found the Lord, and Jerry Lee Lewis married his cousin, a review of the pop music charts before the Beatles arrived is undeniably an odious task. In 1963, the number-one selling popular song was the tepid "Sugar Shack" by an aggregate calling itself "Jimmy Gilmer and the Fireballs," featuring a vocal so flat and pedestrian that it becomes spooky upon repeated listenings. Other number—one records of 1963 were "Go Away Little Girl" by Steve Lawrence of "Steve and Eydie" fame, "Hey Paula" by Paul and Paula (which, admittedly, has a certain ethereal charm), the bondage—advocating "I Will Follow Him" by Little Peggy March, "Blue Velvet" by Bobby Vinton, "Dominique" by the Singing Nun, and "If You Wanna Be Happy" by the wrongly named Jimmy Soul (*Rolling Stone Almanac* 76-81). Do not let the innocuous title of the latter record fool you; the chorus went, "If you wanna be happy for the rest of your life/Never make a pretty woman your wife/From my personal point of view/Get an ugly girl to marry you."

Popular music of the early 1960s thus seems to exemplify perfectly what Theodor Adorno calls "the culture industry." In an infamous passage, Adorno excoriates Tin Pan Alley's product, or "jazz," as he calls it:

The subject which expresses itself expresses precisely this: I am nothing, I am filth, no matter what they do to me, it serves me right....Art is permitted to survive only if it renounces the right to be different....Nothing may exist which is not like the world as it is. Jazz is the false liquidation of art—instead of utopia becoming reality, it disappears from the picture. (132)

In Adorno's view, music produced by the mass culture industry directly reflects hegemonic interests. Such music invades the subject's consciousness, filling it with, at best, white noise, and, at worst, jingoistic thought patterns, so that not only the subject's body but also his or her mind, falls unprovisionally under capital's sway.

Adorno's profoundly pessimistic view of mass culture is now denounced almost ritualistically by Left cultural critics for being "undialectical," but his theoretical framework outlines quite well the soporific commercialized consciousness purveyed on the airwaves in the early 1960s. This music was designed to comfort, not confront; to fit into the background of a subject's life, framing the subject's perception of the everyday world and integrating that perception with the ideologies of common sense—"nothing may exist which is not like the world as it is."

Girl Group records were at first dismissed in the years after they were made as product indistinguishable from capitalist hegemony by a nascent rock critical establishment still immersed in the "revolutionary"—i.e. formalist—aesthetics of the late 1960s rock music scene. This position lost its hegemony with the passing of the urgency of privileging such music; when the counterculture died, it was no longer necessary to characterize all rock 'n' roll up to 1967 as teenage manipulation. Since that time, Girl Group music has usually been celebrated as an expression of joyous innocence and naive desire that the United States supposedly started losing around the time of Kennedy's assassination. At best, the Girl Group sound is represented as being "proto-feminist" in the vaguest of terms. For instance, Greil Marcus, in his aforementioned essay on the Girl Groups, suggests that these singers, who were so dependent on their producers and their record companies, derived some of the power many hear in their music from "the struggle...of the singer—a young girl, black, likely as not—against the domination of her white male producer" (160). He goes on to add that "still, it was a music of celebration—of simple joy, of innocence, of sex, of life itself..." (160), a utopian music: "That the crassest conditions the recording industry has been able to contrive led to an emotionally rich music is a good chapter in a thesis on Art and Capitalism, but it happened" (161). But how did it happen? I would like to account for the Girl Group sound in some more substantial way.

Unfortunately, that way cannot lead along the methodological path Dick Hebdige sketches out in his influential *Subculture: The Meaning of Style. Subculture*, while unquestionably one of the most sophisticated recent attempts to account for pop music's effects in current theoretical terms, cannot "see" the dialectical nature of music not overtly "subversive." In a position suggestively reminiscent of the aforementioned late 60s position and also interestingly congruent with Adorno's privileging of high modernist art, Hebdige defines subversive music as formally innovative music linked to distinct subcultural style. Pop music without "experimental" credentials and without a subculture attached to it is product indistinguishable from capitalist hegemony. A modernist/post-modernist accounting that ultimately relies on a theory of the avante-garde does not do very well when faced with a product like the Girl Groups; or rather, the Girl Groups do not do very well when faced with it. The older language of rock criticism as represented here by Geil Marcus offers, through its "appreciations" of popular music, a better entrance into the dialectics of cultural artifacts seemingly at one with the Adornian "culture industry" than Hebdigean style analysis.

We can perhaps find an entryway into the contradictions of Girl group music through the work of Phil Spector, commonly acknowledged as the dominant producer in the genre, because his work's bombastic exaggeration stretches those contradictions to their breaking point. Spector's productions are instantly recognizable due to his distinctive use of a technique he called the "Wall of Sound." From "Da Doo Ron Ron" in 1962 (where he hit his stride) to "River Deep, Mountain High" in 1966, all of his work was characterized by a massive, literally unfathomable concatenation of instruments piled one on the other; no instrument was ever individually distinct if Spector could help it. Spector once described this baroque method as the creation of "little symphonies for the kids." And like a symphony composer, he spent hundreds of hours in the studio arranging and perfecting the sound of each release.

"Walking in the Rain," by the Ronnettes, three black women whom Spector discovered singing as amateurs in a New York City high school, exemplifies his approach. The song begins with a peal of thunder, followed by the sound of rain falling. The Ronnettes come in behind the rain with a gentle refrain of nonsense syllables—"Doo Doo Doo Doo Doo Doo." Also introduced is an insistent organ note banged over and over again. Then another roll of thunder and Veronica Bennett begins her lead vocal: "I want him and I need him, and someday—whoa—oh—oh—I'll meet him." As with most Girl Group music, the song will speak of The Boy—in this case, The Boy who will love walking in the rain. Behind the Ronnettes' voices, the thunder and rain continue, along with drums and bells and maybe a clavichord—after the first thirty seconds it becomes difficult if not impossible to tell what instruments are being used in the song. Spector commonly had as many as forty musicians playing on a cut, with perhaps four people playing the same guitar part and three people playing the drum part and so on.

The critic Ed Ward explains Phil Spector's productions as "thousands of instruments and singers labor[ing] together for the common good" (240), suggesting an evocation of socialism as the basis for the utopia he hears in the song. However, the objective position of Spector belies the notion; as Jim Miller says, he "was free to create his own utopia of love, dance, and fun in a world where he was in complete control" (47). The possessive is the key here. This utopia is of Spector's devising and for Spector's desires, at least in Spector's own conception of it. What Spector did brilliantly, I think, was not to create an illusory paradise in the self-contained world of pop music; he did not create a space where, as Adorno says, "nothing may exist which is not like the world as it is." In that case, Spector's music could not be distinguished from the bland radio fare that often surrounded it. No, what Spector did was set up a tension between the most overblown, exaggerated, almost parodic version of the culture industry's music possible—his "Wall of Sound"—and the lonely voices which pierce its layers.

For example, "Walking in the Rain" took Spector hundreds of hours of studio work to assemble, but the Ronnette's vocal was apparently the result of only one take (Miller 45) and the freshness and clarity of their performance contrasts strongly with the listener's experience of the Wall of Sound. Jim Miller again: "Each time I listen, I scan the backdrop of instruments, hoping to throw into relief what by design is only dimly perceived. . ."(46). This sound is the noise of capitalism, that nagging Muzak that nags until you accede to its crude seduction, but that grants you the luxury of acceding without being cognizant of the process. In fact, in "Walking in the Rain," even the natural world becomes incorporated into this Muzak in a staggeringly blunt manner—one can only wonder at the grandiose literalness of a mind compelled to add the sound of rain to a song of rain. This sound is both an enforcement and an exposure of "the world as it is;" an enforcement, because it lends empirical evidence to the listener's experience of the "Wall of Sound" as a natural entity, but an exposure because, at the same time, the sound of ersatz thunder and rain remind the listener that this sound is just a shoddy and contrived imitation of a "natural experience."

Against the "Wall of Sound" are poised the voices of the Ronnettes. Two members of the group sing a backup refrain of nonsense syllables throughout "Walking in the Rain," humming a lullaby of incoherence in opposition to the covertly totalitarian noise that surrounds them. Outside of the noise of Spector's machine, the singer's lullaby restores, in its inchoate preverbalness, a sense of infantile pleasure. On this murmured mantra of free space, Veronica Bennett builds with the imperfect instrument that is her voice. Apparently one of the reasons that Spector considered the Ronnettes his favorite group was the quality he heard in Bennett's voice. The sound is thin, even when she is well within her limited range. And when she ventures toward her upper register, she invariably wobbles around the notes she tries to hit. The cracks in her voice only serve to further emphasize the contrast between the Ronnette's transparently flawed spontaneity and the perfect and perfectly opaque "symphony" around them.

If the Ronnette's represent the highwater mark of the Girl Group music, the Shangri-Las represent its ebb tide. In their work, the form plays itself out—there is no place left for the music to go after this group exposes the limitations of Girl Group ideology. Unlike most other Girl Group music, the Shangri-Las trademark was a (for a time) gritty social realism set within an odd musical mix of rock 'n' roll beats, ersatz strings, and sound effects—"little soap operas for kids," as Ed Ward paraphrases Spector's famous formulation (243). Songs like "Leader of the Pack," "Remember (Walking in the Sand)," "I Can Never Go Home Anymore," and "Out in the Streets," told little fables addressing the travails of teenage girls. And unlike earlier

Girl Group songs, these stories began sometime after the boy has been captured—which of course was where the real problems began. As the name "Shangri-La" may ironically imply, this music desconstructed the consummnated paradise that most Girl Group music yearned for, locating only disillusionment behind the utopian facade.

The original Shangri-Las were four white working-class teenage girls who met at Andrew Jackson High School in Queens and began singing together. Their eventual producer, George "Shadow" Morton, discovered them singing at amateur events in and around Queens and decided they were right for the kind of productions he had in mind. He added to their distinctively nasal harmonies a soap opera style music, replete with string arrangements and sound effects. Morton got Jeff Barry and Ellie Greenwich to write songs tailored for the group. The songwriters worked closely with the Shangri-Las. The middle-class Barry and Greenwich had some trouble with the group, as Greenwich recalls:

The girls were a very nice bunch of street urchins I called them...At the beginning we did not get along—they were kind of crude and having to deal with them on a daily basis used to get me very uptight—with their gestures, and language, and chewing the gum, and the stockings ripped up their leg. We would say 'Not nice, you must be ladies,' and they would say, 'We don't want to be ladies...'. (Betrock 102-03).

Like the Ronnettes, the Shangri-Las were plucked out of high school to be molded into puppets acting out the designs of their betters.

"Out in the Streets," the Shangri-Las' fourth single, was written by Barry and Greenwich and tells the story of a woman who has made her "Boy" unhappy through domesticity. The Shangri-Las deliver a tough, impassioned vocal in their distinctive Queens accents. Shadow Morton adds a spooky, echoing quality to the mix, with sombre bell-like sounds and a soaring string section for the chorus. Mary Weiss, the lead vocalist, sings of the charge in her boy since he left his life in the streets; his kisses tell her that "something's died" because his heart is still "out in the street." The narrator then identifies this change—"He grew up running free/ He grew up—and then he met me." The end result of the desire for The Boy is the chain of domesticity.

Not only the lyrics, but also the music helps create this pessimism. Unlike Spector, who worked in his instrumentation against the utopian impulses expressed in the female voices he used, Morton complements the dystopian lyrics of the Shangri-Las; Spector, in "Walking in the Rain," is careful to set Veronica Bennett's thin voice against a veritable mountain of sound, but Morton makes "Out in the Streets" sound empty, using a drum, strings, and bells sparingly in an echoing mix. The Ronnettes' voices support Bennett in her fragile desire with a constantly repeated nonsense chorus, but the Shangri-Las' voices support Weiss by adding their despair to hers—interweaving and repeating the chorus line, "His heart is out in the street," to add emphasis and unity to Weiss's perceptions. We can see here how the communal nature of the Girl Group form—that is, the vision of community possibly engendered by the sound of a group harmonizing—is "neutral" in a certain sense. While it indeed enforces an impression of solidarity in the listener, this impression can be turned to more than one end. In other words, I think that it would be misguided to claim that Girl Group harmonizing unproblematically evokes a communal utopia; while it may be that this evocation is always one of its functions, the solidarity of such harmonizing also serves, at least in the Shangri-Las music, to underscore the speaker's hopelessness. The culture industry does its work again, confirming that nothing can change "the world as it is."

The thematic of "Out in the Streets"—girl meets boy and things fall apart—represents the last gasp of the Girl Group genre because, having reached this point in its exploitation of the psyche and culture of the early to mid-60s American female teenager, the form has exhausted the possibilities available to its discourse. The narrator has posed the question in a way that allows no chance of happiness for her—she must sacrifice herself for the happiness of her man. Not only does "The Boy" in the song see her as captor, she sees herself that way.

The Shangri-Las' realization and subsequent deconstruction of the utopian desires that fuel Girl Group music indicates the reason that most Girl Group songs never obtain "The Boy." To attain "The Boy" is to attain marriage and family, which returns the singer to the oppression she desires to escape. The insistence on the joy of desire only serves to underscore the hopelessness of the singer's objective situation. The limited parameters of working class life belie any but the most utopian of yearnings. The beauty of unlimited desire is its always contradictory appearance in a barren field, for, of course, a utopian desire can never by definition be fulfilled.

The pure and aching desire heard in this music delineates not simply innocence, but despair; you might as well imagine paradise if all you can do is imagine. The limited progression of the Self in Girl Group music goes like this: family to adolescent longing to family again. There is only one pathetically brief instant of freedom—that moment in adolescence when the girl locates her Self in relation to the Other in the person of the Boy, but before she says "yes" to that Other. To say "yes" in Girl Group music is to fall out of the free space of utopia into real social structure and, thus, into the mundane reality of working class life. The pleasure of Girl Group music is purified because it is so brief—the trajectories of these women's lives allows little time for free play.

I would like to conclude with a song that in many ways epitomizes the Girl Group sound. The record, entitled "Party Lights," was issued by a small company called Chancellor Records in May, 1962, and it eventually rose to number five on the Billboard charts. The performer was an unknown by the name of Claudine Clark, a young black woman from Macon, Georgia who virtually disappeared from pop music's annals after making this one record (Betrock 78). "Party Lights" tells the story of a teenage girl whose mother will not allow her to attend a party: "Everybody in the crowd is there," sings Clark, "But you won't let me make the scene." The narrator never does get to do more than watch the multi-colored party lights from her window; the closest she comes to a liberatory moment is her wailing entreaty "C'mon Mama!" after the second verse, echoed by an impassioned King Curtis style saxophone break.

We can read the adolescent's conflict with her mother as a ploy on the culture industry's part to both manufacture and exploit the concerns of the teenage market, a ploy which will generate its own dialectical response later on, when the same teenagers take themselves far more seriously as a cohesive group than capitalism ever intended. In 1962, however, this development has not yet unfolded; we are left, in "Party Lights" with "simple" desire. We cannot go to the party or even see it, necessarily; we can only view the lights that refer to it and imagine what will be there. "They're doing the Twist, the Bop, the Mashed Potato, too/ And I'm here looking like you," the narrator sings to her mother, presaging the day when she will always "look" (in both senses of the word) like a wife and parent. For now, the singer at least has something to desire, even if she cannot see or experience that thing.

While I am willing to agree with Adorno that some of the music business's product is more or less pablum for the populace (although it is not always clear that the populace accepts such pablum in the spirit intended), I think it should be possible to distinguish certain mass cultural products from capitalist hegemony not necessarily on the grounds of their formal innovation, but through complicating their historical positions. The Girl Group sound's utopia turns out to be a libidinal expression at odds with the totalizing forces that seek to contain its implicit critique. The Girl Groups hold up the mirror to see not "the world as it is" but rather, the world as it would be if. . .

Works Cited

Adorno, Theodor. *Prisms*. Cambridge: MIT Press, 1967.

Betrock, Alan. *Girl Groups: The Story of a Sound*. New York: Delilah, 1982.

Clark, Claudine. "Party Lights." *Wonder Women, Volume One*. Rhino Records 55.

Hebdige, Dick. *Subculture: The Meaning of Style*. New York: Methuen, 1979.

Marcus, Greil. "The Girl Groups."*Rolling Stone Illustrated History of Rock and Roll*. Ed. Jim Miller. 2nd ed. New York: Random House, 1980: 160-161.

Miller, Jim. "The Fabulous Ronnettes Featuring Veronica." *Stranded*. Ed. Greil Marcus. New York: Knopf, 1979: 40-48.

Rolling Stone editors. *Rolling Stone Rock Almanac*. New York: Collier Books, 1983.

Ronnettes, The. *The Fabulous Ronnettes*. Phil Spector International, Super 2307-3.

Shangri-Las, The. *Golden Hits of the Shangri-Las*. Phillips, 6336-215.

Shaw, Greg. "Brill Building Pop." *Rolling Stone Illustrated History of Rock and Roll*. Ed. Jim Miller. 2nd ed. New York: Random House, 1980: 120-127.

Spector, Phil. *Phil Spector's Top Twenty*. Phil Spector International, 2301-13.

Ward, Ed. "The Fifties and Before." *Rock of Ages*. New York: Summit Books, 1986: 17-246.

Forbidden Fruits and Unholy Lusts:
Illicit Sex in Black American Literature

Sandra Y. Govan

Contrary to current popular opinion, neither Alice Walker nor Gloria Naylor "started it." The pronoun refers to the public presentation or disclosure of sexual deviancy, sexual promiscuity, illicit sexual activity, or violent and unlicensed sexual misconduct within Black American communities. Neither Walker nor Naylor originated a new motif; they cannot be charged with being the first to present to the reading public disclosures of sexual deviancy or unsanctioned sexual activity. They are simply part of a tradition, albeit one we have overlooked in discomfort, choosen to ignore, or denied in blind self-righteousness.

An examination of early texts in the canon clearly shows that "unholy lust" is not an uncommon theme and that the idea of unsanctioned sex, frequently but not always in a master/slave or black/white context, is part and parcel of these early texts and permeates the tradition. Not only is this a recurrent pattern apparent in the 19th century, it doesn't require a particularly erotic imagination to note this same pattern appearing both explicitly and implicitly in modern and contemporary texts. No longer veiled behind the delicate, careful, polite Victorian prose of our foremothers and forefathers, illicit sex or tabooed sexual desire is out of the closet and into the streets—or into the printed page—in all its vivid possibilities. At any rate, that is the premise of this essay which sprang, to be candid, from the query of a student who wanted to know whether the "weird sex" she was then reading was a theme in Black literature.[1]

Those of us who teach the slave narrative regularly focus on the narratives of Frederick Douglas and Linda Brent as representative texts. Typically, teachers discuss the ways in which these narratives conform to the identifiable patterns of Black autobiography,[2] we may talk about the various "authenticating strategies" in the text,[3] or the rhetorical power of each text. Some of us may even discuss gender difference in male and female narrative strategy. What we seldom discuss in detail is the sexual erotica of both texts. To be sure, we note the "birth" of the "mulatto class" and we allude to the forced sexual liaisons between master and slave woman, but I doubt that many teachers really focus on the sexual tension in these works.

Recall, for instance, Douglass' 1845 *Narrative*. Reread the early segment when he describes his initiation into slavery, an identifiable archetypal motif wherein the slave narrator shares his abrupt realization of his slave status. He was a child; he had previously lived with his grandmother on the outskirts of the plantation; he had never witnessed a beating. What he "witnessed" was Captain Anthony's punishment of his Aunt Hester for the crime of being "found in the company of Lloyd's Ned," a slave of another plantation. Had his Master, Douglas expounded, "been a man of pure morals himself, he might have been thought interested in protecting the innocence of my aunt; but those who knew him will not suspect him of any such virtue" (52). Because Douglas couched his observations in ironic understatement, many readers may not recognize that Captain Anthony was also a jealous sadist. He would take Aunt Hester, tie her semi-nude to a joist with her arms above her head, and "whip upon her naked back till she was literally covered with blood" (51). Douglass says that Anthony "at times seem[ed] to take great pleasure" in these whippings; no tears, words, or prayers "from his gory victim" deterred him. Note that the following description is an almost textbook example of sadomasochism:

The louder she screamed, the harder he whipped; and where the blood ran fastest, there he whipped longest. He would whip her to make her scream, and whip her to make her hush; and not until overcome by fatigue, would he cease to swing the blood-clotted cowskin. (51)

Two quick observations. First, Anthony clearly enjoys his task. As his whip is curling about the naked flesh of Hester, ripping into her tender breasts as well as scoring her "naked back," his "fatigue" or exhaustion comes as much from sexual release as it does from physical exertion. Secondly, Aunt Hester either loved pain or loved Lloyd's Ned entirely too much for Douglass claims he "often" heard her "heart-rending shrieks" at the dawn of day. It seems a clear cut case of a white man who wants "his own" black woman getting bested, sexually, by a black man while the black woman "love" object suffers because of their lust.

Turning to Brent's *Incidents in the Life of a Slave Girl* (1861), we find a stronger emphasis on "licentiousness," on the "corruption" of young slave girls by white men, on the "foul wrongs" endured by slave women "begetting," if you will, mulatto children by white fathers. Black girls are "violated" with impunity and those who, like Brent, tried desperately to hold to the ideals of the "cult of true womanhood" (wherein women maintain their piety, purity, morality, virtue & chastity, and yet remain "submissive and domestic")[4] had an uphill struggle against the "licentiousness and fear" rampant in an atmosphere of "all—pervading corruption" produced by slavery (51). Brent approaches what she and her 19th century audience considered the indelicate topic of perverse lust with all the delicacy she could manage. Slave women have their "purity" violated; the word "rape" is never mentioned. Occasionally, these women are bribed or tempted with presents;

should these methods fail, the lash or starvation can follow. In any event, they mostly live in a "cage of obscene birds" and their "submission" is compelled (52-53).

Apart, however, from detailing the travails of the slave woman, Brent expends tremendous energy detailing how slavery—sexual profligacy in slavery—dramatically affects not only slaves but whites as well. White wives are often embittered and crippled by jealousy, their normal humanity stripped from them by the continual affrontery of recognizing but being unable to acknowledge the bastard children of their husbands. White children of slaveholding families are also affected. "The slaveholder's sons are, of course, vitiated, even while boys, by the unclean influences everywhere around them. Nor do the master's daughters escape" (52). Brent reveals how one such daughter had "selected one of the meanest slaves" on the plantation to father her father's first grandchild. This is not love but lust, illicit sexual conduct, unlicensed and unbridled sexuality deriving from pure power relationships and not from genuine human feeling.

When Brent, at age fifteen, yields to the flattering attentions of a white "lover" (the black man who had courted her had been driven away by her master), and bears his child, she does so solely because she wants some control of her sexual identity. Mr. Sands is not her master and he is not married, significant virtues in a situation with few redeeming options. He was also an educated "gentleman" and thus even more "agreeable to the pride and feelings of a slave, if her miserable situation has left her any pride or sentiment." It seemed to Brent "less degrading to give one's self than to submit to compulsion." "There [was]," she felt, "something akin to freedom in having a lover who has no control over you, except that which he gains by kindness and attachment" (55). Brent also recognized that she was violating moral codes sanctioned by her family and her Christian beliefs. She asks her "virtuous reader[s]" for pardon, explaining that they simply did not know "what it is to be a slave; to be entirely unprotected by law or custom" (56). While she knew she "did wrong," and felt her loss of virtue intensely, she also felt "that the slave woman ought not to be judged by the same standard as others" because of the conditions of chattel slavery (56). Such conditions make possible some incredible moral paradoxes. Brent describes several but like Douglass, she points unflinchingly to the hypocrisy shadowing southern religiousity. "If a pastor has offspring by a woman not his wife, the church dismiss him, if she is a white woman; but if she is colored, it does not hinder his continuing to be their good sheperd" (77).

Early Afro-American novelists, borrowing liberally from slave narratives to construct their plots, depict scenes from slave life, and expound upon themes they thought the public needed to hear. Such novelists also made a point of indicting sexual immorality in the American South. In every version of *Clotel* (1853),[5] whose protagonist is alleged at first to be the slave offspring of Thomas Jefferson, William Wells Brown treats not only the "tragic mulatto" as character and the unplanned creation of a whole "new race" in America, but also levels his finger at the social and moral consequences of unrestrained lust. In the novels, "beautiful" quadroon and mulatto women are "revered" and "loved" by their white suitors/masters. They are given homes in delicate bowers apart from the real world where they have an almost ideal near-marital relationship. Then, by social dictate, the white lover marries a white woman, his race and caste; his cast aside black lover begins to suffer in earnest. Often these women are readmitted to slavery at the meanest levels because of the jealousy of a white wife or mother-in-law who discovers the unlicensed, though accepted and supported by the white patriarchy, sexual liaison. The husband/lover wants it all—his white wife and his black/quadroon lover. Brown argues that he cannot have it all without paying a terrible price. His marriage is destroyed by an absence of trust and his black family is sold away before his eyes. Because of his "sensitivity," this pivotal player in an American tragedy may be consumed by guilt and by failure to act on his conscience. This scenario occurs in Brown's fictitious recreation of slavery because he strives to touch any responsive chord in a largely white audience. However, neither the Douglass nor Brent narratives showed many white males who suffered as severely as Brown's white men; nor did Brown dwell on the feelings of these men. Rather, he emphasized what became of the women and children the men betrayed.

Frances Harper's *Iola LeRoy* (1893) and Pauline Hopkin's *Contending Forces* (1900) focus more on "uplifting the race" after Reconstruction, but both novels also take an obligatory swipe at unsanctioned illicit sex and consequent immorality that results. Harper's protagonist, Iola, is the quintessential lovely quadroon who only discovers upon the death of her white father that she is legally a slave. Naturally, she is sold at auction by mean-spirited relatives and spends the early part of the novel fending off, as best she can, all insults to her womanhood. Iola's case strongly resembles that made for Clotel/Isabella in the *Clotel* saga. While Harper does not repeat Brown's dictim, both authors use the slave auction to illustrate how the "parts" of a beautiful mulatto were packaged. What follows is Brown's description of the evaluation of slave women "...the bones, sinews, blood, and nerves of a young girl of eighteen were sold for $500; her moral character for $200; her superior intellect for $100; a warranty of her devoted Christianity for $300; her ability to make a good prayer for $200; and *her chastity for $700 more*" (*Clotelle*, 9).[6] That Iola is not "violated," with a subsequent loss of her virtue, is only because the Civil War intervenes. Through the timely intercession of a slave benefactor, who has himself escaped from the plantation to Union lines, Iola is rescued from the foul and odious clutches of her newest master to spend the rest of the war safely as a nurse for the Union army.

In *Contending Forces*, the plot is more ingenious, or more contrived, depending on perspective. A base white man covets his new neighbor's wife. It doesn't help that the neighbor, Charles Montfort, has recently arrived from the West Indies with plans to gradually free his slaves. The "bad" and jealous neighbor, Anson Pollack, decides Grace Montfort has too much color to her cheek and her dark hair is a trifle too curly—the tell-tale taint of black blood. He contrives to have Montfort killed and to take Grace to satisfy his lust. His nefarious scheme succeeds up to a point—Montfort dies but Grace kills herself before she can be ravished. Their children, however, are sold away and the rest of the convoluted plot follows them. Of consequence to my argument is that the "colored" descendants of both Pollack and Montfort meet years later, and, surprise, villany is inherited in the genes. John Langley, the son of a bastard black child fathered by Pollack, plans to marry the sister of his best friend, while also attempting to seduce and make his mistress, by blackmail, her best friend Sappho, who is engaged to his best friend. The friend and fiancee are Will and Dora Smith, the grandchildren of the Montforts. In a reversal of the typical "bad" or tainted black blood, it is Langley's villainous white blood which drives him to entertain these ideas of illicit sexual relationships. Ultimately, he pays for his perfidy with his life, something that never happened in the narratives or to white suitors of black women.

Contemporary historical novels that look at slavery and Reconstruction do so with all the verve available to the modern novelists. Themes and plot lines implicitly suggested or delicately alluded to in early texts are today treated with forthright dispatch. Sherley Anne Williams' *Dessa Rose* (1986) for instance, explicitly describes in one segment the forbidden liaisons between slave men and white women. When asked what he did as a slave, Nathan says succinctly, "loved pretty white womens like" Rufel, the lonely white reluctant benefactor who has given sanctuary to escaped slaves. Just before he confidently makes love to her, he describes vividly his initiation into various forms of sex by "Miz Lorraine"-a single, older, white woman with a "wild nature" who took her "belly warmers from among the lowest of the low" (168-169). "Freakish" Miz Lorraine trained her young slave lovers, teaching them about the joys of oral copulation and terrors of making love, with death ever close at hand, to a white woman, truly forbidden fruit. If a slave sex partner ever initiated sexual activity, if she ever lost the feel of control, the slave could be sold or worse; Miz. Lorraine, who swore each "lover" to silence, could scream rape.

Octavia Butler's *Kindred* (1979), is a grim fantasy wherein science fiction mediates upon black history. It proceeds from the premise of a modern woman pulled back and forth across time and space to emerge periodically in 1830s Maryland and the origins of her family line. Dana Franklin and Alice, her great great forebearer several times removed are the proverbial flip sides of the same coin. Dana must help mother, nurture, teach, and raise young Rufus Weylin, the white child later destined to become the male progenitor of her family tree because of his forced attentions to Alice. (This relationship is another one of those black man/white man/black woman triangles; Alice has a black lover. Jean Toomer also plays with the loaded triangle through Louisa's story in *Cane* [1923]). In any event, when Alice dies, Rufus, intellectually attracted to Dana, now expects from her not only intellectual stimulation but the same sexual intimacy he demanded and coerced from

Alice. And this from a woman who had been his surrogate mother!! Talk about Oedipal complexes and perverted urges—Rufus did hate his father and tried like hell to seduce Dana.

Morrison's *Beloved* (1987) gives us insight into what destroyed the relationship between Sethe and Halle, her slave husband. It seems that shortly before the family and some selected others made their escape attempt, Sethe is attacked and Halle must watch the sexual humiliation and desecration of his wife from a hiding place as two young white men attack her, suckling her breast as if she were an animal, stealing her milk while their school teacher uncle merely observes. Though pregnant, Sethe is whipped with a cowhide. But Paul D. also has a tale of sexual perversion to relate. While a prisoner chained with forty-six other slaves, Paul D and the others are forced to perform oral copulation, as "breakfast," on the white men who guard them. Those who rebelled, died. "Occasionally, a kneeling man chose gunshot in his head as the price, maybe, of taking a bit of foreskin with him to Jesus" (108). And before *Beloved* there was Cholly Breedlove's "tender" drunken rape of his daughter Pecola in *The Bluest Eye* (1972).

Black autobiography is another genre where illicit sex is illustrated. That, however, is another discussion. Suffice it to say that Langston Hughes' *Big Sea* (1940), while virtually ignoring his own sexuality and sexual experiences, quickly sketches the plight of two young African prostitutes who become victims of a gang rape or "gang bang." For all their "service" or "labor," these two women are never paid, just used by the crew in the hold of the steamship. And then there's Maya Angelou's *Caged Bird* (1970). Here, you recall, Maya remains silent for four years following her rape, at eight years old, by the boyfriend of her mother. Later, as a teenager she thinks herself some kind of abnormal sexual freak and so solicits a sexual relationship with a young man just to prove to herself that there is "nothing wrong" with her.

Returning to fiction, I could also mention James Baldwin and the sexual tension that animates his works. At fifteen, I first read *Another Country* (1962), almost solely for the titilation factor (the Chicago Public school system had debated banning the book for its "sex and violence" so naturally...). I found the violent and sordid "love" story of Rufus and Leona—a black man and southern white woman—both compelling and vivid; soon the whole novel, complex though it was, had my undivided attention. But Baldwin hooked me first with his tale of illicit sex. In other works, few readers can ignore the rape and sexual degradation of Deborah, Gabriel's first wife, or miss the suggestion of homosexual erotica that connects young John Grimes to Elisha in *Go Tell it on the Mountain* (1953); and incest is part of the text of *Just Above My Head* (1979).

There is, of course, more than a suggestion of dangerous sexual energy in Wright's *Native Son* (1940). Bigger Thomas murders Mary Dalton purely because he fears being caught with forbidden fruit in his hands. Quite literally, he has been carrying a drunken Mary in his arms and becomes sexually stimulated by the feel of her lips against his, the scent of her hair and skin, and the feel of her breasts in his hands (83-84). What Wright calls "hysterical terror" seizes him when blind Mrs. Dalton enters the room and we all know what happens next. Later, to protect his secret, Bigger kills Bessie, his black girlfriend. But before he kills her, to relieve his own tension and because of "insistent and demanding" desire, he forces an "inert, unresisting" Bessie into the position for intercourse. Then, despite her urgent pleas for him to stop, he proceeds to yield to the demands of his body and his needs, and riding "roughshod over her whimpering protests," he rapes her (218-19). Here again we're told that fear drives Bigger but there is an ironic juxtaposition between the little death of sexual copulation and the big one of Bessie's murder.

Wright's *Eight Men* (1961) contains two stories where sexual tension is the dominant element of the story. "The Man Who Killed a Shadow" focuses on two ordinarily insignificant characters—Saul, a black male in his thirties and married, and a nameless, single, forty-year-old white librarian. In the larger scheme of things, neither is an important character in their respective world and both are deemed "shadows." The white woman is a stereotype personified, a sexless nonentity, a white shadow. However, she apparently sees Wright's male protagonist as a way of ending her virginity. Saul is a janitor who does his work thoroughly. The librarian, for no obvious reason, complains to his boss that he has not cleaned under her desk. Shortly thereafter, she demands that Saul come and look under her desk, as if to see what he has not cleaned. When Saul looks, he is shocked. "His mind protested against what his eyes saw, and then his senses leaped in wonder. She was sitting with her knees sprawled apart and her dress was drawn halfway up her legs...her white legs whose thighs thickened as they went to a V clothed in tight, sheer pink panties..." (163). Her sexual overtures, coded as they are by race and caste, drive Saul to "protect himself" by preventing any further intimation of sexual energy from her. Ironically, she dies still a virgin.

The second story, "Man of All Work," is by contrast almost funny although, as usual, framed by Wright's grim humor. In this tale, an unemployed black husband, Carl, dons his sick wife's clothes to find work as a cook and housekeeper to earn money. What he encounters, apart from an observant child who notices immediately the physical differences between "Lucy" and Bertha, the former maid, is the kind of sexual harassment many black domestic workers endured while laboring in white houses. Mrs. David Fairchild knows that her husband has a penchant for young and attractive black maids. She calls her new maid into the bathroom to bathe her back while she discusses her husband's tendencies, warning the "maid" to "just push him away" should he "bother" her (111). The stifled sexual tension generated as our man-in-maid's clothing suffers through this bath would be hilarious, were it not for the implicit sexual/racial violence resonating through the scene. Later, Mr. Fairchild makes the predictable pass just as his wife returns for lunch. She gets her gun, resolves to shoot—not her husband but the maid!—and actually winds up hitting Wright's disguised hero. At this point, neither husband nor wife are as yet aware of the gender switch. I shall not reveal all; go and reread.

In *Invisible Man* (1952), Ralph Ellison goes beyond the suggestion of sexual tension to consummation of perverted unsanctioned sex. Consider the Trueblood/Norton episode. If you recall, Ellison's nameless black protagonist takes Mr. Norton, a wealthy white philanthropist for a ride. Norton asks him to stop at what seems to be a picturesque old fashioned cabin where he meets the sharecropper who resides there with his family, Jim Trueblood. His is the eerie case of a black father who, during a dream, commits incest upon his daughter, raping her, while his wife sleeps on the other side of the bed! This was the "weird sex" my student alluded to. Central to the tale is Norton's response to the story, one which the white villagers repeatedly encourage Jim Trueblood to tell. Norton, it seems, desires his own fair yet unattainable daughter, but must settle for the vicarious sexual satisfaction of hearing how Trueblood "did it." A clear cut case of unholy lust.

Having recounted telling episodes from some of the earlier works that inform the canon, I realize that I still have not gotten to most of contemporary women writers who stand accused of putting the dirty linen in the public's eye by speaking directly to issues of sexual violence, sexual abuse, abnormal or illicit sexual behavior. Nor have I talked about modern African-American male writers who also utilize perverse sexuality as an underlying element in their works. Consider, for example, the mysterious and erotic Minnie the Moocher from Ishmael Reed's *The Last Days of Louisiana Red* (1974). Reed satirically describes Minnie as a "strong, glamorous female...[or] a classical emotional vamp...." Minnie is "like the Black Widow spider that draws its prey, loves it, then drains it. Only she doesn't drain it physically, she drains it emotionally" (34, 36). There are also the tangled sexual relationships found in some of Ernest Gaines fiction—see *Catherine Carmier* (1964) for instance.

I've cited a few Toni Morrison novels but I have not yet discussed Ntzake Shange, Gayl Jones, Ann Allen Shockley, nor the women I began with, Gloria Naylor and Alice Walker. My belief is that closer examination of early texts within the canon and other modern texts by men and women writers should exonerate the accused and make the point sufficiently clear; literary treatment of illicit sex is neither a recent occurrence nor a contemporary by-product of the radical feminist movement. Nonetheless, since works by these authors have been decried for their depictions of shocking or abhorrent sexual tensions between men and women, most often indicted for presenting "negative images of black men," it follows that at least a cursory glance at some novels from the 1970s and 1980s is appropriate.

Anyone looking for heavily accentuated sexuality to undergird a tale— normal or abnormal, licensed or unlicensed sexuality—has only to look at Shange's *Colored Girls* (1975), Shockley's *Say Jesus and Come to Me* (1982), Gayle Jones' *Corregidora* (1975), and *Eva's Man* (1976), Walker's *The Third Life of Grange Copeland* (1970) or *The Color Purple* (1982), and some would say, Naylor's *The Women of Brewster Place* (1982). And unlike a thesis I once heard propounded at a conference, I do not think *Purple* is "as instructive as a how-to-sex manual" merely because Shug Avery explains clitoral function to Celie or because she teaches her to feel genuine orgasmic response, as opposed to feeling only as if someone had simply done "his business" on her (68). Nor is *Purple* the first time Walker flirted with the idea of incest, sexual violence, aberrant or abhorrent sexual conduct or child abuse in Black life. I would direct attention to the complex relationships of father and son, Grange and Brownfield Copeland, to the women in their lives—both to their martyred wives and to the mother and daughter pair of whores, Fat Josie and Lorene, whom both men have utilized.[7] I would also encourage a careful rereading of Walker's "The Child Who Favored Daughter" from *In Love and Trouble, Stories of Black Women* (1967).

"Daughter" resonates with overt yet parodoxically suppressed sexual energy. Curiously, the story is seldom discussed because of a palpable pain radiating from its core, pain so horrifying it makes most readers want to bury it deeply and ignore its message for how do we "explicate" in the face of such raw emotion? In an era where crimes of violence against women permeate the society how do we as teachers surmount the brutality to teach this tale as mere fiction? In the story, set in the South of the sixties, issues of race and caste are mixed together with the twin taboos of brother/sister-father/daughter incestuous urges and ugly family violence. The child who favors Daughter, the father's sister, is doomed in this tale because of twisted obsessive love. The nameless father, who has seen his beloved sister give herself to too many men including white men, attacks his only daughter for being a "replica." Not only has she taken a lover, that lover is white. A misogynist who has always anticipated "evil and deception" from women, the father has consequently mistreated all the women in his life, including his wife, fearing "imaginary overtures" from white men. He beats his child with a harness; then having brutally beaten her clothes half off and subsequently seen her half naked, he is consumed by "unnamable desire." Motivated by both lust and jealousy ("Jealousy is being nervous about something that has never, and probably won't ever, belong to you" [42]), he attacks his child, cuts her bare breasts from her chest and casts "what he finds in his hands" to the dogs (45).

In *For Colored Girls*, Ntozake Shange's choreopoem, several vignettes show the vagaries of male/female relationships shrouded in sexual feeling. The Lady in Red tells two poignant tales. The most striking is the dreadful saga of Beau Willie Brown who drops his child from a window as a twisted act of revenge against his wife; the second recounts the bittersweet story of a painted and perfumed woman who, almost immediately following intercourse with strange men she seduces, puts them out of her bed and her house, records her sexual exploits in a diary, and subsequently cries herself to sleep, alone. Initially, there were scathing reviews condemning *Colored Girls* wherein critics seldom looked at the ironies and paradoxes created by women themselves; instead, reviewers were outraged by the alleged savage treatment of black men. Few attempted to see any semblance of balance in Shange's presentation or to note the social pressures she sketched which, in part, affected the behavior of her "characters."

Ann Shockley's *Say Jesus* breaks precedent by presenting the taboo issue of lesbianism as the principal plot rather than subplot. Her protagonist, a charismatic female minister named Mrytle Black, is a well developed, emotionally complex and rounded character whose lovers are women. Apart from the issues of black and white feminists working together and of homophobia and strained male/female relationships, Shockley raises also ethical questions—just as male ministers occasionally stray by using the pulpit for sexual conquests, Mrytle uses her position to select sexual partners from among vulnerable members of various church congregations. Any minister caught violating the moral tenets of church and society would be subject censure. But, when the minister is lesbian, the risks in exposure are magnified because society condemns homosexuality as perversion.

Gayle Jones's, *Corregidora* and the second novel, *Eva's Man* present explicit, often violent sexual encounters. The family line of Ursa Corregidora originated because of the perverse lusts freely exercised by a Portuguese slave master. On his isolated plantation without regard to social sanction this man made his slaves prostitutes and committed incest upon their offspring. For generations, their story has been passed down because collective memory will not allow this part of history, painful though it is, to be forgotten or erased from record. And in *Eva's Man*, the psychosexual energy almost overwhelms. Eva Medina, narrating from her cell in the psychiatric prison, is there not just for killing a man but for castrating him, then wrapping his penis in a silk handkerchief and placing it back inside his trousers (117). As partial explanation for her psychotic rage which led to the bizzare murder, Jones treats frankly Eva's warped yet fundamentally typical sexual history, the psychologically and sometimes physically abusive sexual experiences which have tormented her since her childhood. Unquestionably, from Eva's current stifled sexual urges to the realistic flashbacks depicting her participation in sexual acts, violent, often demeaning expressions of sexuality *is* both text and subtext of the story.

Gloria Naylor currently has three major works to her credit. *Mama Day* (1988), utilizes the supernatural to frame the story of the power of love and lust to affect lives in Willow Springs. *Linden Hills* (1985) also makes some strong statements about lust and perverted love among the black middle class residents of the Linden Hills community. But it was *The Women of Brewster Place* (1982), those bruised blues women, that projected Naylor into the first tier of black contemporary writers. The vivid and brutal gang rape of Lorraine in the story "The Two" is one of the most chilling descriptions in literature. That the rapists "justify" their action on the ground that Lorraine is lesbian and has never known sex with a man adds to the horror.

Arthur P. Davis has argued that contemporary Black women writers (he cites Morrison, Walker, Shange, and Jones), have seemingly developed "anti-black male sentiments," or an "anti-male attitude" which he identifies as akin to a kind of "line" writing, similar to that adopted by writers adhering to a particular political "line" (4). He goes on to argue that this "new development" in Afro-American literature is not merely a "battle of the sexes" and that the portrayal of such "ugly Afro-Americans" is not simply the portrayal of "just [a] few sick individuals found in every society" but somehow "representative of present-day Afro-American men" (4). To his credit, Davis does not participate in a mindless villification of these women writers; instead, he returns to the canon in search of some possible reasons for the resentment women writers (and readers)[8] ostensibly feel. One possibility, he suggests, is the warped depictions of black women in the novels by black men— a subject few male critics examine.

Whether or not we are witnessing a literary "war between the sexes," the literary treatment of unsanctioned and illicit sex, is not, as I've indicated, new. Perhaps because the sexual violence in contemporary tales, especially those told by black women novelists, is particularly graphic and powerfully fixed in the imagination, we think of these writers as being the first to probe this area. But again, what we have is not so much a new tact as it is an "unapologetic foregrounding of the madness" which has marked our past and "infected" our present.[9] The specter of unholy lust, illicit sex, suppressed erotica, and unlicensed sexual violence, acknowledged or not, permeates both our history and, sadly, our society. That such themes recur in our literature should be recognized as necessary revelations, as psychological insight into individuals and the culture which produced and "sustains" them.

Notes

[1]The student was a freshman enrolled in UNC-Charlotte's University Transitional Opportunities Program (Summer 1988), a "bridge" program to aid incoming black students adjust to college work. Her observation about the Trueblood segment in *Invisible Man* forced me to try to place that episode within the context of canon. The ensuing class discussion led to this essay, originally presented in shorter form as a paper delivered before the 1988 Popular Culture Association national meeting.

[2]There are several recurring patterns in slave narratives. Among them are: loss of innocence, formal initiation into slavery, the quest for education, vivid recounting of everyday experience of slavery, pointed discussion of slaveholder's immorality and religious hypocrisy, an awareness of audience, the North as haven. Both slave narratives and black autobiography in general served a function as historical record, detailing the particular experience of American chattel slavery. The individual experience, though important, was subplanted by the necessity to relate the group experience. For further reading see John Blassigame's "Black Autobiographies as History and Literature," in *The Black Scholar* (Dec. 1973-Jan, 1974), 2-9; see also Stephen Butterfield's *Black Autobiography in America*. Amherst, Mass: University of Massachusetts Press, 1974.

[3]Robert B. Stepto argues that the documentation which often accompanied fugitive slave narratives, the prefaces, letters, afterwords, testimonials and such, served primarily as other "voices" which the slave narrators used to help authenticate their texts. He also contends that the appended documents "collectively create something close to a dialogue—of forms as well as voices"...illustrating "an eclective narrative form" (178). See "Narration, Authentication, and Authorial Control in Frederick Douglass'*Narrative of 1845*" in *Afro-American Literature: The Reconstruction of Instruction.* Eds. Dexter Fisher and Robert B. Stepto. New York: MLA 1979.

[4]"True Womanhood" was a behavioral proscription that upper class 19th century white women were supposed to follow in the early to mid-nineteenth century. As defined by Barbara Welter, its four "cardinal virtues" were "piety, purity, submissiveness and domesticity" (104). See "The Cult of True Womanhood, 1820-1860," in *Women and Womanhood in America.* Ed. Ronald W. Hogeland. Lexington, Mass: D.C. Heath, 1973.

[5]Brown wrote what might be called the "Clotel saga," revising the story of *Clotel* several times, each time removing his protagonist further from the politically damaging indictment that she was Thomas Jefferson's daughter. In the next version, *Clotelle*, his mulatto heroine's name becomes Isabella, some unnamed Senator's slave offspring; her daughter is Clotelle.

[6]A nearly identical descriptive passage appears in the original *Clotel*. Clotel stands on the auction block, her appearance creating a "sensation" for her "complexion [is] as white as most of those...waiting...to become her purchasers." Brown concludes the description of the auction with overt comment. "This was a Southern auction, at which the bones, muscles, sinew, blood, and nerves of a young lady of sixteen were sold for five hundred dollars; her moral character for two hundred; her improved intellect for one hundred; her Christianity for three hundred; and her chastity and virtue for four hundred dollars more" (42-43).

[7]In *The Third Life of Grange Copeland*, Grange saw Josie regularly, despite his marriage to Margaret. Brownfield, his son, "balls" both Josie and her daughter, Lorene.

[8]Several black women students in my Early Black American Literature class were annoyed, even outraged, by the constant emphasis on the light skinned beautiful tragic mulatto found in the works of Brown and Harper. They could not appreciate my "appeal to a white audience" argument; they felt betrayed by writers whom they saw caving in to stereotypic portrayal of dark skinned characters, particularly dark skinned women. And even though Harper presents a dark woman as a positive role model, the attention given Iola and her family dominates the text. Needless to say, the darker the student, the more keenly she felt the issue. White students in the class (this was a large, virtually half and half class) did not see the issue as an issue. Ironically, they identified with and sympathized with these heroines and could not feel the emotional weight of color bias.

[9]An observation by UNC-Chapel Hill professor Dr. Trudier Harris after reading an earlier draft of this essay.

Works Cited

Angelou, Maya. *I Know Why the Caged Bird Sings.* New York: Random House, 1970.

Baldwin, James. *Go Tell it on the Mountain.* New York: Knopf, 1953.

80   Sexual Politics and Popular Culture

———— *Just Above My Head.* New York: Dial, 1979.

Brent, Linda (Harriet James psyodum). *Incidents in the Life of a Slave Girl.* 1861. New York: HBJ, 1973.

Brown, William Wells. *Clotel, or the President's Daughter.* 1853. New York: MacMillan, 1970.

———— *Clotelle, or the Colored Heroine.* 1867. Miami, FL.: Mnemosyne, 1967.

Butler, Octavia. *Kindred.* Garden City, NJ.: Doubleday, 1979.

Butterfield, Stephen. *Black Autobiography in America.* Amherst, MA.: University of Massachusetts Press, 1974.

Davis, Arthur P. "The Black Woman Strikes Back: Background of the Anti-Male Attitude of Current Female Writers." *MAWA Review* 2 (June 1986):4-7.

Douglass, Frederick. *The Narrative of the Life of Frederick Douglass, An American Slave.* 1845. New York: Penguin, 1982.

Ellison, Ralph. *Invisible Man.* New York: Random House, 1952.

Gaines, Ernest. *Catherine Carmier.* 1964. San Francisco: North Point Press, 1981.

Harper, Frances E.W. *Iola LeRoy or the Shadows Uplifted.* 1893. New York: AMS Press, 1971.

Hopkins, Pauline E. *Contending Forces.* Boston: Colored Co-operative Publishing Co., 1900.

Hughes, Langston. *The Big Sea.* 1940. New York: Hill and Wang, 1968.

Jones, Gayl. *Corregidora.* New York: Random House, 1975.

———— *Eva's Man.* New York: Random House, 1976.

Morrison, Toni. *Beloved.* New York: Knopf, 1987.

Morrison, Toni. *The Bluest Eye.* New York: Holt, 1970.

Naylor, Gloria. *Mama Day.* New York: Tichnor and Fields, 1988.

———— *Linden Hills.* New York: Tichnor and Fields, 1985.

———— *,The Women of Brewster Place.* New York: Viking, 1982.

Reed, Ishmael. *The Last Days of Louisiana Red.* New York: Random House, 1974.

Shange, Ntozake. *For Colored Girls Who Have Considered Suicide When the Rainbow is Enuf.* New York: MacMillan, 1975.

Shockley, Ann. *Say Jesus and Come to Me.* New York: Avon, 1982.

Stepto, Robert B. "Narration, Authentication, and Authorial Control in Frederick Douglass' *Narrative* of 1845." *Afro-American Literature: The Reconstruction of Instruction.* Eds. Dexter Fisher and Robert Stepto. New York: MLA, 1979. 178—191.

Toomer, Jean. *Cane.* 1923. Liveright, 1975.

Walker, Alice. "The Child Who Favored Daughter." *In Love and Trouble: Stories of Black Women.* New York: Harcourt, 1967.

———— *The Color Purple.* New York, Harcourt, 1982.

———— *The Third Life of Grange Copeland.* New York: Harcourt, 1970.

Welter, Barbara. "The Cult of True Womanhood, 1820—1860." *Women and Womanhood in America.* Ed. Ronald W. Hogeland. Lexington, MA.: Heath, 1973. 103—113.

Williams, Sherley Anne. *Dessa Rose.* New York: William Morrow, 1986.

Wright, Richard. *Eight Men.* 1961. New York: Pyramid, 1969.

———— "The Man Who Killed a Sparrow" in *Eight Men.*

———— "Man of All Work" in *Eight Men.*

———— *Native Son.* 1940. New York: Harper, 1966.

As Her Hand Crept Slowly Up Her Thigh:
Ann Bannon and the Politics of Pulp

Suzanna Danuta Walters

Lesbian pulp novels are not typically the stuff of literary criticism, even in this time of post-structuralist anything goes. And the methodologies and theoretical approaches common to literary criticism—be it reception theory or ideology critique or even deconstruction—seem somehow inadequate or inappropriate to so marginalized and low-brow a cultural product. Typically, even cultural analysis that looks at this sort of popular culture does so with a language and technique that, while often insightful, serves to distance the reader from the "popular" content of the object. In other words, the potentially subversive stuff of popular culture is rendered abstract and safe through its aestheticization in high culture criticism.

The attempt here is not, of course, to discard criticism altogether but rather to re-position its relevance to the objects being analyzed. Too often feminist critics, in attempting to keep up with the newest in "post"-thought, lose sight of our own (feminist) insights about the relationship between theory and methodology: analyzing "objects" that come out of our own experience as women.

To understand the lesbian novels of Ann Bannon then, we must do more than randomly apply a critical method upon a text. Our critical method should, it seems to me, be developed to ask questions that are linked to the reality of these novels as part of *lesbian* culture. To instrumentally apply a method of analysis to a lesbian text without at the very least sensitizing that method to its lesbian object is to miss the point.

A sensitized and political method might experience these novels as expressive of the textures and tastes that comprise the lived experience of lesbians. For all their wild improbability, these novels are records, traces of an existence deeply submerged and suppressed. The radical sensuousness of these pulps mitigates against an analysis that imposes discrete formal categories on a subcultural artifact that cries out for indiscretion. I am making an argument, clearly, for an original reading of Bannon's books that is guided more by explicit feminist concerns than by a set of formalist codes.

That my political interpretation is guided by feminist concerns will be readily apparent in the pages to come. The themes of desire and sexuality are not arbitrary categories of analysis but rather derive from my own positioned—and political—reading as well as from the social context in which

81

Reprinted from *Social Text* with the permission of the author.

these novels were written as well as received. For a political interpretation means fundamentally that we contextualize all cultural production. Precisely because Bannon's novels are *lesbian* fiction with central and sexual *lesbian* characters makes them of interest in the context of a homophobic, patriarchal society—ours, as well as the '50s she describes. This analysis, then, should be seen as a political intervention upon a text and upon a culture that renders those thematics both possible and problematic.

In order to treat these novels as cultural products rich with the sedimentations of history, we begin this analysis by placing these novels in a cultural and historical context that will hopefully enable us to read Bannon with a deeper sense of her own historical specificity.

Ann Bannon's *Beebo Brinker* series[1] have recently found fame as part of a revived interest in lesbian pulp novels of the '50s and early '60s. This interest is connected both to recent debates within feminism (e.g. the sex debates) as well as to a critical concern with popular genre novels. In 1983 Naiad Press reprinted five of her books as "lesbian classics," omitting her sixth because of its dominant heterosexual focus. Along with Vin Packer/ Ann Aldrich, Valerie Taylor, Paula Christian and others, Bannon's books constituted a sort of industry within an industry: lesbian pulps written by women within a thriving lesbian pulp industry dominated largely by male authors, and written for a voyeuristic male audience.

The development of the lesbian pulp market must also be seen in the context of the huge growth of the paperback book industry that had begun in 1939 and was really taking off by the '50s. Lesbian pulps meant big money for publishers like Fawcett Gold Medal, the leading publisher of lesbian paperbacks. In 1957 Reed Marr's *Women Without Men* was one of the ten best selling paperbacks of the year among *all* publishing houses[2] and Ann Bannon's books were not only big sellers but were translated into other languages as well. These books were generally sold where other paperbacks were sold: drugstores, supermarkets, etc., but, as Joan Nestle points out, they were clearly "marked":

Finding, buying and keeping the paperbacks was a political act. Called trash by the literary world and pornography by the commercial world, these books were often hidden away on the pulp racks of the more sleazy drugstores. To pick the books out, carry them to the counter and face the other shoppers and the cashier was often tantamount to a coming out declaration.[3]

These pulps are clearly different from the more overtly sexual material that constituted itself as pornography for men, using lesbian sexuality as quite traditional voyeuristic titillation. The Bannon pulps not only distinguished themselves through their female *authorship* but through their female *audience* as well; an audience that was reading as much for pleasure of self-confirmation as it was for the pleasure of the text.

Little, in fact, is known about this audience, the readers who hunted for these books in their local drugstore or who cautiously borrowed them from friends.[4] We can guess, though, that these popularly written pulps reached a different class of lesbians than, for example, did the 1928 tale of aristocratic lesbian damnation written by Radclyffe Hall, *The Well of Loneliness*. While Hall wrote of the trials and tribulations of to-the-manor-born deviants, Bannon and her colleagues spun emphatic tales of working class lesbian love and lust. *The Well of Loneliness* refers to the high-society lesbian salon and many of Hall's characters were obvious stand-ins for "real" people in the 1920s high culture lesbian crowd. Bannon's books, on the other hand, refer to Village gay subcultural life, and the characters are not "famous people" with regal country estates but elevator operators and medical secretaries trying to make ends meet.

What separates these pulps from the male pornographic lesbian genre is thus a complex of factors, including gender of the author, intended and/ or actual audience and, of course, content. For it is not only that these novels tend to be less explicit sexually than the male-authored ones, but that the construction of sexuality and sexual preference is itself constituted differently from both the male version of this genre as well as from the dominant culture.

Interestingly, too, these novels do not fit into the more traditional mode of female romance which Ann Snitow has discussed as "...pornography for women, in which sex is bathed in romance, diffused, always implied rather than enacted at all."[5] Snitow's description of the female pornographic genre of the Harlequin as desexualized and decontextualized ("waiting and yearning") could not be more at odds with the "sex in context" style of the Bannon books.[6]

While it is vital to understand the conditions of literary production and distribution it is equally important to situate these novels in the cultural context of '50s lesbian life, a context that encompassed both the growth of gay communities such as Greenwich Village as well as the often violent backlash that accompanied that new gay identity and visibility. Much has been written about the anti-homosexual, politically repressive '50s and I need not recount that history here. What is important to recognize, in addition to the general context of the McCarthyite fifties, was the specific configuration of the pre-Stonewall gay culture. In some senses, lesbian life in the '50s can be seen as an ambiguous battle between two somewhat opposing forces. On the one hand, we had the appearance of new organizations such as the Mattachine Society and the Daughters of Bilitis which ostensibly attempted the assimilation of gay women into the mainstream culture by attacking stereotypical and "negative" images of lesbians. Yet these organizations often found themselves at odds with the "other" lesbians—the bar dykes, often working-class women whose affectional preference included the engagement in "butch/fem" interactions. Butch/fem lesbians were seen by much of the leadership of DOB as helping to perpetuate negative stereotypes about lesbians and thus contributing to their own marginalization.

These lesbian pulps, then, occupied an ambiguous space in this debate. More often then not set in the lesbian bar subculture of Greenwich Village, these novels often conflicted with the image of the "nice" lesbian (a regular girl just like you and me) promoted by the homophile organizations. But the lesbian pulps could not be ignored by these organizations and their journals (including the pioneering *Ladder*, whose own ambivalence on the assimilation vs. subculture question provides yet another example of the dominant tensions of '50s lesbian life), because not only were they read voraciously but, as Libby Smith argues they:

> ...were crucial to lesbians during those years, simply as a recognition of their existence... they fulfilled certain functions: For example, they confirmed that lesbians did exist, and helped readers develop a positive identity while lesbians were otherwise said to be sick, when they were described at all. They also sometimes conveyed a sense of lesbian culture, and sometimes helpful lesbians find others like themselves.[7]

Thus, these novels played a multi-layered role in lesbian culture, existing as description, as witness, as evidence, as connection, as representation and, of course, as pleasure.

In recent years, thanks to the work of Gene Damon (Barbara Grier) and the Lesbian Archives, we have gained a bit more knowledge of the authors who always wrote under a least one pseudonym. Ann Bannon (not, of course, her real name) turns out to have been a married woman when she wrote her first lesbian novel at the age of 22. That she lived a sort of double life not unfamiliar to her readers is clear from a recent interview with Bannon where she claims that, "...everyone in my daily life thought I was a very nice, young conventional wife and mother. They really didn't know what was going on in my head or my emotions and that was sort of how I got away with it."[8] In the interview, Bannon recounts her early years as a young wife and mother in Philadelphia, and her forays into New York's gay bars. One feels the powerful *ethnographic* sense to these novels as we imagine this woman observing gay life in the '50s through the eyes of one both outside that culture and within it as well. She continued writing (although she broke off for a period of time when her children were young), and eventually received a doctorate. She is no longer married and teaches college English in the California State University system and is, needless to say, quite astonished at her new status as feminist cult hero.

The Lesbian Text and the Pulp Novel

One of the first issues we must confront when analyzing these books has to do with the nature and constitution of a lesbian text. What is it that marks off a particular body of work as "lesbian"? And here we have competing views, for some critics tend to define the lesbian text more broadly than others, in terms of a women—identified *sensibility* from Adrienne Rich's *lesbian continuum* to the *ecriture feminine* of the French feminists. In my definition, though, I follow Catherine Stimpson, who stresses the *sexuality* of the lesbian writer, character and author:

She is a woman who finds other women erotically attractive and gratifying. Of course a lesbian is more than her body, more than her flesh, but lesbianism partakes of the body, partakes of the flesh. That carnality distinguishes it from gestures of political sympathy with homosexuals and from affectionate friendships in which women enjoy each other, support each other, and commingle a sense of identity and well-being. Lesbianism represents a commitment of skin, blood, breast, and bone. If female and male gay writings have their differences, it is not only because one takes Sappho and the other Walt Whitman as its great precursor. They simply do not spring from the same physical presence in the world.[9]

And if it is this carnality which distinguishes the lesbian text, then Ann Bannon's pulp novels are most emphatically included. Bannon insists on uncoded lesbian sexuality, devoid of either the elaborate codings of a Woolf or Stein or the tedious use of nature metaphors to describe female to female sex. Yet Stimpson claims that the explicit lesbian writer pays a dear price for her refusal to encode her passion:

As if making an implicit, perhaps unconscious pact with her culture, the lesbian writer who rejects both silence and excessive coding can claim the right to write for the public in exchange for adopting the narrative of damnation.[10]

Does this describe the work of Ann Bannon or is Stimpson actually projecting her own class and aesthetic values (or those of feminist literary criticism) by describing a situation that is perhaps only applicable to what is considered to be of high literary quality? Bannon's work, it seems to me, escapes the narrative of damnation not only through the complexity of its content and characterization, but through its use of the "low" genre of the pulp/romantic paperback. As Jeff Weinstein says:

Bannon took the soft porn/illicit—love genre and, without denying the reader's expectation of simplistic, unlikely plot and routinely passionate characters, opened up the form to allow a serious study of three women coming to grips with their attraction to women.[11]

Perhaps the conventions of "literature" prevent the high art lesbian writer from making a happy ending, but the conventions of the low genre novel reverse our expectations by insisting that lesbians, too, must walk off into the sunset or, in this case, the twilight. While the genre insists on its conventions to maintain its read-ability, Bannon quietly subverts or overflows the form by insisting on its universality. The anonymity of the pulp genre only adds to this sense of universality. Because the characters are so broadly drawn, so caricatured, we are urged to identify not so much with the individual (could anyone *really* be as butch—cool as Beebo?) but with the situation itself, the cultural milieu. For example, we are asked not to experience the butch—Beebo—as such, but the butch as the site of sexual power, and accordingly, social contradictions. Thus it is not a question of Bannon simply *transcending* the genre (going beyond it to create more "honest" art), but rather using the conventions of the pulp genre to turn it in on itself, to offer itself fully up to the lesbian reader.

So it is not simply a matter of the controversial content overflowing the restrictive and schematic form of the genre. Rather, we are talking here of a more paradoxical process whereby a traditionally masculinist form is used and, in the process, somewhat transformed, by women for whom the language of high culture is neither an option nor resonant with their lived experience:

> Potboilers used simple exaggeration to accomplish their tasks, but when Bannon exploits melodramatic conventions something unusual happens: they become realistic. . . . Melodrama does throw its arms around the arenas of daily 50s gay struggle: not in the courts or battlefield, but the dormitories, apartments, and bars. No high—cultural language existed to play out 'lesbian heartbreak' so Bannon has backed into a kind of gay realism of her time.[12]

In addition, we can find significance in Bannon's choice to use a serial form with continuing and developing characters. In the first place, the 50s serial novel has as its referent the emergence of TV as the dominant form of media. These types of novels were clearly playing off of the new and booming TV audience that was becoming hooked on "installment" entertainment. One immediately feels the visualness of the novels; the soap-operaish quality that derives from the use of limited physical space, "event" orientation, interlocking story lines, etc. They read like TV. There is also a class dimension reflected in the choice of this form, in the historical relationship between the penny press installment series and the working-class audience who gained their first acquaintance with "literature" through this medium. These connections are not simply gratuitous, but in fact place these novels in a context that reveals their class location, both historically—in relation to earlier forms of serial entertainment—and currently, as it relates to mass media influenced popular culture.

There is also, I believe, a more subliminal or hidden dimension to this choice. In producing a serial in which lesbian characters live, work, love and grow old together, Bannon was implicitly challenging the prevailing belief that homosexual life was brief, episodic, and more often than not resulted in early death. By showing characters moving in both fictional time and space, as well as real time and space (the period of time in which she wrote the books) Bannon insisted on the continuity of lesbian love, while everything in her culture was speaking of its quick and ugly demise. Remember, the contemporary soap opera is the paean par excellence to the immortality of heterosexual romance. . . . These novels, then, combine the powerful politics of a clearly lesbian text with the formulaic conventions of a pulp potboiler to produce a series that challenges our usual assumptions of *both* genres.

The Dialogue with Desire

This challenge is largely played out in the arena of sexuality and desire. Indeed, because of the focus in these books on sexuality and desire as the realization of preference, they in some way prefigure the contemporary debates within the feminist community as well as offer a competing perspective from, for example, Radclyffe Hall whose writing suggests:

...that the stigma of homosexuality is tolerable as long as the erotic desire that distinguishes it remains repressed. The conclusion—that a released eros will provoke the destructive potential of the stigma—placed Hall in that Western cultural tradition that links sex and death. In addition, she is attributing to lesbianism a conventional belief about female sexuality in general; that women prefer love and romance to physical consummation.[13]

For Bannon, the lesbian *is* sex, her difference as manifested in desire is what makes her a lesbian; indeed, what makes her a person. In Bannon's world, it is the lesbians who *repress* their desire, who suffer from what we would now call "internalized homophobia", that bear the greatest burden. The character Vega, in *Journey to a Woman*, is actually visibly scarred from her own self-hatred, an interesting reversal of Hall's Stephen Gordon whose scar is the mark of her deviancy. For Bannon, the scar is the mark of self-hatred; deviancy is its own mark: desire.

So we are talking, then, of the construction—or signification—of lesbian sexuality in the novels. And there seems to be a primary contradiction that develops throughout the five novels, a contradiction that can reveal to us the "second narrative" or "second voice" that lurks beneath the surface and that is partially obscured by the homophobic ideological context in which these novels were written. It is this contradiction, or rather, *dialogue*, that we now turn to. I propose to analyze these novels in terms of an ongoing dialogue between the voice of determinism (the '50s voice, the voice of biology, of psychology, of Freud, of the Fathers, of self-hatred) and the voice of choice (the voice of precocious feminism, of activity, of power, of agency, of lesbian identity). And desire exists here as a sort of "third term" that traverses the dialogue as it encodes them into the body. The power of desire is such in these novels that it urges choice along, nudging it past the narrow determinisms that threaten to negate it. Desire gives choice meaning, it gives it a body, it gangs up on determinism and KO's it in the last instance. Sort of like tag-team semiotics.

For, on the one hand, Bannon was clearly embedded in, and thus reflected, the '50s reading of homosexuality, even the most liberal of which was deeply flawed by the prevalence of both a pop Freudianism and homophobic culture. Bannon cannot escape the conclusion that homosexuality is something one is born with; it is inherent within the person and then only waits for the antinomous options of repression or self-discovery. In some sense, then, the depiction of lesbianism is a discovery and, for Bannon, an *acceptance*, of what was "always there."

This first voice of *biological* determinism is joined by a second *psychological* determinist voice that centers on the role of fathers in determining their daughter's sexuality. Mothers, incidentally, are conspicuously absent from these novels—both Laura's and Beebo's mothers died young and they were raised by fathers who then figure significantly in the novels. Beebo was raised on a farm where she was treated "as a boy" by an adoring but weak-willed father. Laura virtually accuses her father of causing her homosexuality in their confrontation scene where both his incestuous desires and his past abuse of her are revealed to the reader.

So we have this "born with it" biologic ideology coexisting alongside the psychologizing ideology of "Daddy done it to me"—either by treating me like a boy (Beebo) or by desiring me (Laura). While these ideological constructions of lesbian identity may seem at odds, I would claim that together they constitute the first narrative: the narrative of determinism. For, while they give different answers for the causes of homosexuality, they are both (a) monocausal and (b) deterministic and essentialist. Now, again, the reasons for doing this are not the "fault" of the inadequate author, but rather can be found in both the cultural limitations under which she wrote as well as the limitations of a genre novel which must have a psychologistic and developmental focus, preferably one revealed to us as the motivating force behind the characters' previously bewildering actions.

Does this narrative of determinism exist as the sole discourse on lesbianism in these books or is there, in fact, a second voice that can be discerned that renders the conservative determinism problematic and contestable? It seems to me that the active sexuality in the books as the *realization* of preference (i.e. the characters fully realize their lesbianism through sex itself, not through thinking about it, or analyzing it, or experiencing it in "meaningful relationships") operates as a sort of encoding of sexual *choice* and thus at least a partial repudiation of the determinist arguments. Bannon had to encode this choice. She could not write a lesbian-feminist celebratory romp; lesbian-feminism as such did not exist and the 50s was not a great time for romping.

In addition, it is important to remember that the question of *choice* in sexuality, and the politics of that choice, is itself a product of the development of competing ideologies of homosexuality. The '80s now makes it possible for us to ask this question of choice; it would not really have been possible to speak of the choice of the desired object when Ann Bannon wrote these novels.

As Joan Nestle says:

There are sad moments, ugly moments in these books; they do not follow the eighties lesbian feminist scripts. They were written in a different time by a housewife who hung out in the village still not sure which one of these characters she was....The most prevailing literary metaphor for Lesbian life was walking in the shadows. These novels ironically were blinking lights in the time of judgement....[14]

But if they were blinking lights, they were beckoning the reader into a subculture that flashed lust and desire at every Village streetcorner. The presence of an active and directed sexuality in these books both explodes the genre as well as redirects the content away from the overt determinism to a more complex mixture of determinism, choice and sexual politics:

Physical attraction and love may merge, but lust can happily flower without—and in spite of—love. Passion is part and parcel of the potboiler, to be sure, but where before had anyone seen such firm, promiscuous, demanding, heartfelt *lust* originating from women, lesbian or not?[15]

One could even see these books as a sort of "how-to" of lesbian lust, and Bannon as the Horatio Alger of the bar set. These books are travel guides to the seamy side of Village life, inviting the reader to venture into the bars and coffeeshops and test her skills with the ladies. From these books, one could learn the terminology, dress codes, and etiquette necessary to negotiate the lesbian subculture. And one could even pick up a good line or two in the process.

In attempting to flesh out the "second narrative" or "second voice" of these novels, I have tried to analyze the texts in terms of a number of themes or tropes, themes within which this dialogue is carried out. These themes that I have constructed come not from some dictionary of correct literary metaphors nor do they come from the "discovery" of the "real" Ann Bannon. These themes are *constructions* or, more precisely, *interventions* of a specific political sort that comes from a conscious and active political interpretation. They are themes that are central to lesbian culture and its fictional representation. Underlying this interpretation is surely an attempt to uncover the ideological inferences of the text, but to do so in a way that stresses not the uniformity of the ideological message but rather its variability, its multiplicity. The focus, then, is on *contradiction* in the text. These contradictions, this panoply of voices, can reveal to us much about the contradictions that real, live '50s lesbians lived and struggled with in the not so distant past. And, yes, there is a larger question to be dealt with here. For these novels not only speak to us of lived history, but carry on a dialogue with high culture critics everywhere who would rather pore over Woolf one more time than dirty their hands with pop cult smut. But be assured, the point here is not to insert Bannon into the feminist canon or to assert a claim to "Art." The point, rather, is to read subversively and politically that which was read by many women—often subversively and politically.

Etiology of Homosexuality: Desire as the Realization of Preference

As noted earlier, there is clearly a voice in here that responds to the question: "why are you a homosexual?" with a combination of biological and psychological determinism. In *I Am A Woman*, the "daddy done it to me" theme hits us hard as it does in *Journey to a Woman* and in *Beebo*

Brinker. This assertion of the inherency of homosexuality is in itself uninteresting and most clearly the reflection of the dominant ideology of the times. What *is* interesting, however, is the presence of a number of alternative discourses on the origins of homosexuality. Yet these alternative explanations do not completely nullify the determinism, and often exist side-by-side with it. In *Woman in the Shadows,* Laura asserts that a homosexual is made, not born, yet she does this in the context of a conversation with a black man in which she tries to create an analogy between her situation and his:

"What makes you normal, Milo?"
"I was born that way. Don't tell me you were *born* queer! Ha!" And he was sarcastic now.
"I was made that way," she said calmly.
"By who?" he asked skeptically.
"A lot of people. My father. A girl named Beth. Myself. Fate."[16]

In *Journey to a Woman* we again hear the dual voices. Beth has met up with Laura's father and is amazed that he doesn't hate her for what she "did to" his daughter and he responds:

"For what *you* did to her?" He gave a scornful little laugh that turned against himself. "If I were guiltless myself I could despise anyone I pleased. I could blame anyone I pleased. But I'm not guiltless." His words made her feel braver. "If it hadn't been you it would have been someone else, Beth. You know that, of course. Laura is a Lesbian. Sooner or later she would have understood that, whether with your help or without it."[17]

The determinism is clearly there, yet there is a strange and suggestive anti-romanticism to his words that not only muddy the waters of determinism, but challenge another dominant ideology of homosexuality: that of the "evil seductress."

But the real challenge to this determinist voice is to be found in the discourse on pleasure and desire that so delightfully pervades these novels. This discourse crops up in many different forms, but at this point I will focus on the ways in which the presence of an active and passionate desire transgresses the bounds of destiny and constitutes a distinct and perhaps radical voice in the debate on the origins of sexual preference. For even if the explicit moral tone of the books claims a biologistic destiny, the actions speak to desire as the *realization* of preference. Throughout the books, the assurance of preference comes through sex with another woman. By foregrounding the overflowing of desire, Bannon not only gives the women power as sexual actors, but, interestingly enough, places herself in opposition to contemporary lesbian novels that foreground internal self-discovery and political choice. In these novels, the body speaks:

There was not time to wonder whether the happiness was purely physical. She didn't stop to think about her ambivalent feelings for Nina, about how Nina might look in the daylight. . . . There was no daylight, no night, no time, nothing but that moment on the bed with Nina in her arms. Beth was unable to think ahead or to care what happened. Nina's voice came softly out of the dawn to her. "You're gay, Beth." she said positively. "I know." It came as a wild wonderful relief, just to know for sure after years of tormented wondering.[18]

The realization of one's sexual preference comes not through psychological self-discovery nor through the retrospective moralizing that serves as the determinist argument. These may be *explanations* for behavior but only in an abstract sense that is rarely acted out in the novels. Sex and unbound desire is what works on us, as it works on the characters. As Beebo says in response to Venus' question: "Beebo, are you sorry you're gay? Are you bitter about it?" "Yes," Beebo said, and Venus frowned. "All day long, when you go off to the studio, I'm sorry as hell. At night, I get down on my knees and give thanks."[19]

Gay Pride / Gay Culture / Gay Politics

The discourses on desire at times suggest a more overt politics and ideology of homosexuality. And, again, there are competing voices, each acting on us in particular ways. It is within this dialogue that we will find some of the more revealing statements on the implications of homosexual life. An achingly funny scene in *Odd Girl Out*—Bannon's first novel—initiates the voice of pride and self-respect:

Laura sat up and pulled away from her. "I don't care what he thinks. I don't care, I'm not ashamed. Are we doing something dirty or wicked to be ashamed of? are we, Beth?"
"No." She shut her eyes and said slowly, "But other people don't understand that Laura. We have to keep it secret—absolutely secret. People will say we're queer—"
"But we're *not*! I know what queer is. I've seen people—"
"Laura, we're just as queer as the ones who *look* queer," Beth said sharply, looking at her. "We're doing the same damn thing. Now, let's not kid ourselves. Let's be honest with each other, at least." Her own deception shut her up.
Laura sat and stared at her with a horrified face. "Beth—" she quavered, shaking her head. "No. . .no. . ."
Beth grasped her hands. "I'm sorry. Oh, I'm sorry, that was a terrible way to say it. I'm just so damn upset. I—"
"Are we really—" She couldn't say the word. "Are we Beth?"
"Yes."
Laura was mute for a minute, and then she said, "All right. Then we are." She set her chin. "That still doesn't make it dirty or wicked."
"No." Beth smiled ruefully at her and kissed her hands. "It just makes it illegal."[20]

Here, and throughout the novels, we get a clear sense of the social and legal implications of homosexuality, and there is a tension always between the desire to win acceptance in the straight world and a valorization of marginality. This tension is often manifested through the question of "the closet." Yet the question of "out" or "in" needs to be raised differently in these novels than we would raise it today. For example, Beebo is in the closet in the sense that she did not declare herself as a lesbian to the "outside world" or at least at work. But, within her own subculture, which is where we see her the most, she is clearly out. Similarly, Beebo is treated as if she was an out character—she bears the burden for her homosexuality by virtue of her butch appearance. Perhaps Bannon is trying to say that no matter whether we're butch or fem, out or in, we are all subject to the same stigmatization as lesbians (in the last instance). Venus gets away with passing and is not only frowned upon, but seen in the end as pathetic. It is clear, in addition, that Venus' passing at least in part derives from her superior class position. Beebo—the most marginalized both by class (she is an elevator operator) and by sex (she looks "like a man") is also the most sympathetic and articulate character: the bodily presence of contradiction:

"I wanted Venus and I got her, but I'm not sure having her is worth the shame and secrecy of it. I'm strong and tall as a boy, but I'm not as free as a man. I wanted to be gentle and loving with women, but I can't be feminine."[21]

This ambivalence about gender roles is continually expressed, most persistently by Beebo. But we also get a powerful sense of gay *culture* in these books, and it is this cultural aspect that perhaps provides the most radical voice, for it is here that one feels the sense of collective struggle and shared history that defies the limitations of soap-opera-ish love stories. One of the most powerful examples of the celebration of gay culture comes from the use of the bar as initiation rite. Each major female character experiences the power of knowing that there are others like yourself; the power of knowing that one is desired and can desire back. Here, the *gay* culture is seen as "civilized" and the *dominant* culture as "savage," quite a reversal of the traditional derision of the gay bar scene:

And then she looked around the room again, and suddenly she saw a girl with her arm around another girl at a table not far away. Her heart jumped. A pair of boys at the bar were whispering urgently to each other. *Gay,* Laura thought to herself. *Is that what they call it? Gay?* she was acutely uncomfortable now. It was as if she were a child of civilization, reared among the savages, who suddenly found herself among the civilized. She recognized them as her own. And yet she had adopted the traits of another race and she was embarrassed and lost with her own kind.[22]

Beebo also experiences the self-recognition through witnessing, through the tasting of lesbian culture:

She would sit and gaze for hours at the girls in the bars or passing in the streets. She wanted to talk to them, to see what they were like....Looking at one, she would think, *She knows how it feels to want what I want. I could make her happy. I know it.*[23]

The power of the gaze is clear here: a woman looking at another woman with desire. In the world of Ann Bannon, the gaze is undeniably female and, moreover, is intimately connected both with a collective culture or subculture as well as with the power to desire.

Butch/Fem

The portrayal of butch/fem in Bannon's novels is both fascinating and frustrating. The few critics who have examined her work have tended to dismiss the characters as "typical" '50s role-playing lesbians, the implication being that we of the politically correct '80s write more "realistic" and affirming characterizations in our novels. But in the past few years the (still-raging) "sex debates" within feminism has served as a catalyst for a re-evaluation of the meaning and practice of butch/fem[24]—both in its historical form and as it is experienced by present day lesbians. Without getting into that debate, suffice it to say that this re-evaluation has enabled me to read Bannon differently, with more complexity and allowing for more variability of meaning.

Butch/fem as it operates in these novels is something more—or other— than the symbolic reflection of societal limitations on homosexual practice. Butch/fem operates in Bannon's novels such that it subverts our everyday notions of role-playing while at the same time inscribing power and choice in the bodies of both the butch and the fem women. The central point, I believe, about the use of butch/fem here is that it is highly contextual and interactive. The movement of one character from expressing "butch" characteristics to acting "fem" arises in their interaction with other women. The status of butch or fem is played out as changeable, rather than a static and given aspect of personality. This contextual and interactive presentation of butch/fem implies that these "roles" are something other than the dominant culture acting on us and through us, but perhaps significant indicators of choice, sexual play and power. Bannon's portrayal of butch/ fem seems to agree with the experiences of many lesbians who came out in the '50s and were involved in butch/fem bar culture:

Butch-fem relationships, as I experienced them, were complex erotic statements, not phony heterosexual replicas. They were filled with a deeply Lesbian language of stance, dress, gesture, loving, courage, and autonomy.[25]

For example, Beth is described very much like Beebo: masculine, short hair, boyish, in charge, etc. But this "butch" ends up getting married and, in the very end, living with another "butch"—Beebo. This is a reversal of much of the traditional reading of butch/fem which interprets them as highly dichotomous representations of sexual oppositions. Beth is portrayed as butch in relation to Laura but is also seen as desirable to men as well as to a butch woman. To what extent does this mutability of roles indicate that the women have some measure of control over their sexual choices and that butch/fem role playing has to do with a contextual interaction with the "Other"?

This scene between Jack and Laura describes both the contextual nature of butch/fem as well as the way it is used as part of the initiation into gay subculture:

"What are you?"
Laura stated at him over the rim of her glass. "What am I?" she repeated, confusedly. "Do I have to be anything? I don't know."
...Jack grinned at her. "You're a boy," he said.
"With Marcie, anyway. My friend won't like that."
Laura put her glass down. "I'm a girl," she said. "Don't look at me that way."
Jack put his head back and laughed. "Correction," he said. "You're a girl. Why don't you move down here where you don't have to be either?"[26]

Not only is there a real playfulness to this discussion of butch/fem but there is a recognition of the liberating quality of "gay space" rather than an emphasis on the seaminess of subcultural life. Laura is invited to join in, to be part of the Village scene where the mutability of gender roles is acknowledged and even celebrated.

Later on in the same book, we get a sense of the relationship between "butchiness," outness, and economic and social reality:

"What does she do?" Laura asked rather shyly.
"Who? Beebo?"
"She must get money somewhere. She has to pay the rent like everybody else."
"She runs an elevator. In the Grubb Building. They think she's a boy."
"My God—an *elevator.*" It seemed wrong, even ludicrous. Beebo had too much between her ears to fritter her youth away running an elevator. "What does she do *that* for?"
"She doesn't have to wear a skirt."
Laura was stunned. It was pathetic, even shameful. For the first time she saw Beebo not as an overwhelming, handsome, self-assured individual, but as a very human being with a little more pride and fear and weakness than she ever permitted to show.[27]

The butchiness of Beebo is reflected in her choice of work but, ironically, this makes Laura see her in more "human" terms. In the *Beebo Brinker* book, Beebo tells Jack that she always wanted to be a doctor and realizes that her lesbianism limits her career and economic choices:

"You're saying I didn't have the guts to fight them," she said, speaking without resentment. "It isn't that, Jack. I did fight them, with all I've got. I'm tired of it, that's all. You can't fight everybody all the time and still have room in your life to study and think and learn.[27]

Again, Bannon never allows us to escape the realities of homophobia. Her world is one where passionate lesbian sexuality and culture exists side-by-side with the hardships of being gay in a repressive heterosexual society.

Later on in the book, Beebo is trying to explain to Jack about the feelings that she was having before she left home. Most of the conversation centers around Beebo's "masculinity"—that she didn't look or act like "other girls." But every example she brings up to convince herself of her masculinity only confirms for us her feminism: "Jack, long before I knew anything about sex, I knew I wanted to be tall and strong and wear pants and ride horses and have a career...and never marry a man or learn to cook or raise babies. Never."[28] She goes on to further convince herself of her masculinity by making the claim to sexual desire ("...big and hot and anxious...")[29] that she identifies with maleness. This contradicts the identification of butchness with masculinity and in fact refers to the type of social relations that have constituted power, active sexuality, and economic independence as male prerogatives.

The exploration of butch/fem in these novels provides for the emergence of the voice of choice in its refusal to succumb to easy stereotypes and glib characterizations. Indeed, one could claim that there is an incipient feminism in this portrayal, as Joan Nestle attests to:

I believe...that many Lesbians, pre-Stonewall, were feminists, but the primary way this feminism, this autonomy of sexual and social identities, was expressed was precisely in the form of sexual adventuring that now appears so oppressive.[31]

Female Sexual Prowess/Power/Promiscuity

We seem always to be returning to issues of sexuality and desire, and it is to Bannon's credit that she insists that sex not serve as metaphor but be explored as sex itself. Rarely do we find books, even pulps, that celebrate female sexual power at all. And even rarer is the examination of that power in the context of lesbian sex. For the issue here is not how loving or intuitive or sensitive the character may be in her lovemaking (a la lesbian-feminist novels) but how *good* she is and the various aspects of power and desire that spark particular pleasures in particular women. Throughout the Bannon books, we are treated to voluptuous and passionate sex scenes that raise a host of issues, some of which we have discussed above.

One such issue has to do with female sexual prowess and how it is often linked to wild and transgressive sexuality. Now, clearly, the theme of illicitness is a staple of pulp fiction, both heterosexual and homosexual. Yet the connection of this illicitness with female-to-female sex in the context of a text that virtually eliminates the voyeuristic male gaze, renders this illicitness doubly transgressive. In addition, the implication for the contemporary debates on s/m are obvious and startling given the historical context in which these novels were written. This becomes increasingly evident in the relationship between Laura and Beebo. Laura is tormented by her "wild, animal" desire for Beebo and comes to realize that her desire is intimately connected to Beebo's dominance and sexual skills:

Laura looked at her and found herself caught by Beebo's spell again. Beebo was born to lose her temper. She looked wonderful when she did. It exasperated Laura to feel a bare animal desire for her at times like this. ...She looked at Beebo with embarrassed desire and to make her shame complete, Beebo saw it. And she knew she was in command again, even if only for an hour or so. ...Beebo shifted support of her leaning body from her arms to Laura, lifted up Laura's angry helpless face and kissed it. "Why aren't you like this all the time?" she asked. And Laura startled her when she echoed, "Why aren't *you* like this all the time?" "Like what, baby? Drunk?" "No...," Laura hesitated. She didn't quite understand what she meant herself.[32]

The ambiguity of sexual desire is stressed, yet Laura's suspicion that this kind of interaction might not be the healthiest thing in the world for her does not stop her actions. In fact, the novels are saturated with scenes of women saying yes to lust and being much more circumspect with love:

"Why is it that you're such an angel in bed and a bitch out of bed?" Laura snapped. For an answer, Beebo only lay on her back and laughed at her. Laura looked at her lithe body and after a moment she had to turn away to keep from lying down beside her. "I don't even like you, Beebo," she said harshly, hoping it would hurt. "I don't know why I can't keep away from you." "It's because I'm such an angel in bed, Bo-peep," Beebo said. "That's all you care about. That's all you want from me."[33]

Bannon gives us a rare glimpse into a world of lesbian sexual power, when women take and are taken *by each other*. Active sexuality is celebrated and, contrary to the ruling '50s ideologies, women are shown to be ruled as much by their bodies as by their emotions.

Rejection of Patriarchal Family and the Ideology of Maternalism

Catherine Stimpson claims that, in the lesbian realist novels, "...even though the lesbian may have children whom she loves, she must reject the patriarchal family, which the stigma against her helps to maintain, if she is to reject repression as well."[34] Both explicitly and implicitly—both within the text and in the texts relation to its external referents—Bannon presents a radical and forward-thinking rejection of the patriarchal family and the dominant ideologies surrounding motherhood.

In the first place, Beth leaves her marriage and her two children to go in search of her old flame, Laura. Now, in almost every genre—from high modernism to our own beloved smut—a woman who leaves her children is the ultimate signifier of transgression: she must be punished. The amazing thing about the Bannon books is that Beth not only doesn't get punished (she ends up living happily ever after with Beebo) but the issue of leaving her children is never made an issue, it's never foregrounded. She has some remorse, she briefly agonizes, and she goes on with her life with women. In this scene, Beth is preparing to leave Charlie and he is attempting to make her stay. This scene is packed with frustrated housewife angst, budding feminism, claiming of lesbian identity, and the desire to be free of the family:

"...I want to get closer to myself, I want to *know* myself, Charlie. I don't even know who I am. Or *what* I am." "You're *my wife!*" he said sharply, as if that were the argument to end them all, to end all of her doubts with one stroke. "I'm myself!" she cried, rising to her feet again, her fists knotted at her sides.[35]

Charlie is amazed that she plans to leave the kids with him: "He was truly shocked; it blasted all his favorite concepts of motherhood to see her behave this way."[36] Beth then comes up with a precociously feminist statement: "I want them," she cried, "but I want my freedom more...."[37] This feminist statement is not without its provisos though. Beth goes on to say that she wasn't a good mother anyway and, going by her behavior at the beginning of the book, we don't exactly question this.

Nonetheless, the critique of the family comes through loud and clear, particularly in the way the marriage of Laura and Jack is handled. Now, this is a problematic situation, because, on the one hand, their marriage can clearly be read as a reconstitution of the patriarchal family and thus at least a partial repudiation of the anti-family stance taken by Beth earlier on. While I think it is true that Jack Mann (really!) often serves as the hook to bring the wayward lesbians back into the clutches of dominant culture, I think his presence as a *gay* person is much more significant. Jack's role as the kind of Village welcome wagon relates more to the realities of gay subcultural life in the '50s than anything else; e.g. it was far more likely that one would meet up with a savvy gay man than with a gay woman in those days. In addition, although Jack may help the women acclimate themselves to the gay world, he does so in a benign and passive way; it is the women who are the actors and, however useful Jack's advice may be, the resolutions are always between each other.

The marriage at the end remains contradictory, especially after the scene where Jack is pushing Laura to marry him and, in the process, telling her of the evils of homosexual life and the benefits of wedded bliss. Yet the fact remains that these are two committed homosexuals marrying each other and neither of them renounces their homosexuality for the marriage, although it is interesting to note that Jack does seem to renounce *his* active sexuality, a telling reversal of roles in traditional heterosexual marriages. The two do have a baby—but it is a strange parody of a nuclear family: a faggot and a dyke and an artificially inseminated produced baby. Anyway you look at it, this is no happy '50s nuclear family resolution. And Jack is no run-of-the-mill patriarchal figure but a highly ambiguous man who serves as confidante to the women but is shown to be vulnerable and troubled by his own penchant for feckless young men.

Beebo adds her name to the critique of the family in the final book, when Venus deserts her and gives in to career concerns and husbandly pressures. Venus here not only valorizes Beebo's gayness but even hints at the kind of proto-feminist yearnings that Beth expressed in *Journey to a Woman*:

"Beebo, you knew what you were early in life. Some of us don't find out till after we've committed ourselves to a man and children. You're one hundred percent gay. You never doubt it. You breathe such easy contempt for me. But, darling, believe me, you're the lucky one. You knew yourself in time to save yourself from housewifery and husbands—things the rest of us have to live with."[38]

Venus is here pitied for her entrapment in the nuclear family and for the loss of the sexual pleasure she was only able to share with another woman. In Bannon's world, the nuclear family is deconstructed and a new sort of homosexual hybrid is constructed in its place.

It is time now to pose what is perhaps the most important question for a cultural critic who lives not only *for* marginality but is *of* it: how can we interpret this text so that its most liberatory moments are revealed to us; how can we construct the subversive reading?; how can we claim our cultural heritage without hoisting up a new and restrictive canon of legitimacy? Has the above actually been an attempt to add one more lost feminist to the burgeoning critical canon? Have I now rescued Bannon from the clutches of the smut-brokers and safely delivered her to the (co-op) doorsteps of the friendly neighborhood Literary Critic? I hope not, for it is precisely in Bannon's smuttiness and pulp sensibility that the subversiveness is located. These kinds of books must be examined for the popular culture that they are, rather than for what moments of high culture motifs we may discern within them. So often we find that the few critics who manage to read such stuff are still attempting to "get past" the "banalities" in order to dig out the "real" meaning. This assumes a unitary truth that reveals to us the meaning of a particular novel. The interpretation I have just done is intended to reveal as well, but reveal not "truth" or even "meaning" but the workings of a contradictory and ambiguous desire. More profoundly, the interpretation elaborates the workings of desire not as a transcendent force but in a specific historical and gendered set of social relations; a necessary corrective, I believe, to certain post-structuralist theories of desire.

Read these books, then, as cultural history, as political intervention, as sign-system. But read them as smut too. At the same time. And see what happens.

Acknowledgment

Special thanks to the MassCult Research Group of the Graduate Center-City University of New York, and to the Lesbian Herstory Archives. Thanks also to Ara for her creative visualizations of Beebo Brinker.

Notes

[1]The following is a brief summary of the plots of the five novels. In *Odd Girl*

Out (1957) Laura and Beth meet at college. They have an affair. Beth then falls in love with Charlie—a college boy—and they get involved. Laura tries to get Beth to leave Charlie, but they remain together and Laura leaves college alone. *I Am A Woman* (1959) opens up with Laura after she has left school and gotten a job in NYC at a doctor's office. Laura meets Jack Mann (who is gay), and goes to her first gay bar where she meets Beebo Brinker and goes home with her. Laura continues to see Beebo but has a crush on her straight roommate Marcie. After a bad visit from her father (who attempts to seduce her), Laura disappears for a couple of days, only to turn up at Beebo's where they walk off together in the lamplight. *Woman In Shadows* (1959) is Bannon's darkest novel and includes a faked rape (Beebo's), a dog murder, a slide into alcoholism (also Beebo's) and a tortured affair between Laura and a Black woman who pretends she is an Indian. In the end, Jack and Laura get married and Laura gets artificially inseminated. In *Journey to a Woman* (1960) Beth is married to Charlie and they have two children. Beth has an affair with a woman named Vega and leaves Charlie to go hunting for Laura. After a liaison with Nina, a writer of lesbian novels, Beth finally finds Laura who is by now married to Jack and has a daughter. Beth and Laura make love but realize it's over for them. Vega goes to Beth's hotel and shoots herself and Charlie bails Beth out of jail and wants her to return with him, but she refuses. Beebo and Beth realize they are in love and go off together. *Beebo Brinker* (1962) is actually the first book in the series chronologically and it starts out with Jack's story. He meets up with Beebo, who has just left home on the farm for the big city. Beebo goes to work as a pizza delivery person, and gets involved with a woman (Paula) for the first time. Beebo meets Venus Bogardus, a famous movie star, and eventually goes off with her to California. Beebo, forced to go back to New York when rumors begin to spread about their relationship, returns to the open arms of Paula.

[2]Gene Damon, "The Lesbian Paperback," *Tangents*, June 1966, p. 5.

[3]Joan Nestle, "'Desire So Big It Had To Be Brave': Ann Bannon's Lesbian Novels," (unpublished article, January 1983), p. 2.

[4]The recent work of the Buffalo Lesbian Oral History Project should shed some much-needed light on the "everyday life" (and reading habits!) of working-class lesbians.

[5]Ann Barr Snitow, "Mass Market Romance: Pornography for Women is Different," in *Powers of Desire* ed. Ann Snitow, Christine Stansell and Sharon Thompson (New York: Monthly Review Press, 1983), p. 257.

[6]A careful reading of the two other significant feminist works on romance (Tania Modleski's *Loving With a Vengeance* Modleski: Hamden, Conn: Archon Books, 1982 and Janice Radway's *Reading the Romance* Radway: Chapel Hill: University of North Carolina Press, 1984) gives support to the position that argues for a clear distinction to be drawn between Bannon's lesbian pulp and heterosexual romances.

[7]Libby Smith, "Lesbian Pulp Novels 1955-1968," (unpublished article, Department of History/Graduate Division, University of Pennsylvania, 1984), pp. 2-3.

[8]Maida Tilchen, "Ann Bannon: The Mystery Solved," interview with Ann Bannon in "Gay Community News," 8 January 1983, p. 10.

[9]Catherine Stimpson, "Zero Degree Deviancy: The Lesbian Novels in English" in *Writing and Sexual Difference* ed. Elizabeth Abel (Chicago: University of Chicago Press, 1982), p. 244.

[10]Ibid.

[11]Jeff Weinstein, "In Praise of Pulp," *Voice Literary Supplement* October 1983, p. 9.

[12]Ibid.

[13]Stimpson, pp. 250-251.

[14]Nestle, pp. 4-5.

[15]Weinstein, p. 10.

[16]Ann Bannon, *Women in the Shadows* (Fawcett Gold Medal, 1959; A Volute Book/Naiad Press, 1983), p. 159.

[17]Ann Bannon, *Journey to a Woman* (Fawcett Gold Medal, 1960; A Volute Book/ Naiad Press, 1983), p. 94.

[18]Ibid., p. 121.

[19]Ann Bannon, *Beebo Brinker* (Fawcett Gold Medal, 1962; A Volute Book/Naiad Press, 1983), p. 153.

[20]Ann Bannon, *Odd Girl Out* (Fawcett Gold Medal, 1957; A Volute Book/Naiad Press, 1983), p. 121.

[21]*Beebo Brinker*, p. 168.

[22]Ann Bannon, *I Am A Woman* (Fawcett Gold Medal, 1959; A Volute Book/ Naiad Press, 1983), p. 36.

[23]*Beebo Brinker*, pp. 46-47.

[24]Joan Nestle's work, in particular, attempts to address the question of butch/ fem in a highly personal and non-judgmental fashion. In "Butch-Fem Relationships: Sexual Courage in the 1950s," (*Heresies* #2), Nestle rightly takes feminists to task for ignoring or even denigrating this vital part of lesbian history and culture.

[25]Joan Nestle, "Butch-Fem Relationships: Sexual Courage in the 1950s," *Heresies* #2, p. 21.

[26]*I Am A Woman*, pp. 66-67.

[27]Ibid., p. 163.

[28]*Beebo Brinkerr*, p. 20.

[29]Ibid., p. 50.

[30]Ibid., p. 51.

[31]Nestle, "Butch-Fem Relationships," p. 23.

[32]*Women in the Shadows*, p. 64.

[33]*I Am A Woman*, p. 141.

[34]Stimpson, p. 253.

[35]*Journey to a Woman*, p. 79.

[36]Ibid., p. 80.

[37]Ibid.

[38]*Beebo Brinker*, p. 193.

Works Cited

Bannon, Ann. *Beebo Brinker*. Fawcett Gold Medal, 1962; a Volute Book/Naiad Press, 1983.

Bannon, Ann. *I Am A Woman*. Fawcett Gold Medal, 1959; a Volute Book/Naiad Press, 1983.

Bannon, Ann. *Journey to a Woman*. Fawcett Gold Medal, 1960; a Volute Book/ Naiad Press, 1983.

Bannon, Ann. *Odd Girl Out*. Fawcett Gold Medal, 1957; a Volute Book/Naiad Press, 1983.

Bannon, Ann. *Women in the Shadows.* Fawcett Gold Medal, 1959; a Volute Book/ Naiad Press, 1983.

Damon, Gene. "The Lesbian Paperback." *Tangents,* June 1966.

Nestle, Joan. "Butch-Fem Relationships: Sexual Courage in the 1950s." Heresies 2.

Nestle, Joan. "Desire So Big it Had to be Brave: Ann Bannon's Lesbian Novels." (unpublished article, January 1983).

Smith, Libby. "Lesbian Pulp Novels, 1955-1968." (unpublished article, Department of History/Graduate Division, University of Pennsylvania, 1984).

Snitow, Ann Barr. "Mass Market Romance: Pornography for Women is Different." *Powers of Desire.* eds. Ann Snitow, Christine Stansell and Sharon Thompson. New York: Monthly Review Press, 1983.

Stimpson, Catherine. "Zero Degree Deviancy: The Lesbian Novels in English." *Writing and Sexual Difference.* ed. Elizabeth Abel. Chicago: University of Chicago Press, 1982.

Tilchen, Maida. "Ann Bannon: The Mystery Solved." Interview with Ann Bannon in *Gay Community News* (January 8, 1983), p. 10.

Weinstein, Jeff. "In Praise of Pulp." *Voice Literary Supplement,* October 1983, p. 9.

Just Say No:
Repression, Anti-Sex and the New Film

Linda Singer

It should come as no surprise that the AIDS epidemic, and the cultural discourse surrounding it has produced, at least for the time being, a change in the terms of sexual exchange, and with it, a change in erotic climate. The eighties have ushered in a new sexual aesthetic which Richard Goldsmith of the *Village Voice*, has dubbed "the new sobriety," an umbrella term which points toward changes in sexual behavior as well as toward larger shifts in how sexuality is culturally valued, represented and circulated. Abstinence or monogamous domesticated sexuality has become fashionable, or at least respectable again. Sex educators and policy makers rally round the promise that the sexual epidemic can be abated if one is willing to "just say no."

The AIDS epidemic is, of course, not singularly responsible for having revivified the discourse of anti-sex, nor has it been the sole occasion for arousing concern about the relationship between representations of sex and erotic material, and sexual behavior. Long before AIDS became a central social preoccupation, groups from the Moral Majority to Women Against Pornography advocated restrictions on sexual representations and their circulation. Long before AIDS there were voices raised to argue that popular media, from films to television and rock and roll had become too permissive, i.e. too willing to capitalize on the public's desire to consume images of sexuality, images which were questionable on moral and aesthetic grounds. Both the moralistic New Right and the anti-pornography feminists seemed to agree, despite their rather significant differences, that sexual imagery encouraged, even induced, mimetic behavior. The result of this behavioral consequentialist logic, was a strategy focused on targeting undesirable representations, i.e., representations which it was thought or feared resulted in undesirable behavior. Feminists, who are primarily concerned with representations of violence and abuse of women, focus the bulk of their attention on the more marginal pornography and skin trade markets. The New Right, by contrast, focuses on mainstream media, like television and rock and roll.

Because the circulation of sexual representations is governed by the logic of commodity culture, we can expect that the decisions made by those in the industry of producing and circulating such material will be governed by the logic of the market. Part of that logic includes consideration of demographics. The rock and roll industry has been able thus far to most successfully resist, largely by ignoring, the demands for negative labelling, at least in part, because that part of the population which is represented by the New Right, is not a significant segment of their market to begin with. This is far less true for television, where advertisers aim primarily at familial households, and thus are concerned about appearing indifferent to familially based concerns about the welfare of children. Consequently, television has been far more vulnerable or responsive to the regulation of sexual images in general, regulations dominated by a self-imposed aesthetic of restraint and indirection with the ways sexual issues are represented.

The film industry, since the days of the Hays code, has been sensitive to how and what kinds of sexuality are represented. In an effort to avoid external intervention, the industry currently employs an internal regulatory system, which rates and marks films for sex and violence. But the film industry's attempts to accommodate the revived anti-sex discourse is complicated by the law, of the commodity market which demands accommodation to a diverse and polyvalent/contradictory consumer psychology. With respect to the consumption of sexual imagery, market patterns are often contradictory. On the one hand, public opinion surveys consistently reflect a perception that there is too much sex and violence in popular media. On the other hand, such offerings are often the most popular, as reflected in television ratings and movie box office receipts. Teenagers, for example, are often especially loathe to patronize films with G and PG ratings. Furthermore, the public has become accustomed to seeing sex at the movies, at least in some form. Certain traditional Hollywood genre, like western, from which representations of sexuality were almost always entirely absent, are not very popular with contemporary filmgoers. And sexual scenes have become a regular element in other film genres like science fiction and war stories which traditionally also avoided sexual motifs. John Wayne never took his boots off. Sylvester Stallone does (a lot). He also takes a lot more off.

In general, therefore, the film industry's accommodations to the anti-sex discourse have not taken the form of explicit excision. Most Hollywood films include some representations of sexual activity. A conspicuous counter-example is the recent yuppie comedy *Broadcast News*. In that case, sex is resisted not on moral grounds, but because the protagonist, a news producer played by Holly Hunter, is simply too busy. The displacement of sex onto work is also an element in the sexual economy represented in *Baby Boom*, where sex between the corporate co-habitants is carefully scheduled and timed.

Baby Boom also operationalizes another strategy of accommodation that has become a recurring theme in several recent Hollywood films, namely the domestification of sex in reproduction. In *Baby Boom* the protagonist inherits the baby that changes her life from that of NY corporate consultant to country entrepreneur. Much of the comedic effect in this film is supposed to flow from the character's ineptitude and unpreparedness for motherhood. Her work in a male dominated competitive corporate milieu has not encouraged or rewarded the development of her nurturing skills. Similarly, Hollywood has attempted to exploit conditions of unlikely parenthood for comedic effect in *For Keeps* and *She's Having a Baby*, where the parents are teenagers, and the very popular *Three Men and A Baby*, the American remake of the French film *Three Men and A Cradle*, which was also very popular. Paternity/fatherhood is a source of interest, perhaps, because it is so exotic. (Remember the success of Dustin Hoffman as primary parent in *Kramer Vs. Kramer*). Even Woody Allen, no great sentimentalist on this score has included father-son scenes in several films, including *Manhattan*, *Radio Days* and *Hannah and Her Sisters*.

These representations of paternal activity have a double strategic edge in terms of the contemporary sexual economy. On the one hand, they work to valorize paternity at a time when more and more men are choosing to desert their families, and are failing to contribute to the support of their children. On the other hand, they re-enforce the traditional double standard by virtue of which anything men do, even or maybe especially when it is gender atypical, is infinitely interesting. Watching women mother except ineptly, is not so terribly interesting because it is so socially ubiquitous. Men engaged in active parenting is interesting because it is not. At a time when there is social urgency attached to limiting multiple and unregulated sexual exchanges, there is social utility in valorizing fatherhood, and at least attempting to glamorize the familial organization of sexuality.

A more complicated, and if box office is any indication, successful example of accommodating the anxiety induced by the sexual epidemic is *Fatal Attraction*. I want to examine *Fatal Attraction* at some length for several reasons. First, its popularity suggests it hit some kind of nerve and thus may serve as some sort of impressionistic barometer of the sex-pol climate in the age of epidemic. Secondly, its tropic function is being confirmed through replication. Television offered several major productions with similar themes and titles (like *Deadly Attraction* and *Fatal Infatuation*), reflecting the mass media logic that there is never too much of a good thing.

The questions I wish to raise about *Fatal Attraction* all revolve around the nature and significance of the kind of pleasure this film induced for its substantial audience. What is so attractive, at this particular time, about a film in which sexual attraction is also figured as fatal? For whom or what is attraction fatal, and what larger utilities are accommodated or recuperated thereby? What is the effect of eroticizing the connection between pleasure and danger? What, if anything, is ideologically significant about the ways in which *Fatal Attraction* mobilizes and organizes its audiences' desires and satisfactions?

The question of pleasure and object relations in the cinema, as elsewhere, is an extremely complex question and one to which I cannot possibly do justice in this context. Nevertheless, if you will pardon the pun, I want to take a stab at it and suggest that at least part of why *Fatal Attraction* was so interesting to the large number of Americans who were willing to invest time and money in it, was the way this film managed a nexus of contemporary sexual anxieties surrounding changes in the family, alternation in the cultural theory and practice of femininity, and transformations in the erotic climate induced by the contemporary sexual epidemic, which raises the risks entailed in sexual exchanges. One way to summarize this shift in the erotic economy was suggested by Arthur and Marilouise Kroker, who characterize the contemporary sexual hegemony as an aesthetic of "panic sex," in which sexuality is increasingly represented as a site of "disaccumulation, loss and sacrifice." Panic sex operates affectively "between a melancholy sense of fatalism and a triumphant sense of immunity." Representationally, this hegemony works to produce eroticism as a "scene of a violent and frenzied implosion where sexual activity is coded by the logic of extremism, where consciousness is marked by an intense fear of ruined surfaces... (I)t is just the hint of catastrophe that makes sex bearable." (*Panic Sex in America*, p. 14)

The intuition I tend to elaborate is that *Fatal Attraction*'s success is attributable, at least in part, to the ways it represents and resolves the forms of sexual anxiety it both exploits and produces. The whole economy and narrative development of *Fatal Attraction* work to link sex and loss—loss of stability, security, respect, family and property. At one point, the image of the daughter's dead pet rabbit is offered to us as a carnal image of sacrifice, a motif also represented through the recurring imagery of spilled blood. The narrative unfolds in the direction of increasing catastrophe. The temporal economy of the film works to conflate the pleasures attached to sexual adventurism, restricting their representations to the first reel. After that the fun is definitely over, and the rest of the film devoted to expanding the concentric circles of consequences following from a husband's one night stand with another woman. As the plot unfolds, representations of pleasure are progressively displaced by images of panic, hysteria, destruction and eventually death. *Fatal Attraction* develops as a narrative of sexual panic, but in a way that also produces pleasure for its audience.

Fatal Attraction works to create its specific forms of pleasure in danger by figuring sexual catastrophe in a way that both draws upon and manages the anxieties induced by contemporary sexual conditions. One major mechanism operative in achieving this effect is that of displacement. Within the diegetic logic of the film, social factors, like the decline in nuclear families, the changing position of women, AIDS, are displaced entirely from the frame of reference, and are instead condensed into individuals whose conflicts can then be resolved within an atomistic dramatic framework. But the operations of displacement and condensation also transfigure those anxieties, and thereby the terms of their recuperation. In the case of *Fatal Attraction* the effect is to make the anxieties more manageable and thereby more susceptible to a satisfying resolution, either by being eliminated or by being re-directed in ways that are more productive viz, the existing systems of social utility.

Fatal Attraction is not the only film that attempted to draw upon the connection between pleasure and danger operative in situations of sexual catastrophe. Some of the other recent entries in the mainstream genre of "dangerous sex" films include *Body Heat, The Postman Always Rings Twice* (a remake), *Thief of Hearts, Angel Heart, No Way Out, Black Widow,* and *Falling in Love.* None of these films was nearly as successful at the box office as was *Fatal Attraction.* The film in this group to which it is closest in terms of subject matter is *Falling in Love.* Both films figure sexual catastrophe in terms of the dissolution of what otherwise seem to be well-functioning marriages. I think a quick comparison will provide some clues to the specific representational strategies that help account of the former's success, and which, I think also constitute the core of its ideological significance as a discourse influencing contemporary sexual politics.

In *Falling in Love,* a series of chance encounters between two middle class suburban commuters results in an attraction that eventually disrupts both their marriages. Moreover, the infatuation that comes to take hold of their situation functions without benefit of coitus as lubricant or motive. Both characters are represented as guilty about the prospect of infidelity. Their behavior toward one another is callow, almost adolescent in its awkwardness and indirection. Neither one is living life in the fast lane, but are rather contrasted with peers who cannot understand their reticence in pursuing one another more directly. Both are shown as otherwise devoted to their spouse and in the case of the DeNiro character, his children. Neither one is to blame. Whatever it is that draws them out of their marriages and towards one another is vague, unstable, and thereby produces an anxiety that cannot be contained, resolved or relieved. *Falling in Love,* ended up leaving its audience uneasy, having tapped into a circuitry of anxiety about marital stability and the dynamics of desire that it cannot or does not suture.

Fatal Attraction also opens with images of a well running nuclear family. The couple, played by Michael Douglas and Anne Archer, and their young daughter are healthy, attractive and well dressed. Their apartment is clean and well furnished, and by Hollywood standards is scaled small enough to encourage belief in its verisimilitude. The initial sequence shows Douglas and Archer preparing for an evening out, which suggests both that they have an interesting social life, and also allows the couple to engage in gestures that reveal sexual interest between them. Douglas is shown to be a warm and attentive father. As a lawyer, he is also a representative of middle-class respectability and stability. His identification with the law will later become a figure of irony, as this position will be shown to offer little protection against a force that will eventually threaten not only his well being but the stability of his family as well.

The effect of this opening sequence is to establish the familial economy as a diegetic threshold, an image of stability designed to elicit an identificatory or desirous investment from the audience. It also works to position sexual threat as a force from without, and as a gratuitous, hence unjustified, invasion by the alien or outsider, rather than as a dynamic already operative within the family. By eliciting audience belief in the family's stability, the film mobilizes the audience's investments in the form of a desire for the restitution of the family and the organization of desire it represents, a desire that the film fulfills with its closing shot of the framed family portrait, an image of the family romance recuperated.

The film is capable of satisfying its audiences' desire for the restitution of the family because that which threatens family stability is figured as a singular alien force from without. In *Fatal Attraction*, the family is positioned as the major target of sexual risk, the major victim of the economy of pleasure in danger. Within its diegetic logic, that which threatens the family takes the form of a woman, specifically the "other woman" who disrupts a stable erotic economy by challenging the wife's claim to undivided sexual possession of her husband. In this case, the other woman is an attractive, unmarried New York career woman played by Glenn Close. This construction of sexual threat in the form of an aggressive transgressive female sexuality is certainly not a new diegetic strategy. But in the case of *Fatal Attraction* the figure of female transgression is put to some rather historically specific ideological and narrative use value that I think is worth elaborating as a way of understanding this film's mass appeal.

Dramatically, the figure of Alex provides a kind clarity that was lacking in *Falling in Love*. In *Fatal Attraction*, even if there are no heroes, there is a villain, and therefore a specifiable site of disruption and threat subject to specific mechanisms of containment and eventual elimination. Because sexual threat is figured as a sexually predatory woman, audience sympathies can be mobilized on behalf of the male character who comes to occupy the position of victim, and on behalf of the order of family and law with which he is symbolically linked.

Because I think the construction and development of the character of Alex is crucial to the way the film organizes its audience's expectations, I want to examine it at some length. The establishing shots of Alex work to glamourize her, and thus position her as a culturally decipherable object of desire. She is attractively dressed and beautifully lit. We see her first when Douglas does, at the cocktail party where they engage in brief flirtation, and thus we are encouraged to see her as he does. In this sequence she is shown as poised, confident, as a woman who is accustomed to the attention of men. Her persona is further glamorized when she is shown working for a publisher with which Douglas has legal business. These stylistic and contextual codes establish Alex in terms of the contemporary stereotype of the new age career woman—independent, successful, and sexually sophisticated. The appropriation of this contemporary cultural fiction has dual effects. On the one hand, it makes Douglas' interest in her understandable, even forgivable. After all, this was a desirable woman, desirable in part because she is positioned as an alternative to the traditional full-time wife and mother he has at home, desirable, in other words, because she is not like his woman. Given the way the character of Alex is established, neither Douglas, nor the audience can be expected to foresee the disastrous consequences that follow from Douglas' submission to desire. The problem or risk as figured by *Fatal Attraction* is not Douglas' desire, as such, but its object. His mistake was to have picked the wrong woman. In the logic established by the film, such an error is understandable because the objects are women, creatures of appearance which, in this case, are ultimately deceiving.

This factor allows for Douglas, and the male position he comes to represent, to be removed from the primary sphere of culpability for marital infidelity and its more disastrous social consequences on the one hand. On the other hand, it allows the film to engage in some feminist backlash and misogynist tactics, by offering a woman that the film will make it all too easy to hate, by placing the blame for familial destabilization clearly on the backs of non-traditional women. Certainly this film does not invent feminist backlash. But it does exploit it by developing a narrative logic such that the solution to the problem will appear to be the elimination of woman, or at least of a particular kind of woman. The strategic beauty of this solution, from a hegemonic perspective, is that even though the male character is positioned as the victim, it is the transgressive woman that pays the price. Even though *Fatal Attraction* mobilizes audience sympathy on behalf of the man and the family he represents, it is the women in this film, both Alex and the betrayed wife, that suffer the consequences. Furthermore, this suffering is presented in a way that the audience is induced to take pleasure in it. On the two occasions I saw this film, the scene of Alex's death at the hands of another woman was greeted with tremendous satisfaction.

Part of the pleasure at this climactic moment, to which I will return later, is dependent upon the way in which the character of Alex is transformed from that of being an object of desire to that of castrating predator. This transformation begins with the encounter which results in their one night stand. Given the way this encounter is written and staged, Alex appears to be so much in charge of the situation that every one of her moves appears to be calculated. Douglas' character is made to appear callow, almost innocent by comparison. He represents his interest in her as clearly supplemental. He assures her of the quality of his marriage, which elicits her ironic comment, "then what are you doing here with me?" When he agrees to go home with her, he is operating under that assumption that she understands and agrees to the limited conditions of their involvement. Though both parties acknowledge the importance of discretion, i.e., secrecy about such matters, that part of the bargain is the one which Alex eventually chooses to betray.

The transformation of Alex from glamorous vixen to terrifying bitch begins almost as soon as the two leave the restaurant and return to her loft apartment. Its location within New York's meat market district links Alex with the economy of the sexual meat market. The disarray in her apartment clearly marks her as the nondomestic type, in sharp contrast with the kind of home that Douglas' wife, who is away for the weekend, has provided for him. Her sexual habits also mark her as transgressive, as she begins moving in on Douglas in the elevator, an encounter that culminates in the infamous sex in the sink sequence. This is hardly the good housekeeping kitchen. The appearance of the knife in this sequence also functions as an image of foreboding. It is an instrument that the female protagonist, true to the masochistic tropes of femininity, initially wields on herself in a suicide attempt the morning after when Douglas is getting ready to leave. The knife, as we will later discover, will eventually be aimed at other targets.

As the plot develops, Alex becomes progressively detached from any orienting or stabilizing milieu. There are no more scenes of Alex at work. The film gives us no indication that she has any other interpersonal connections with friends or family. Her wardrobe changes as well. To visually mark her progress toward increasingly predatory behavior, Close begins dressing in black leather, which, at least according to Hollywood stylistic codes, is apparently the preferred fabric choice of sadists. Because Alex appears to belong nowhere, she seems to appear everywhere, in subway stations, on the telephone, and eventually at the male protagonists' apartment, under the guise of a prospective buyer for their condo. When the family moves to the suburbs, she follows them, and begins to shift her attention to the wife and daughter. The course of events works to construct Alex as a threat that is ever more polymorphous and present, an uncontained, unbound female agent in a masculinist social order.

Because the logic/motivation behind Close's pursuit of Douglas remains ambiguous within the diegesis, it is thereby also made to seem all the more terrifying and irrational. At one point, Alex tells Douglas that she is pregnant and that the child is his. Although the film provides ample occasion for the viewer to question its truth, the issue is never diegetically clarified or resolved. Given the forms of deceit of which Alex is shown to be amply capable, the viewer is left with the impression that she very well might by lying about this as well. At another point in the same conversation, she rails at Douglas that she is not just a one night stand. But nothing we have seen from Close and her way of approaching Douglas would suggest she could have expected more from him. Given the directness with which she pursued him, her moral outrage is made to seem irrational, and excessive. By keeping her motivation ambiguous, the logic of the film works to position Alex as an excessive alien threat, to the family, stability, and rationality itself. The development of this anxious economy induces along with it a desire for her elimination, a desire the diegesis satisfies in the final sequence when Alex is, quite completely, eliminated.

Part of what is interesting about *Fatal Attraction* is the way it displaces the threat to masculinity onto a contest between women. Ultimately it is the betrayed wife who must come to the defense of the household. This is because she and not her husband has become Alex's eventual target. The final showdown in the bathroom is the culmination of a series of sequences in which Alex moves in on Douglas' family. The women have been positioned oppositionally from the beginning of the film: housewife vs. career woman, dark haired vs. light haired, married vs. single, mother vs. childless. At one point Alex says she wants the child she is supposedly carrying, and thus all of the sudden seems to want everything the wife has, despite the fact that we are given every indication prior to this that Alex very deliberately is leading another kind of life. When Alex goes after Douglas' wife and child, the transparent logic of this replacement makes her seem all the more insane. On the other hand, it also has the effect of letting the Douglas character off the hook. The really serious consequences of his transgression will accrue to others, and to the innocent.

By the time Alex confronts her rival, the threat Alex poses is literally overflowing, as the water leaks through the floor to the ceiling below, threatening the integrity of the house's structure. By this time, everything in the situation calls for her elimination. In the economy of justice established by the film, it is only appropriate that she who is really threatened, she who represents the stability of the family and the world of "good women" should be the one to eliminate Alex and the threat she poses. On the two occasions I saw the film, the moment of Alex's demise was greeted with great pleasure from the audience. Indeed the film has worked carefully to produce that effect, and anticipates it, by allowing the the camera to linger on Alex's bloody body, which is now dressed in a white sweat shirt ensemble that makes her body look almost naked, revealed, bloodied (perhaps evoking menstrual blood, indicating Alex was not even pregnant after all). The audience's pleasure at Alex's elimination is further stoked by the film's final image, a close-up of a family portrait which assures us that the order represented by the family has been restored.

The figuring of the threat to the family as a female homewrecker, is certainly not new to Hollywood film (indeed the word "homewrecker" is a term almost exclusively applied to women). This construction has persisted as a satisfying fiction because it serves several ideological and psychological functions. Most significantly, in this context, the fiction of the female figuration of sexual temptation helps assure men of their sexual mobility, while also allowing them the assumption of their wife's fidelity, through her containment and conflation within the family. (That is why in this film the wife must stand as protector of the family. She is the family, or stands in the place of it, especially when, in this case it is the only social space the character of the wife is shown to occupy. Though Anne Archer is represented as attractive, she is never shown operating as an independent sexual agent). Through the consumption of such images, men can empower themselves with this fiction of the perpetual accessibility of women outside the family, without having to confront the anxiety about its loss within.

For women spectators, by contrast, I think this fiction works quite differently. The figure of the "other woman" becomes associated not with the promise of plentitude/excess but rather explicitly with the threat of loss. The other woman is made other to and for women. She threatens loss of the woman's key possession—her man. As rival, the other woman can function as a projective screen for a variety of anxieties, resentments and angers, because she is a symptom or emblem of male marital discontent, which is also likely to be perceived as a real threat to women. The figure of the other woman allows the woman spectator to displace her fears of male marital discontent onto women who come to be blamed as its cause. This allows for a reading where it is female and not male transgression that is responsible for the dissolution of marriage and the family. The utility of this kind of fiction for the maintenance of male hegemony cannot be overemphasized, especially at a time in history when the nuclear family is in a state of decline or at least transformation, and contemporary conditions motivate a repackaging of the family as the latest safe sex prophylactic device. The genius of *Fatal Attraction* is the way it works to displace this anxiety onto the bodies and presence of women, especially women who occupy non-traditional roles.

Even though Alex is figured as threatening and therefore as an object of anxiety and/or contempt she is also made to seem attractive. In doing so, the film also works to eroticize and glamorize the threat she represents. Alex is a figure of sex laced with danger. For the audience, of course, this is pleasure at a safe distance. Such a figure is a very fitting one for the era of sexual epidemic allowing for the appropriation of pleasure in danger, while at the same time promising that the threat it represents will also ultimately be contained, neutralized or eliminated. In this way, *Fatal Attraction* provides for its audience a resolution of the anxiety it induces, a resolution that takes a form which is very well suited to the current mood—militaristic combat. *Fatal Attraction* offers what to many is the pleasurable fiction that we can directly combat the forces which threaten us. It also promises that we can do that by directing our combative mechanisms at socially acceptable targets, the bodies of women, and that furthermore the agents of this combat will also be female.

According to the story told by this film, attraction is fatal in the end to and for women. It is they who pay the ultimate price for male transgressions, and they are also the ones who will have to clean up the mess afterward. *Fatal Attraction* can be read as a cautionary tale, or as an exercise in cost—benefit management of sexual risk. Read from the perspective of a female spectator, this indeed is a cautionary tale, alerting us not only to the risks we are all likely to want to displace, but also to the need to be protected from that which also often poses as protection.

On a Soapbox:
All My Children and AIDS Education

Diane M. Calhoun-French

Since its premier in 1970, a hallmark of Agnes Nixon's successful ABC daytime serial *All My Children* has been its commitment to increased viewer awareness and understanding of contemporary social issues: in its early days, the peace movement of the Vietnam era, and in subsequent years such subjects as sexual harassment, drunk driving, the plight of the homeless, and drug and alcohol abuse. It is, therefore, not surprising that *All My Children* was among the first soap operas to introduce a major AIDS storyline, nor that its treatment has been one of the most realistic, thorough, and sustained in daytime drama. Despite its ground-breaking successes with this story, however, *All My Children* ultimately failed at its self-appointed task of AIDS education and wanted courage, at the least, to deal with the unrelentingly harsh reality of AIDS. Moreover, I believe that the nature of its failure has ironically reinforced some of the very attitudes and beliefs about AIDS which writers and producers intended to debunk.

The spectre of AIDS first rears its head in *All My Children's* mythical Pine Valley when rehabilitated drug addict and long-time series character Mark Dalton discovers that Fred Parker—an addict with whom he once shared a needle—has died of AIDS. Fearing the worst, Mark is tested—with the hoped-for result of an HIV-negative reading. In the meantime, a new female character and her son—Cindy and Scott—move into Pine Valley and into the home of Dr. Angela Hubbard. Cindy, it is subsequently revealed, is Cindy Parker, estranged wife of Fred. Hearing of her husband's illness and death, Cindy tests for AIDS and learns that she has contracted the disease. As word of the diagnosis spreads, the townspeople react predictably: some with fear and threats, others with sympathy and support. Foremost among the latter is Stuart Chandler, the "special" twin brother of wealthy Adam Chandler who had spent much of his life institutionalized as a mental patient. Despite Cindy's illness and Stuart's "simplicity," they fall in love, spend an idyllic, ultra-romantic honeymoon in Paris, and set up housekeeping in the picturesque gatehouse on the Chandler estate. As she battles a number of opportunistic infections, Cindy becomes involved in various support and advocacy groups, and, at one point in the later stages of her illness, seeks and finally abandons alternative medical treatments. Aware that the end is near, Stuart determines to find Cindy's sister, from whom she has been

112

estranged since her first marriage, convinced that Cindy will die more peacefully if she is reconciled with her only sibling. And, indeed, such proves to be the case. Cindy dies, having bid serene farewells to her husband, her son, and her sister.

On the positive side, there are many things to commend in *All My Children*'s treatment. It is significant, first and foremost, that the producers resisted the temptation to abandon the storyline when it became too painful and the character of Cindy Chandler too popular. That many critics and viewers expected them to do so is clear from the number of times the producers reiterated their determination to see Cindy's story through to the end. And, of course, the writers could have resorted to any number of ploys and still stayed within the boundaries of the medically possible: having Cindy die ironically by some other means, sending her off-stage to die, or simply having her disappear. Happily, they resorted to none of these unsatisfactory plot devices.

All My Children is also to be congratulated on the number and variety of sub-stories which formed a part of this larger plot. Their extended narrative probed the multifaceted personal, social, political, and medical phenomenon that is AIDS. On the personal side, viewers empathized with a woman working through the stages of a terminal illness and watched her family and friends react with generally believable mixtures of fear, anger, confusion, and grief. *All My Children* also spanned the spectrum of societal reactions to the introduction of AIDS into a small community. There is public harassment of both the person with AIDS and the woman who dares to employ her as a hairdresser, and insensitive treatment at the hands of law enforcement and hospital personnel who act out of fear and ignorance. Cindy's son is even discriminated against by schoolmates and their parents. Support groups are developed for PWA's (*All My Children* was careful to introduce and use this preferred terminology) and the social services provided by a pastoral network explored at some length.* One sub-plot involved bogus holistic healers, another the controversy surrounding the establishment of a special AIDS hospice, and a third the exploitation of PWA's by sensation-seeking media.

All My Children writers demonstrated particular insight with their depiction of the political exploitation AIDS hysteria is ripe for. In her volume entitled *AIDS and Its Metaphors* Susan Sontag writes that "the AIDS epidemic serves as an ideal projection for First World political paranoia," (62) which would have "us" fear the pollution of our physically (as well as morally) pure society by undesirable and contagious aliens. *All My Children*'s head vigilante, who is willing to burn out—in fact, burn up—a woman with AIDS, very much embodies such a frightening neo—Nazi perspective, listing

---

*A group of (apparently) real clergy from several denominations discussed their consortium, the "Interfaith Pastoral Care Services," in a scene remarkable both for its straight informational content and its extraordinary, uninterrupted length.

both Blacks and PWA's in his delineation of the threats to Pine Valley society "decent" people must guard against.

All My Children also succeeds in educating its viewers to a number of important facts about AIDS: its routes of transmission (and the fact that it cannot be spread by casual contact), its most usual symptomology and the primary opportunistic infections and diseases which characterize it, and the psychological effects on persons who have been exposed.

All these things considered, certainly All My Children can be said to have achieved some important goals with the Cindy Parker story. In the pre-C. Everett Koop era of AIDS education, it did tell viewers that one couldn't get the disease by kissing or being shampooed by an infected person; it did roundly denounce all forms of discrimination against PWA's; and, most importantly, it did transform AIDS from a staggering mass of statistics into a human story by eliciting viewer empathy for a decidedly appealing character.

However, having praised All My Children for all the things it did right, let me characterize where I believe it went wrong, especially as the AIDS story moved toward its conclusion in February of 1989. My first dissatisfaction occurred shortly after All My Children announced that it was inaugurating a major AIDS plot when it became clear that a new series character was to be stricken with the disease. Now, wearing my viewer's—not my critic's—hat, I was loath to relinquish one of my favorite characters to a terminal disease and story line. Nevertheless, the story would have driven home the psychological truth that all of us know or will know someone who has AIDS much more compellingly if a PWA had been identified from among existing series characters. Clearly that would have been possible, since the cast included both an IV drug user and a number of hospital personnel, not to mention a plethora of illness and accident victims who had received blood transfusions in the course of one crisis or another. Instead, All My Children resorted to the emotionally cheap ploy of bringing in a new character specifically to sicken and die. There are many, I'm sure, who would criticize All My Children for choosing a heterosexual woman as their person-with-AIDS since AIDS has been, in America though not elsewhere, primarily a disease of homosexual and bisexual males. And indeed, although certain males in Cindy's support group were obviously characterized as homosexuals, the sexuality of PWA's and accompanying homophobia was never a sustained issue. However, it might be argued on the other side that since women represent the fastest growing group of people with AIDS, (Facts, 1) All My Children performed a useful function in reminding viewers that this disease strikes women and men alike. Ultimately, it seems to me, the real problem here was not the gender of the character chosen, but the nature of the individual portrayed—and so, my second criticism of All My Children's story: its muddying of the issues of AIDS and sexuality and even AIDS and sex.

From the outset, Cindy Chandler is depicted as an asexual being—sometimes overtly, more often by implication. She looks stereotypically angelic and virginal, with long, straight, fine blond hair, which she tends to wear in childlike coiffures. She rarely wears make-up, and her clothes, on the few occasions when she dresses up, tend to be grown-up variations of little girl prettiness. In one scene, during which Stuart calls her a princess, she descends a staircase to appropriately childlike strains wearing a full-skirted print dress with a high collar and a large bow at the back. The man whom she marries, Stuart Chandler, is similarly childlike. A highly protean character—such as one often finds in soapland—Stuart has been gradually transformed from a dangerous mental patient into a supremely wise fool (without the benefit of any real medical treatment). Like Cindy, he is presented as asexual—a romantic, overgrown child. Although they often kiss one another, Stuart and Cindy are seen only in *romantic* embraces— never passionate ones—and *never* in bed—not even talking, in what is favorite soap opera territory for heart-to-heart conversations. Their courtship and marriage are constantly symbolized by such emblems as carousel horses and brass rings and accompanied by a concertina rendition of "Love Makes the World Go Round."

The significance of all this is twofold. First, by continually depicting Cindy as "the innocent," *All My Children* perpetuates by implication a notion still prevalent in America when AIDS is spoken of—that there are "the guilty" who deserve to get AIDS and the innocent who will always get it too as long as the guilty are not properly segregated, identified, or destroyed. Indeed, this suggestion is aggravated by the writers' defining Cindy's innocence as sexual innocence, since AIDS is a disease linked in the popular imagination with sexual "misconduct" in any of its several manifestations. What the writers have done—unwittingly, I believe—is exactly what our culture has unfortunately done: turned what is a medical problem into a social/political one. In an earlier work entitled *Illness as Metaphor* Susan Sontag warns of the results when illness stops being thought of as simply illness and, "encumbered by the trappings of metaphor," (5) starts being thought of as something more. The consequences of such thinking, of course, may be devastating for all those associated with the "something more," as they have been for homosexual males in this country.

Thus, instead of creating sympathy for all PWA's, as *All My Children* seems to have intended, the program has done the opposite on an unconscious level, suggesting that the sexually "deviant" (homosexuals, sexually active singles, etc.) deserve, or at least must accept the possibility of, AIDS—a view at the heart of all who believe that abstinence is the only form of prevention which ought to be advocated in public AIDS education.

The second consequence of the asexual, purely romantic treatment of Cindy's and Stuart's marriage is that *All My Children* completely skirts the issue of safe sex. This is unsatisfactory from two perspectives. First, like other AIDS education, which tends to reticence when specific sexual practices are at issue, *All My Children* fails to give important information which ought to be included in any viable education effort. Secondly, it reinforces the moral idea that abstinence is the preferred method of protection. There is a scene during which another female PWA in Cindy's support group asks Stuart to speak to her fiancé about what kind of safe sex she and her new husband will be able to engage in (only after marriage, of course). While Stuart readily agrees to talk to him, implying that he and Cindy are as sexually active as any normal married couple, everything in the presentation of Cindy and Stuart and their relationship—as I have already demonstrated—argues otherwise. And the message again seems to be "just say no." An irony (and danger) of all this, of course, is that in every one of *All My Children*'s other story lines, it is business as usual where sex is concerned. No one seems to think twice about sleeping with anyone else, no one worries about condoms or other protections, and no one ever mentions AIDS. In terms of viewer education efforts, there is clearly some unfortunate doublethink here—akin to the same kind of doublethink that permeates soap world: "although sex outside of marriage is wrong, it's OK because everybody does it."

A third flaw in *All My Children*'s AIDS story was the sentimentalized depiction of Cindy Chandler's death. As anyone knows who has read or seen a realistic description of AIDS patients in the last stages of their illness, AIDS, like cancer, is characterized by a "hard death." And, indeed, in an episode some months before her death, Cindy is shown at the bedside of a dying PWA whose chronic, terrible pain shows in his ravaged face and labored breathing. Cindy's death, by contrast, is very clearly romanticized. After she enters the hospital for the last time and it is clear her death is imminent, Cindy's former employer and co-worker from the beauty parlor arrive with their "tools" to give her a psychological lift. She emerges from their ministrations with delicate pearl earrings and an ultra-feminine ruffled nightgown, her hair glistening and swept off her face with a pink ribbon— an altogether lovely, if fragile, creation. In the scenes which follow, as she drifts gently in and out of consciousness, she bids tender farewells to friends and family and she and Stuart reminisce about their idyllic courtship and marriage—all to appropriately sentimental melodies. With a final reprise of "Love Makes the World Go Round," Cindy slips easily away—only to materialize at the doorway of her sleeping son's room. Scott awakens to find his mother bending over him, wearing a simple flowered dress and looking as she always looked. After telling him that she loves him and that "everything will be all right," Cindy walks to the door, turns for one last look and vanishes.

Clearly, Cindy's is a version of the idealized death Susan Sontag describes in *Illness as Metaphor*. Beginning with the contention that tuberculosis preoccupied the nineteenth-century as cancer does the twentieth, Sontag describes the "beatific...ennobling, placid" (16-17) death popularly associated with tuberculosis and the "hard" death popularly associated with cancer wherein the dying person is "robbed of all capacities of self-transcendence, humiliated by fear and agony." (107) She further demonstrates how the mythologies of these diseases and the "deaths" which eventuate from them affect cultural attitudes toward patients who are stricken with them—often negatively. Clearly this problem is at the heart of *All My Children*'s superimposition of a romantic death onto a realistic one. This treatment denigrates the PWA as Sontag claims cancer patients have been denigrated; *i.e.*, suggesting by omission and substitution that there is something undignified, shameful, less than human about one kind of death and, by extension, one kind of "die-er." This is especially unfortunate with AIDS, since—by virtue of the primary circumstances of its transmission in this country—it is a disease already associated with shame and guilt.

My final disappointment with *All My Children*'s Cindy Parker story occurred when writers introduced the Karen Parker story. As early as nine months before Cindy's death, references begin to be made to an estranged older sister, Karen, whom Cindy steadfastly refuses to discuss or contact. Regular viewers understand immediately, of course, that such dialogue anticipates the off-stage character's arrival on the scene. And, as I have already explained, she does arrive in time to reconcile with Cindy before her death. Although Karen is not a twin sister, she is identical in appearance (which is not surprising since both characters are played by Emmy-winning actress Ellen Wheeler). Two things indicate that *All My Children* writers and producers did not anticipate this development when they began the AIDS story. First, there is the testimony of Ellen Wheeler, who discussed her short-term role and contract shortly after she assumed the role. And second, there is the discrepancy created by the Parker surname. Supposedly, Cindy's name is Parker by marriage. Why, then, is her sister's name also Parker? Clearly because giving her that name made Stuart's secret search for her possible. Had the writers intended to keep Ellen Wheeler on from the start as a new character after Cindy's death, surely they would have made more careful preparation from the outset.

All this illustrates the bind in which *All My Children* found itself with this story and why writers must add to their failure at AIDS education the failure to do an emotionally credible AIDS story. I have already criticized the writers for undercutting the potential emotional impact of this plot by making the AIDS character a new cast member with whom the audience had not developed a strong emotional bond. This same sort of emotional erosion happened with the introduction of Karen Parker. Once the audience had developed a deep identification with and affection for Cindy, the writers had a significant opportunity to make viewers feel the loss of a loved one to AIDS (as we have all grieved at one time or another for the loss of beloved characters in television, film, and fiction). Instead, they lacked the courage to confront the ultimate truth about AIDS. Cindy dies, but not before she is *already* resurrected in the person of a sister who looks exactly like her. Consequently, the viewer is deprived of a valuable vicarious experience and left instead with a cheap sleight of hand which trivializes what might have been a poignant and moving climax.

Certainly *All My Children* made a strenuous effort to develop an emotionally and factually credible AIDS story. But they fell short on both counts—sometimes by substituting one version of reality for another and sometimes by omitting certain truths too important to be left out. In the process, they propagated negative attitudes toward PWA's in the sub-text of a story which intended exactly the opposite. They perpetuated the attachment of sexual guilt and innocence to a medical condition, and, in their retreat from the hard death of AIDS, implied that such an end was shameful and disgusting. There are probably many reasons why *All My Children*'s good intentions went awry. One is surely economic: viewers determine which characters come and which characters go and what happens to them. And soap viewers usually want fantasy, not reality. The strong taboos still operating in soapland provide a second explanation. While there are token homosexuals (almost always male) and the rare incest scare, daytime drama still worries about offending the sensibilities of its viewer. And it isn't surprising, then, that having made its foray into the world of sexually transmitted diseases, *All My Children* has retreated to safer territory where the only consequence of sex one worries about is the unintended pregnancy. A final reason why *All My Children* was never able to disengage AIDS-as-disease from AIDS-as-moral-judgment can be sought in the value system which undergirds all popular social melodrama. As John Cawelti observes in *Adventure, Mystery, and Romance*, the notion of a "benevolent moral order in the universe" is a central organizing principle of the "moral fantasy" (262) of melodrama. Such a moral fantasy demands vindication of the good and punishment of the evil, and it permeates the world of daytime drama. Perhaps, then, it would be impossible for any soap opera to separate questions of guilt, innocence, and morality from consideration of a sexually transmissible disease. After all, in the Pine Valleys of television land, it is usually characters' sexual attitudes and conduct which locate them on the continuum of good and evil, and it is often illness which punishes or purges those who fall toward the wrong pole. Ultimately, perhaps, *All My Children* should not have tackled a topic so resonant with social, political, and cultural implications—not when the cost of distortion will be measured in negative attitudes toward people who can least afford to be victims of them. Ultimately, perhaps *no* soap is ready to deal with any issue like AIDS which demands more realistic treatment than this genre is yet prepared to deliver.

Works Cited

John G. Cawelti, *Adventure, Mystery, and Romance: Formula Stories as Art and Popular Culture* (Chicago: The University of Chicago Press, 1976), p. 262.

Facts on Women and AIDS (New York: NOW Legal Defense and Education Fund, 1988), p. [1].

Susan Sontag, *AIDS and Its Metaphors* (New York: Farrar, Straus and Giroux, 1988)
———— *Illness as Metaphor* (New York: Farrar, Straus and Giroux, 1988).

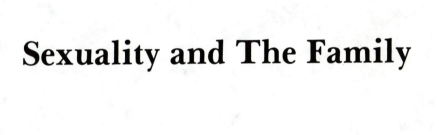

Sexuality and The Family

Identity Crisis:
The African Connection
In African American Sitcom Characters

Minabere Ibelema

Besides concerns with representation and coverage, studies and critical appraisal of African Americans in the media have focused on their portrayal from the early years of film at the turn of the century, through radio a few decades later, to television in the 1980s. The thrust of these studies is that their portrayal has been negative and stereotypical.[1] Among the stereotypes identified by critics and researchers are the shiftless Negro, the happy-go-lucky singer/dancer, the street-smart hustler, the buffoon, the fat, docile mammy, the matriarch, and the lecherous black man.[2]

These stereotypes have evolved through the various media and apparently reflect deep-rooted societal attitude towards African Americans. Some scholars have traced some of the stereotypes to Euro-American perception of Africans and African culture. Anthropologist Elliot P. Skinner, for instance, sees a link between the negative portrayal of Africa and the views held of black Americans by white Americans. "This portrayal has meaning for American society in that the presence of blacks in America serves to underscore the supportive myths about Africa," Skinner has been quoted as saying (Artis, pp. 48-49). If this is the case, then the portrayal of African Americans in relation to their African cultural identity may be revealing of the nature and impetus of media stereotyping.

But in spite of the potential insight, little has been done to examine the overt portrayal of blacks in the media with regard to their expression or projection of identity with African culture. Even studies and critical appraisals of the television program *Roots* glossed over this element apparently because, as a mini-series, it could not have established a pattern from which to draw larger conclusions.[3] This study explores the African connection in the characterization of African Americans by examining how the theme of African cultural identity is dealt with in television situation comedies.

Three specific questions are examined: (1) How frequently is identity with African culture an episodic theme in situation comedies featuring major African American characters? (2) Is development of that theme, taken as a whole, supportive or dissuasive of such identity? And (3) What theoretical perspectives best explain the supportive or dissuasive portrayal?

Research Method and Rationale

Situation comedies or 'sitcoms' were chosen for this study for several reasons. First, they are the most popular form of programming (*World Almanac*, 357). Second, of all dramatic programs (night and daytime soaps, cop shows, adventure series, mysteries) sitcoms have the highest African American representation (Reid). For instance, compared to other dramatic forms, there have been more sitcom programs that revolve around African American characters. Third, contrary to popular belief, as David Marc notes, sitcoms tend to be more reflective of societal tendencies than any other dramatic form. Given these considerations then, an examination of sitcoms is as good a beginning as any for the study of the subject of this paper.

The programs examined are *Sanford and Son, What's Happening, The Jeffersons, Diff'rent Strokes, Facts of Life*, and *Gimme a Break*. All but one of these programs feature blacks as the main characters. The exception, *Facts of Life*, has one major black character.

Data for this paper were gathered first by perusing the synopses of every episode of the programs. Episodes dealing with racial or ethnic identity were selected and viewed for the critique. Scripts for episodes that for logistical or contractual reasons could not be viewed were obtained and perused. Thus, the research data do not represent casual references to issues of identity; they represent only treatment of the topic as an episodic theme.

Frequency of Identity as Episodic Theme

Very few episodes of the programs explore African American identity with Africa as a primary or secondary storyline. No episode of *Gimme a Break* deals with racial or ethnic identity. Only one episode of *What's Happening*, deals with a racial theme[4] and none deals with cultural identity with Africa. *The Jeffersons* has one episode that deals with African ancestry and *Facts of Life* has one on African identity. Another episode of *Facts of Life* explores interracial dating. *Diff'rent Strokes* has one episode dealing directly with African identity and *Sanford and Son* has two.

Nature of Portrayal

There is a definite pattern in all the episodes on African or racial identity. First, concern with African identity results from a personal crisis. The African American character does not project his African cultural identity in normal times. Overt awareness and projection are triggered by an event or in moments of self-doubt. Secondly, the character begins to engage in uncharacteristic behavior, rejects most social norms, and acts in exaggeratedly strange ways. In other words, overt awareness and expression of African identity is portrayed as a form of personal revolution and social rebellion. Thirdly, the character is confronted with 'evidence' that convinces him that assertion of African identity is not necessary. Fourthly and finally, the character reverts to his old ways, and the identity crisis is over.

One of the two episodes of *Sanford and Son* dealing with African identity is the most illustrative of this pattern of portrayal. In that episode, entitled "Lamont goes African," Lamont Sanford's meeting with a princessly Nigerian woman precipitates a fanatical embrace of his African heritage. He drops the name Lamont in favor of an African name, replaces his Western shirts with 'dashiki' and insists that his father, Fred Sanford, not eat sausage because it contains 'pig poison'. When Lamont comes home for the first time following his cultural conversion and tries to persuade Fred to accept his new identity, the following dialogue ensues:

LAMONT: I'm a black man, right?
FRED: You can say that again. (Laughter)
LAMONT: So I should have a name and a language and clothes that let everybody know I am a black man.
FRED: Listen, people will know you are a black man if your name was Spiro D. Agnew. (Heavy laughter)
LAMONT: We shouldn't even have these names. Do you know any white people with names like Lumumba, or Kasavubu or De Shaka?
FRED: I don't even know no black people with names like that.
LAMONT: That's the point, pop. Black people in America have been cut off from their homeland for so long they don't even know the names of their ancestors.
FRED: My father's name was Sanford, his father's name was Sanford. And their fathers'. We've all been Sanford. Now I've been cut off from my homeland a little over 30 years. (Laughter)
LAMONT: And I suppose that's when your ancestors left Africa, ha?
FRED: No, that's when I left St. Louis. (Heavy laughter)
LAMONT: I'm talking about before that.
FRED: Before that, well, that was ancient history. Don't even bring that up.
LAMONT: Pop, what we called ourselves before we called ourselves Sanford is what is important to black people, because that reflects where we originally came from. And that's why I have chosen a name that leaves no doubt about my origin.
FRED: And what's your original new name?
LAMONT: Kalunda. (Scattered laughter)
FRED: Kaa what? (Laughter)
LAMONT: Kalunda.
FRED: If you think I'm gonna change the sign from Sanford and Son to Sanford and Kalunda, you're crazy. (Laughter) (*Sanford and Son*, "Lamont Goes African," Tandem Productions, 1972.)

After some jesting with the name, Fred said, "It just doesn't sound right for a junk dealer. With a name like that you should be driving an elephant, not a truck" (Heavy laughter).

Fred was unsuccessful in convincing Lamont to shed his new identity, but a subsequent development in the plot did. During a visit by the Nigerian woman, Olaiya, Lamont is irked by Fred's continued skepticism about the "African thing," as Fred calls it, and they both go into a spirited argument.

Olaiya is stunned by Lamont's conduct and chastises him for disrespecting his father, a behavior she says is not tolerated in Africa. Before departing, to underscore her disapproval of Lamont's behavior, Olaiya counsels Lamont:

Brother Kalunda, you have far to go along this path you have chosen for yourself before you reach your destination. Do not mistake Dashiki and sculpture and hairstyle for Africa, because they aren't. Nor can you expect merely to put on that cloth and become such a man as your ancestors were. The clothes you can put on and take off; it is the heart you must change—the heart.

This counsel apparently convinced Lamont that African identity, at least in the forms he was expressing it, was not for him. Soon after Olaiya's departure, Lamont shed his dashiki, and when Fred referred to him as Kalunda, he responded: "The name is Lamont." There was no explicit or implicit commitment by Lamont to 'change the heart,' and subsequent episodes of the program reflected neither an outward expression that Lamont engaged in nor the inward transformation that Olaiya prescribed.

An episode of *Diff'rent Strokes* entitled "Roots" explores the issue of identity with the same pattern of crisis, resolution and normalcy. The two black boys living with a benevolent white millionaire take steps to assert their African cultural identity after being told by their Harlem mate that they were getting indoctrinated into white American culture. They suddenly become aware that their adoptive father takes them to ballets and similar elite cultural events, but not to black ones. The boys adopt African names, insist on eating only ethnic dishes, obtain African cultural artifacts, including decorative masks and drums, mount them all over their rooms, and begin to beat their drums to a deafening frenzy, screaming in the tradition of Tarzan movies. After trying in vain to get the boys to moderate their nascent cultural expressiveness, their adoptive father, Mr. Drummond, turns to a black psychologist for help. The psychologist gets Mr. Drummond to admit that he has done little to expose the boys to black culture and influences and to promise to redress that. And he counsels the boys that "blackness isn't just a matter of what you eat or the way you walk or talk. It's the way you think, feel and conduct your life." (Tandem Productions, 1981, *Diff'rent Strokes*, "Roots"). With the family crisis thus resolved, the boys return to normalcy, the masks and drums all gone.

Another example is an episode of *Facts of Life*. Tootie, the black character among a group of white students, has an identity crisis when her segregationist new boyfriend implied that she may be becoming too 'white.' In the episode entitled "Who Am I?," Tootie begins to assert her cultural differences with her white mates in every way possible. She even refuses to go to a dance contest with a white dance partner with whom she won the contest the previous year and opts instead for her black boyfriend. But during the dance she realizes that the boyfriend is not nearly as good a dancer as her white partner. An ensuing dialogue with the boyfriend convinces Tootie that her nascent concern with her cultural identity is unwarranted. Accordingly, she turns again to her white dance partner and they win the contest again.

The pattern of thematic development in these three episodes is typical of all the episodes dealing with African Americans' identity with their ethnic origin.[5] That is, African American identity with African culture is depicted as a passing fancy that surfaces only in times of cultural identity crisis, rather than as an enduring element of the black psyche. In no episode is the new awareness sustained to the end. In "Lamont Goes African," it is not clear why Olaiya's well-meaning advice to Lamont causes him to abandon his new cultural views. In "Roots," the *Diff'rent Strokes* episode, the adoptive father makes promises to the boys to appease them and so they give up their new cultural commitment—entirely. And in "Who Am I?," Tootie returns to her 'normal' ways for very tenuous reasons. The morale of each story seems to be that nascent identity with African culture is an abnormality, and, like most abnormalities, it can be rectified with appropriate measures or in due course.

It is important to emphasize that in no episode is African (or African-American) culture denigrated. In "Lamont Goes African," for instance, the Nigerian woman is portrayed as beautiful, intelligent, cultured and dignified. Even the skeptical Fred ends up trying on the dashiki and owning that there is substance to the "African thing." Nothing in the portrayal could make a strong case of racism, per se. Yet the portrayal of African Americans' cultural identity with Africa as a transient abnormality begs for explanation.

Theoretical Perspectives on Portrayal

The pattern of portrayal identified here bears some resemblance to a theory of identity evolution first postulated by William E. Cross, Jr. Cross posited that African Americans come to terms with their identity through a process involving five stages: the pre-encounter (or pre-discovery) stage, the encounter (or discovery) stage, the immersion-emersion stage, the internalization stage, and the commitment stage. The programs under analysis imply the first stage, specify the second stage, deal rapidly with the third, and reverse the process before it reaches the fourth and fifth stages in which permanent transformation is attained.[6] While Cross states that progression to the final stage is not automatic and, in fact, that some people revert to pre-encounter characteristics, there is no suggestion that reversion is the dominant or usual tendency. And while there are no figures on the rate at which African Americans come to terms with their identity (internalization-commitment) and it is probably impossible to quantify, studies of groups such as black moslems suggest that those who have the encounter and immersion experience do not typically revert to their pre-encounter outlook (see, e.g. Essien-Udom; Porter and Washington). Thus the portrayal of identity with Africa as a transient phenomenon does not seem to have a basis in reality.

There is probably no one theory that exclusively explains the pattern of portrayal identified here, but two theories seem to be the most plausible, namely, media determinism and cultural assimilation. The dictates of the medium and media producers' inherent belief in the soundness and vitality of the American socio-political and cultural system seem to be the most plausible explanations for the portrayal.

Marshall McLuhan's notorious aphorism that "The medium is the message" provides a general basis for understanding the constraints of the medium on the message. McLuhan's point, in essence, is that every medium places some parameters within which the messenger must work. For this study, the parameters are those of the medium of the situation comedy.

The format of the sitcom is quite rigid. As Sholle notes, "A look at its structure...reveals a fixed form that limits not only possible narratives but possible solutions." Unlike straight dramas, which thrive on what Hollywood calls cliff-hangers, sitcoms have self-contained episodes. Few episodes have storylines that are "To be continued." Therefore, the plot for each episode has to be developed and resolved within the 23 or so minutes of actual body time. That forces a quick resolution to every storyline. And since the episodes are self-contained, writers avoid leaving "unfinished businesses" which will affect the storylines of other episodes. They are especially careful not to introduce a new situation to the situation comedy. That explains, for instance, why Rebecca never goes to bed with Sam (in *Cheers*), and Fred and Lamont always lose whatever wealth comes their way. If Lamont had not abandoned his nascent Africanness, for instance, the 'situation' of *Sanford and Son* would have changed in a way that would have affected future storylines.

In regular drama there is continuity in storyline. For that reason, a theme introduced in one episode is likely to remain with the show indefinitely or for several episodes. In contrast, sitcom episodes tend to be independent of each other. The characters and their situation are the elements of continuity. The storylines are not. The sitcom medium, thus, limits the options for ending its episodes.

Also, since sitcoms thrive on exaggeration, the exaggerated behavior of the transformed characters may be attributed to the medium. In this case, the exaggeration provides a justification for treating the new identity as a passing crisis. Thus the medium not only prescribes the nature of characterization but also justifies a particular resolution.

However, though exaggeration is a common element of comedy, it is not an essential one. As Mel Watkins has noted, for instance, traditional African-American comedy derives more from nuances of delivery than on punchlines. Producers and writers in the programs here did not have to resort to exaggeration. Also, though the medium limits options for ending episodes, it does not specify them. Thus, producers who have reason to modify characters or situations still do so. Therefore, neither the whimsical element of comedy nor the constraint of sitcom plots satisfactorily explains the portrayal of African identity as transient.

A more cogent explanation of the depiction is the media's tendency to portray mainstream American values and tradition as all-serving and self-redeeming. Lee Loevinger's "reflective-projective theory" of mass communication explains this tendency. Loevinger "postulates that mass communications are best understood as mirrors of society that reflect an ambiguous image in which each observer projects or sees his own version of himself and society" (252). Loevinger supports his characterization of the nature of mass communication by arguing that:

A nation or community is formed by common interest and culture—by a common image and vision of itself. But to have a common image or vision, there must be one that is seen, understood, and accepted by most people, not merely by a minority or by an elite. This requires that the social image reflected in the media mirrors be one that truly reflect the masses (p. 256).

While Loevinger's argument is aimed at those who wonder why television is not dominated by elite programming, his point does also explain why African-American expression of African identity is portrayed as rebellious and transient. To let the characters' new identity become permanent would be to suggest that American mainstream values is not good enough for all Americans. That would be a deviation from the collective image in Loevinger's theory. Moreover, as Gans has noted, the media rarely blame American mainstream political and social values for American problems (in the sense that they blame communism for the problems of the Soviet Union, Cuba or Nicaragua, for instance). Rather the media treat them as rectifiable conditions or "as deviant cases, with the implication that American ideals, at least, remain viable" (Gans, 42). Thus, the African American characters' reversion to their old identity serves to reinforce the viability of mainstream values and to uphold the collective mirror. That is, all problems can be redressed in the context of mainstream values, not outside them.

The portrayal of African Americans is also consistent with Milton Myron Gordon's theory of assimilation in America. Gordon posits that the concept of assimilation, rather than that of "the melting pot" or "cultural pluralism," is the dominant tendency in race interaction in the United States. Gordon writes that assimilation is characterized by Anglo-conformity, which has "as a central assumption the desirability of maintaining English institutions (as modified by the American Revolution), the English language, and English-oriented cultural patterns as dominant and standard in American life" (88). That contrasts with the melting pot (in which all cultures contribute to a shared new standard) and cultural pluralism (in which each culture maintains its separate identity in co-existence with others.) The programs seem to encourage Anglo-conformity, with minor trade-offs as necessary.

That minority portrayal is consistent with the goals of assimilation is further supported by stages in minority presence in the media. Cedric Clark has identified four stages in the portrayal of minorities as: (1) non-recognition (when the minority is hardly present in the media), (2) ridicule, (3) regulation (when the group is portrayed in roles that convey adherence to law and order) and (4) respect. These stages may be explained as follows: A minority group is initially ignored in the media because it is not considered a part of the culture. But when that minority can no longer be ignored (for social or political reasons), it is ridiculed to discredit its culture and values. Discrediting of the group's culture induces self-doubt within the group and thus a willingness to be assimilated into the dominant culture.[7] Regulation then would have the effect of conditioning the dominant culture for acceptance of the minority. Having been assimilated, at least to a satisfactory degree, the minority is then respected. This granted, one may add 'maintenance' as a fifth level of portrayal by which assimilation is reinforced. Thus, projection of African identity as a transitory frame of mind may serve to remind African Americans that they have no reason to look beyond their American identity.

It is important to distinguish between this argument and the one that attributes black characterization to the stereotypical images held of blacks. Crediting the idea to Tony Brown, Melbourne S. Cummings writes, for instance, that the characters in most black sitcoms are "appealing precisely because (their) images do not disturb or dispute the overall view of black people generally held in the minds of the viewing American audience." However, the unprecedented popularity of The (unstereotypical) Cosby Show defies this theory. Granted one can dismiss The Cosby Show as an exception. Still, the larger idea that mainstream values, not stereotypes, per se, are the dominant force in program creation and acceptance provides a more compelling explanation of black portrayal on television. Certainly, stereotypes are inherent aspects of cultural values. But as The Cosby Show demonstrates, consistency with other aspects of the values can override stereotypes in determining program acceptance and popularity.

The Cosby Show epitomizes family wholesomeness, fun and comfortable living, in easy combination with individuality, adolescent misadventures, and adult wisdom. These are aspects of the American cultural vision which, without going into a detailed analysis of the factors of program popularity, must be elements of the popularity of The Cosby Show. Moreover, while the program is non-racial in tone and theme, it seems to convey a sense that the American ideal has no regard for race, and perhaps that African Americans are at last an integral part of that ideal. In short, The Cosby Show seems a perfect exemplification of the reflective—projective—mirror theory.

Conclusion

The foregoing findings and analysis suggest two predictions on media portrayal of African Americans. One is that, even if society's stereotypical views of African Americans continue, African Americans increasingly will be portrayed positively—successfully—in the media, if the programs tap into aspects of the American collective self-image that can override the stereotypical views. Conversely, and for the same reasons, African American assertion of African cultural identity is less likely to be endorsed in mainstream entertainment programs. Certainly, it will not be a recurrent theme in such programming.

Acknowledgment

An earlier draft of this paper was presented at the Popular Culture Association Conference, St. Louis, MO., April 5-8, 1989. The author wishes to thank participants in the session on "Black American Identity and Popular Culture" for their very useful suggestions and encouragement. The author wishes to thank also the publicity departments of Columbia Pictures Television (Los Angeles) WRGT-TV, WHIO-TV and WKEF-TV (all of Dayton, Ohio) for their assistance and cooperation.

Notes

[1]Among the studies and reports on stereotypical portrayals are: Thomas Cripps, *Slow Fade to Black: The Negro in American Film (1900-1942)* (New York: Oxford University Press, 1977); United States Civil Rights Commission, "Window Dressing: Women and Minorities in Television," (Washington, D.C.: United States Government Printing Office, 1977), Marilyn Diane Fife, "Black Image in American TV: The First Two Decades," *The Black Scholar,* (Nov. 1974), pp. 7-15. Even empirical research that finds that negative black characters are proportionately not greater than negative white characters still conclude that the net effect of portrayal is more negative for blacks. See, for instance, J.L. Hinton et al, "Tokenism and Improving Imagery for Blacks in TV Drama and Comedy: 1973," *Journal of Broadcasting,* 18 (Fall 1974), pp. 423-432.

[2]Some of these stereotypes are mentioned in the works cited above and also in Robert Toll, *Black Up: The Minstrel Show in 19th Century America* (New York: Oxford University Press, 1974); H.L. Gates, Jr., "Portraits in Black: From Amos 'n' Andy to Coonskin," *Harper,* (June 1976), pp. 16-19; and Melbourne S. Cummings, "The Changing Image of the Black Family on Television," *Journal of Popular Culture,* 22 (Fall 1988), pp. 75—85.

[3]See, for instance, "Forum: Symposium on 'Roots'," *The Black Scholar,* (May 1977), pp. 36-42 and Phillip Vandor, "On the Meaning of 'Roots'," *Journal of Communication,* 4 (Fall 1977), pp. 64-69.

[4]That episode was about a case of reverse—reverse discrimination: Dee is denied a place on her school's cheerleading squad in favor of a less deserving white rival, who is chosen to meet racial quotas.

[5]Participants at a panel of the 1989 Popular Culture Association Conference commented after the presentation of this paper that the sitcoms "Fish" and "Good Times" also have episodes on identity crisis that follow the pattern here.

[6]This writer does not assume that the program producers were aware of Gross's model and actually intended to reflect it in the plots.

[7]One support for this conjecture is a finding that blacks who watch a lot of entertainment programs tend to have lower self-esteem while whites who watch at comparable levels do not: Alexis S. Tan and Gerdean Tan, "Television Use and Self-Esteem: Ethnic Studies in Black and White," *Journal of Communication,* 29 (Winter 1979), pp. 129-135.

Works Cited

Artis, William Jr. "The Tribal Fixation" *Columbia Journalism Review* (Fall 1970): 48-49.

Clark, Cedric. "Television and Social Controls: Some Observations on the Portrayal of Ethnic Minorities." *Television Quarterly* (Spring, 1969): 18-22.

Cross, William E. Jr. "The Negro-to-Black Conversion Experience: Toward a Psychology of Black Liberation,"*Black World* (July 1971): 13-27.

Cummings, Melbourne S. "The Changing Image of the Black Family on Television" *Journal of Popular Culture* 22 (Fall 1988): 75-85.

Essien-Udom, Essien—Udosien. *Black Nationalism: A Search for an Identity in America.* Chicago: University of Chicago Press, 1962.

Gans, Herbert J. *Deciding What's News: A Study of CBS Evening News, NBC Nightly News, Newsweek and Time.* New York: Vintage, 1979.

Gordon, Milton Myron. *Assimilation in American Life: The Role of Race, Religion and National Origins.* New York: Oxford University Press, 1964.

Loevinger, Lee. "The Ambiguous Mirror: The Reflective-Projective Theory of Broadcasting and Mass Communication," Gary Gumpert and Robert Cathcart, eds., *Inter/Media: Interpersonal Communication in a Media World.* New York: Oxford University Press, 1979, pp. 243-260.

Marc, David. *Comic Visions: Television Comedy and American Culture,* Winchester, MA: Unwin Hyman, 1989.

McLuhan, Marshall. *Understanding Media: The Extensions of Man.* New York: McGraw-Hill, 1964.

Porter, Judith R. and Robert E. Washington, "Black Identity and Self-Esteem: A Review of Studies of Black Self-Concept, 1968-1978," *Annual Review of Sociology* 5 (1979): 53-74.

Reid, Pamela Trotman. "Racial Stereotyping on Television: A Comparison of the Behavior of Both Black and White Television Characters." *Journal of Applied Psychology* 64 (October 1979): 465-471.

Sholle, David J. "Critical Studies: From the Theory of Ideology to Power/Knowledge," *Critical Studies in Mass Communication* 5 (1988): 16-41.

Watkins, Mel. "Beyond the Pale," *Channels.* (April/May 1982): 56-60.

——— *World Almanac and Book of Facts,* 1989. New York: World Almanac, 1989.

Not as Tough as It Looks:
Images of Mothering in Popular Culture

Diane Raymond

Somehow the questions raised here did not take on a problem-solving or strategy-laden dimension but rather concerned mothers, mothering, motherhood. As we found them inside of us. No feminist theory of motherhood? Well, we will start to invent one. We start with our hands on our pulses.
>
(Duplessis, 2)

My children cause me the most exquisite suffering of which I have any experience.
>
(Rich, 1)

In *The Dialectic of Sex*, radical feminist Shulamith Firestone argued that women's oppression is rooted in biology. Like conservatives who maintain that there are undeniable biological differences between men and women, she maintains that these differences—more specifically, women's biological capacity to bear and give birth to children—account for the inequalities between men and women. Unlike the conservative, however, Firestone rejects the notion that "biology is destiny" and defends the use of technology to free women from reproduction. Firestone found it unbelievable that anyone would want to *bear* children. The "joy of giving birth" is a patriarchal myth, more akin to "shitting a pumpkin" (198).

When Firestone wrote, only contraception, abortion, and sterilization were widely used. Today, however, embryo transfers, *in vitro* fertilization, embryo freezing, and surrogacy are realities. A woman who begets a child need not bear it, and a woman who bears a child need not rear it. Cloning and artificial placentas may be options in the not-too-distant future, making it possible for women's role in the reproductive process to be as limited as men's. Further, once born, a child would be able to have any number of either sex parent(s), offering virtually limitless alternative family constellations.

Most feminists, however, now reject Firestone's techno-optimism. For some, since it is men who control technology, it will be men who control reproductive technology; "through the years, with widespread use of the technologies, social institutions will be restructured to reflect a new reality—tightened male control over female reproductive processes" (Corea 38). It has become obvious, particularly since the litigations involved in the Baby

131

M case and the more recent decision over "ownership" of frozen embryos, that one cannot assume that new reproductive technologies represent greater freedom for women; "in a system characterized by power imbalance, the greater the asymmetry, the greater the potential abuse of the less powerful group" (Hanmer 444-445). Critics of the new reproductive technologies maintain that these technologies may take from women the one source of power they possess—childbearing—and put it in the hands of men.

Radical feminist Adrienne Rich has distinguished the institution of mothering from the physical and emotional experiences of mothering particular women have. In her now classic work, *Of Woman Born*, she weaves theory and personal experience to construct a view of mothering which removes it from the realm of the ahistorical and asocial. Motherhood ceases to be a private, biological act divorced from a social system. Rather, motherhood

has a history, it has an ideology, it is more fundamental than tribalism or nationalism. My individual private pains as a mother, the individual and seemingly private pains of the mothers around me and before me, whatever our class or colour, the regulation of women's reproductive power by men in every totalitarian system and every socialist revolution, the legal and technical control by men of contraception, fertility, abortion, obstetrics and extrauterine experiments—are all essential to the patriarchal system, as is the negative or suspect status of women who are not mothers. (15)

The debate over mothering continues to rage inside and outside the feminist community. After all, much of the energy of the women's movement has been taken up with the demand that the "private sphere" (of which mothering is an enormous part) be given the full recognition it deserves. At the same time, however, feminists have rejected patriarchal demands to reproduce—"compulsory motherhood"—along with the socialization that accompanies it. Thus, just as feminists must validate what women do and have historically done, they must also condemn the patriarchal co-optation which has sought to appropriate those experiences.

Mothering is central to the lives of all women, whether or not they bear their own children. Thus, an understanding of mothering is essential to feminist theory. Yet there is no unified feminist position on these issues. Some feminist theorists, for example, have gone even further than Firestone to argue that women should refuse to give birth at all. Jeffner Allen argues that birthing children buttresses the patriarchy, saps women's energy, and is evolutionarily unsound. She urges women to "evacuate" mothering.

Others (see, for example, Irigaray) have valorized women's childbearing as one of the few expressions of power women under patriarchy possess. These feminists "embrace motherhood" (Maroney) and decry the loss of female control over the spiritual and physical dimensions of childbirth. French feminist theory in particular has tended to focus on the power of the mother; but this power is not the patriarchal power of dominance and control, but of nurturance and creation. In fact, this sect of feminist theory has maintained that it is men's jealousy of women's power of creation which has led them to devalue women's experience and to seek the power to control reproduction in particular and women in general. Emancipation from the father (patriarchy), they claim, requires the liberation of the mother and the revaluing of women's bodily experiences of creation and of women's relationships with women.

Finally, a third strand (e.g. Held) defends the normative thesis that child *rearing* (if not child *bearing*) must be shared by men and women. According to this view, a biological connection between parent and child is neither necessary nor sufficient to make one a "mother." Rather, the role of mothering is one of nurturing and of caretaking; in this sense, almost anyone can mother. Further, neither biology nor technology *per se* is oppressive in this view; rather, it is how a community interprets those biological factors and uses its technological resources that makes the decisive difference. Mary O'Brien, for example, has argued from a Marxist perspective that women must be integrated into the productive realm and men must be integrated into the realm of reproduction and the care of the next generation. This view has received support from the psychoanalytic community in the writings of feminists like, for example, Nancy Chodorow and Dorothy Dinnerstein who, in *The Mermaid and the Minotaur*, links misogyny to the prevalence of single-sex parenting in Western societies.[2]

Even more recently, some feminists have attempted to explore maternal practice as a vehicle to re-vision ethical theory. Sara Ruddick, for example, has coined the phrase "maternal thinking" to refer to certain kinds of activities like protecting, nurturing, preserving, loving, and helping to grow—in short, to those activities historically and culturally tied to mothering. Her analysis follows from the empirical research of Carol Gilligan and others who have observed differences in men's and women's relational modes. Where men, Gilligan claims, tend to operate from a "rights" perspective, women are most comfortable in what Gilligan calls a "caring" mode, which focuses on responsibilities to others. The traditional family perhaps best exemplifies these "different voices;" while the father works outside the home, teaches rules and fairness, and is the source of disciplinary measure, the mother is the one who comforts and cares, who may bend the rules at times in the interests of compassion and understanding. Though generalizations of the crudest sort, these styles of interaction have traditionally tended to be gender-linked. Ruddick argues, though, that anyone *can* and, from a normative perspective, everyone *should*, mother, even if one never has a biological child. Maternal practice has been undervalued in most societies; not only does it need to be valued fully, but its virtual monopolization by women must also end.

In this paper I shall follow the practice of the majority of feminist theorists and not assume that the notion of "mothering" depends on biology. Instead, I want to explore the ways in which images of mothering appear in popular culture, especially in film. These popular images not only reveal glimpses of our deeply mythic thinking about mothers and mothering; but they also create a popular mythology with new, and possibly, dissonant messages. It is to those messages that I wish to attend. Though I shall reference a number of examples from film and television, my focus here is on three recent popular films: *Baby Boom, The Good Mother,* and *Three Men and A Baby.*

Baby Boom

As *Baby Boom*'s opening credits roll, we catch scenes of New York City with its anxious residents struggling to get to work. Waiting for buses, taxis, and subways; carrying briefcases and cups of coffee; wearing sneakers and three piece suits—all are daily consigned to this demanding rat race. Gradually, as we realize that we are observing more and more women in these throngs of workers, a voice-over announces: "53% of the American workforce is female. . . . As little girls, they were told to marry doctors and lawyers. When they grew up, they became doctors and lawyers."

The music picks up and soon Wall Street is our backdrop. We see Diane Keaton as J.C. Wyatt who is, we are told by our narrator, a woman on the move. She makes six figures a year and lives with an investment banker who, like her, is married to his job. With the last of the credits, the narrator warns us: "One must take it for granted that J.C. has it all. One must never take anything for granted." This notion of "having it all" continues thematically to haunt the film.

At work, J.C., known as "tiger lady" to her co-workers, reels off instructions to her subordinates and is crisply efficient. Later that day, she is offered a partnership in the firm, which she gratefully accepts. But, for the first time, we see her falter. As she is offered the partnership, her legs begin to shake uncontrollably under the table in a nervous reaction. Is this her happiness at accomplishing her long dreamed of goal or is this a visible sign of her ambivalence? Regardless of its meaning, this reaction humanizes (and *feminizes*) J.C. for the viewer; we now realize that she is not "all business," and we cannot help but like her.

Her now-partner paternalistically urges her to think long and hard about the demands on her a partnership will make. It is his wife, he informs J.C., who makes it possible for him to do all he needs to do. Interestingly, he is in the dark about what goes on in the private world of home and family; but he is clear that, whatever *it* is, it provides a measure of stability for him. "A man can be a success and have a personal life. . . I can have it all," he says with some embarrassment. Rather than question his premise, J.C. demurs, "I don't want it all."

That evening, in the luxurious condominium she shares with Steven, her live-in boyfriend, J.C. and he finish up some work in bed; later she circles ads for Vermont estates. He quips: "You in Vermont without a speaker phone would not be a pretty sight." They make love, with before-and-after-shots of the digital clock to let us know how quick it actually was (two minutes) and the camera shows us the longing on her face as he falls immediately off to sleep.

When J.C. later inherits the daughter of a distant relative, her life falls apart. Despite her "six figures," she is unable to find competent childcare. Steven demands that she put Elizabeth, the baby, up for adoption, and J.C. initially has the same desire. But she begins to bond with Elizabeth when the baby comes down with the flu, and she is unable (at the decisive moment) to give up Elizabeth to the provincial, Midwestern couple who want her ("suddenly I saw her in frosted lipstick wearing a Dairy Queen uniform," she explains). Steven, who has made clear his feelings about parenthood, ends the relationship when she returns with Elizabeth, and J.C. moves out.

As Linda Singer points out in her essay in this volume (see pages 102-111), Hollywood filmmakers seem most interested in the aberrant and the exotic. So in *Baby Boom* we see a woman who is, at least initially, a thoroughly inept mother. Though a graduate of Yale and Harvard (and apparently without any of the usual babysitting experience), she is unable to diaper the baby, holds her slung under one arm, and shows none of the tenderness we have come to associate with maternal care.

But what *Baby Boom* makes clear is that one does not need biology to be a mother; one can *learn* mothering. Indeed, J.C. goes from an inept, uncaring woman to a *real* mother. Beginning with her care of Elizabeth and her decision not to abandon her to new parents (would she have done so, we wonder, if the prospective parents had not been so obviously and absurdly wrong for a child?), J.C. becomes Yuppie Supermom, bringing Elizabeth to classes, to the park, and even occasionally to work. But, consistent with our narrator's foreshadowing, J.C. is soon to realize that she cannot have it all.

J.C.'s behavior at work is erratic, and the Tiger Lady has lost her claws. Her office is now full of baby bottles and nursery toys, and co-worker Ken slowly eases her out of her favored position in the firm. After she loses an account to him, he explains: "You've changed. You've lost your concentration. You've gone soft." How can a woman—no, a *mother*—compete in such a cut-throat enterprise? It would seen that the moment that J.C. made the "soft" decision not to give up Elizabeth, every aspect of her life followed suit. It is almost as though J.C. has herself gone through a birthing experience; she has indeed, like the typical postpartum woman, "gone soft." Rather than accept a humiliating demotion, she quits the company, buys a home in Vermont and begins to build a new life for Elizabeth.

The country, it seems, is the place for those who "go soft." For J.C., the boredom and the expense of the constant repairs on her old home drive her to think about trying to market the baby food she has overzealously made for Elizabeth. After some time, with her knowledge of marketing strategy (she is even able to make use of the town library), her line—Country Baby Applesauce—becomes a huge success. Her old company offers her a deal, and she travels back to New York to negotiate with them. In the meantime, though, she had gotten involved with the local veterinarian, played by Sam Shepard.

Back in New York, facing her old building in a pose reminiscent of *Rocky*, J.C. finally decides not to sell her trademark even though the deal would, in the words of one of the negotiators, "make you richer than you've ever dreamed." In an impassioned speech to the board, she announces, "I'm not the tiger lady any more. Now I have a mobile over my desk and a crib in my office. ...I'm doing very well on my own. ...The rat race is going to have to survive with one less rat." In concluding from her own experience, she says "the bottom line is: nobody should have to make those sacrifices" between family and work. Finally, she loses her ardor and begins to talk dreamily about her new relationship: "There's this veterinarian I'm seeing...." She even rolls her eyes at the thought of him. This shift in tone and content serves to "feminize" the rest of her speech, to depoliticize it. This discourse is clearly outside the language of the boardroom; it is woman's language, the discourse of the mother, which is so private that it is unintelligible. Indeed, one man says, "What did she say? She's become a vegetarian?" This solipsism in the boardroom serves two purposes: it makes clear that the mother, contrary to popular views about women returning to the work force, cannot go back, for she has lost her access to the language of the public domain; but it also inverts this very real dynamic of exclusion by suggesting that J.C. is happier (and, let us not forget, richer and more sexually fulfilled) than she ever was. She has *chosen* to opt out.

The final scene of *Baby Boom* is of J.C. and Elizabeth together in a rocking chair. All of the energy of her visit to New York has been defused and J.C. is placid and content. Does she "have it all"? She has a man to love her, a baby, incredible wealth (she has informed the assembled members of the meeting that she can make the money off the line of babyfood independently), a "career" that allows her to stay home and be with her child, and has wrecked revenge on the company that let her go. The final word of the movie is Elizabeth's: "Mama." Though we hear J.C. murmuring to Elizabeth, her words are undecipherable. That "Mama" makes it clear that mothering must be a priority and that the sacrifices it entails are not only worthwhile, but they also actually *pay off.*

The Good Mother

Interestingly, *The Good Mother* also stars Diane Keaton, who plays J.C. in *Baby Boom*. Based on a novel by Sue Miller, *The Good Mother* is the story of a divorced woman's eventual loss of custody of her only child to her ex-husband.

The film begins with a flashback which is also the opening of Miller's book. Anna Dunlop is remembering back to her childhood visits to her grandparents' summer home in Maine. In this flashback, she is really recounting the story of her fascination with her Aunt Babe, a woman considerably younger than Anna's own mother and so more like Anna's peer. Babe is beautiful and reckless. In a family where feelings are carefully reined in and understatement is the norm, Babe is openly angry, glamorous, and unconventional. Anna says, "I adored her." Babe encourages Anna to take risks, to defy authority. When Anna protests "my mother won't let me," Babe responds "You want to grow up to be just like your mother?" In fact, a viewer can only guess at what is implied in Babe's question, since we never see Anna's mother, and this is the only reference to her in the entire film.

Babe, however, becomes pregnant out of wedlock and is peremptorily shipped off to Europe where she gives birth to a child who is immediately put up for adoption. When Babe returns, Anna tells us, she is not the same. Her lightness and gaiety have been replaced with an obvious (though not to the rest of her family!) desperation. She is still reckless and unabashed, but she drinks too much and her provocative behavior with men seems to embarrass everyone, including young Anna. Babe soon drowns in the lake which has become her means of transport to and from her dates with men. Anna reminisces in a voice-over: "I often thought of what she offered me during those summers. ...I wanted to be just like her. I wanted to be a passionate person, I wanted to take risks. And, despite everything that's happened, I feel I really, really had to try."

When we return to the present, though, there is little of Babe in the Anna we see. She is a fairly conventional divorced woman living in Cambridge, Massachusetts with her young daughter Molly. We are told that she had been married for seven years and that that marriage lacked excitement and passion, particularly in the bedroom. "Sex," she confides to her friend Ursula, "was so...nothing." Anna teaches piano (she sheepishly corrects her grandfather when he describes her as a pianist; she is, she says, "more like a piano teacher") and works in a laboratory cleaning glassware. She still visits her grandparents and continues to be intimidated by her overbearing, patriarchal grandfather. She allows her ex-husband, who is now living in Washington, D.C. and remarried to Brenda, a lawyer like him, to stay in her apartment on weekends when he visits Molly.

As *The Good Mother* develops, we see Anna performing a number of tasks for Molly to give us a sense of what sort of mother she is. While making Molly's breakfast (pancakes in the shape of animals!), Molly spills her milk; Anna, though clearly frustrated, does not lose her temper. In the evening she reads to her from a book about the "facts of life," and Anna's explanations are frank and unembarrassed. All in all, Anna strikes the viewer as a "good mother" who is attentive to Molly's needs, keeps her sense of humor, and works very hard at her two jobs so that they can live decently.

After Anna meets Leo Cutter at the laundromat, her life changes. She sleeps with him on their first date, and experiences her sexual awakening with him. Leo is exotic (he even has an accent), bohemian, and they love each other intensely. To Anna, Leo seems all she is not: talented, experienced, self-assured. Leo and she begin to spend more time together, and soon he is sleeping over at Anna's apartment and even occasionally babysitting for Molly when Anna is at work. Molly is clearly comfortable around Leo, and Anna's life goes from modulated to full of passion as she becomes aware of the power of her desire for Leo.

But all this quickly unravels when Anna returns home to discover that her ex-husband is keeping Molly and suing for custody. After retaining a lawyer, Anna and Leo reveal the "indiscretions" which have occurred while Molly was in their care: Leo has allowed Molly, after she asked, to "touch his penis;" this is the catalyst for Molly's father to instigate the hearing. Later, though, we discover that the fact that Anna and Leo once made love while Molly was asleep in their bed also counts as "evidence" of Anna's alleged incompetence as a mother.

While Leo tries to help in whatever ways he can, Anna and her lawyer are actually concocting a strategy to convince the court that Leo was acting on his own and that he "misunderstood" Anna's guidelines. Despite her assurance that she'll stop seeing Leo, the court awards custody to her ex-husband and gives Anna visiting privileges.

At the end of the film, Anna tells us in another voice-over that she sees Molly "every second weekend and all school vacations" and that Molly is doing better with this new arrangement despite a difficult adjustment in the beginning. Though her lawyer has advised her to look for signs of unhappiness in Molly as a first step toward appealing the decision, Anna—ever the "good mother"—tells us that she's relieved at Molly's apparent improvement and refuses to hope for her daughter's misery. She must, Anna realizes, reconstruct her entire life, since she has lost not only Molly but also Leo, whose presence reminds her of her loss. In her bleakest moment, she remembers a statement of her grandmother, "uttered when losing Molly was unthinkable," that "everybody knows you're a good mother, Anna."

Strangely, the ending to the novel is even more demoralized than the film's. In Miller's work, Anna is reduced to following her ex-husband and his new wife and their new baby in their fairly frequent moves around the country in order to be able to see Molly. As a result, she is never able to secure any really meaningful work and she lives for her few moments with Molly. Anna even keeps a second bedroom, despite the financial difficulty and its infrequent usage, to create a sense of normalcy during Molly's occasional visits.

Perhaps the filmmakers of *The Good Mother* decided that mainstream movie audiences would not tolerate such a dismal ending or would question the proportionality (and the reality?) of such a severe punishment. Regardless of the explanation for this slight shift in tone, however, the Anna of the film promises us that she is rebuilding her life; the Anna of the novel is without a life. The novel Anna, too, is alone at the book's end; the film placates us with a parting shot of Anna and Molly together.

What is the message of *The Good Mother*? In one key scene in the film, Anna is enraged with Leo when he suggests to her that she might be more ambitious than she is. She is not like him, she says angrily, and she is tired of people thinking that everyone has to be motivated to the same degree. Whether a slap at the woman's movement or a valorization of the institution of mothering, Anna's speech makes unequivocally clear that her *only* talent is her mothering. Thus, viewers must realize how much *more* devastating is her eventual loss.

Further, the flashback which opens the film (note, too, that the film ends in the same summer home in Maine where it begins) is revealing. Anna's respect and admiration for Babe and for Babe's risk-taking might lead us to expect her to take risks as well. Yet, she fails to stand by Leo in the trial and she is defensive and apologetic to the court and to the social service workers who are assigned to her case. Like Babe, Anna's only "risk-taking" is in her being sexually active. Could one even imagine a comparable "trial" for a man? How are we to understand Anna's statement that "I really, really had to try?" To "try" what? Rather than "try," Anna retreats. Perhaps she means that she tried to be sexual *and* be a "good mother." If this is what she means, then the message is clearly that this cannot be accomplished and women must make a choice. Like Babe, Anna's attempt to find love (in sex?) leaves her dead. Like Babe, Anna must give up her child—yet how can a mother be a mother when childless? So Anna, unlike Babe, cannot rest, but rather must spend her life in powerless, "barren" dependency, following her child and her child's new family.

Three Men and A Baby

Three Men and A Baby is a remake of the French film *Trois Hommes et Un Couffin* (1986) and stars three very popular actors: Tom Selleck (Peter), Steve Guttenberg (Michael), and Ted Danson (Jack). They live together in a very upscale apartment in New York City. Peter is an architect, Michael a cartoonist, and Jack an actor, and their apartment is the "bachelor pad" par excellence. In fact, during the opening credits we see each of the roommates entering and exiting in frenetic (and deliberately sped up) pace with a number of different, very attractive women. A party for Peter's birthday includes hundreds of the "beautiful people," lots of champagne, all the latest technology, and much bed-hopping. Whether all this womanizing is merely to make clear how ill-suited these three bachelors are for the baby soon to arrive; or whether it is to reassure us that, strange as this arrangement is, these men are *not* gay—the very definite message is that Peter, Michael, and Jack are to be envied.

Only Peter has a girlfriend, and their relationship is not a monogamous one. It is doubtful that any movie would ever feature three female roommates who do the kind of bed-hopping these men do. It is even more doubtful whether bed-hopping women would ever be as likeable and sympathetic as are Peter, Michael, and Jack. At the same birthday party, for example, Jack is searching for a bottle of wine to share with his most recently acquired female conquest. "What's a good year for pronging chicks?" he asks his roommates, and, interestingly, receives an immediate answer. But, it is worth noting that, once their sexual prowess is established, the pace slows and the film takes us in a different direction.

Due to a misunderstanding, Peter and Michael assume that a baby left for Jack on their doorstep is the "package" he informs them will be delivered that day. The note which appears with the baby is from the biological mother: "I can't handle this now. Maybe some day you'll both forgive me." Jack is alleged to be the biological father and his roommates never question this claim. Jack is away filming a new movie, and they are unable to reach him.

Like *Baby Boom*, *Three Men and A Baby* entices us by taking us through the stages of the men's growing attachment to Mary, Jack's daughter. They find that they have no idea what size diapers to buy, what sort of baby food is appropriate, even whether Mary has teeth. They are horrified by their first diaper change. They seem to work out an arrangement for shared child care so that each can fulfill his work responsibilities (indeed, at times their roles seem to mimic those of a married couple). Gradually their lives adjust to having her there, and, despite obvious exhaustion, they seem to be enjoying her presence.

There is, however, another "package" which actually contains drugs left by a friend of Jack's to be picked up by two thugs. After a series of miscommunications, Michael and Peter realize what has occurred, but by then the police are involved and it is too late to set things right. Finally, Peter, Michael and Jack end up employing some of their fancy camera equipment to amass evidence against the criminals and turn them over to the police.

This drug subplot gives *Three Men and A Baby* an odd, almost schizophrenic feeling. Is this a movie about "three men and a baby" or is it a movie about "three men, a baby, two bad guys, and some misplaced drugs"? It is almost as though a movie about men and a baby could not simply be about men and a baby. Rather, there must be some dramatic tension, which involves the real *action* of police and thugs. So this film forces us to move between the domestic world of home and children and the public world of crime and danger. Domesticity, it appears, would not be enough.

In *Maternal Thinking* Sara Ruddick maintains, like Dinnerstein and Chodorow, that men should participate in childrearing. The ability to mother is not related, she argues, to gender. Further, she claims that mothering by men has transformative power. "To be sure, by becoming a mother, [a man] will, in many social groups, challenge the ideology of masculinity" (45). *Three Men and A Baby* shows just how naive is Ruddick's claim. These three men only seem *more* masculine in the course of this film. Their devotion to Mary does not "emasculate" or "feminize" in any way; perhaps audiences would not even tolerate such a transformation. But Michael, Peter, and Jack offer no challenge to patriarchy or to the ideology of masculinity. Indeed, they epitomize the "new" man: tough yet tender, made irresistible to women in their attachment to Mary. What better reassurance could we have of masculinity intact than the scene in which Peter lulls Mary to sleep by reading to her from a *Sports Illustrated* description of a boxing match?

Women in *Three Men and A Baby* seem either incapable of or not interested in mothering. First, there is the unseen but felt presence of Sylvia, the baby's biological mother, who has abandoned her child to strangers. Jack's mother is quite taken with Mary, but she refuses to help him care for her: "You were a screw-up," she tells him. "Now you're a father." Peter's occasional lover is indignant that he would assume that, because she is a woman, she'd want to be involved in Mary's care. Finally, their landlady ends up bound and gagged when criminals break into the apartment while she is babysitting for Mary.

Hoffnung has discussed the "limiting effects" of mothering on women's public participation. But while women with children are often isolated from public life, the men in this film seem to suffer no such ill effects. In fact, their attractiveness to women only increases as we, for example, see them playing in the park with Mary while women crowd around them. They bring Mary with them to work; Peter even has a little hard hat for her when he brings her to construction sites.

When Sylvia returns at the end of this film, we cannot help but resent her intrusion. She wants her baby back, and very obviously loves the child. Yet our sympathies are with the men who learned to love this child and accommodated to her needs. We observe their anguish as they pack up Mary's belongings, and we cannot help but note that they know more about Mary's needs and habits than does her own mother.

How does the patriarchy resolve this dilemma? We cannot simply disregard the imperative of biological motherhood. Yet what about "fathers' rights"? Further, how can we deprive Mary of the material comforts she will obviously enjoy in her present home? Sylvia provides the key to the solution: "I have to work. And I can't take care of Mary alone. I need help. I need someone to help me." Realizing that they do not want to be occasional babysitters, Peter, Michael, and Jack propose that Sylvia move in with them.

The last scene of *Three Men and A Baby* is of Peter, Michael, Jack and Sylvia all wheeling Mary in her stroller. Michael has even painted Sylvia's image on the wall with the three of them. In some ways this ending resembles the union of J.C. and her veterinarian in *Baby Boom*. There is however, a relevant difference. J.C. needs a man, and to conclude *Baby Boom* with her still unattached would leave us (and her) frustrated and less able to care for Elizabeth. But men do not need women in this same way, and it is clear in *Three Men* that it is Sylvia who needs a roof over her head and help with Mary. Though on some level we recognize that there are three of them and only one mother, we cannot help but think "she can't do it alone." And it is their charity, their *noblesse oblige*, that allows her to stay; Mary seems to have suffered no ill effects from her mother's absence. With such power, men do not need to fear women's reproductive capabilities.

Conclusion

It is noteworthy that biological motherhood is not a central theme in most of the recent Hollywood films that feature family/parenting arrangements. Of the three films discussed above, only *The Good Mother* features a biological mother, and she alone loses custody of her child. *Baby Boom* and *Three Men and A Baby* introduce us to individuals who seem the unlikeliest candidates imaginable for parenthood. Indeed, from our superior vantage point, we can laugh at their inept early attempts to parent: the pathetic try at diapering; the confusion over the source of a baby's discomfort; the chaos in which traditionally "child-free" households are thrown with the appearance of a child.

Further, the attachment to the child (because it is not rooted in the biological?) is never taken for granted in these films and so must be developed over time; Diane Keaton in *Baby Boom*, for example, is willing to leave newly acquired Elizabeth with the coat checker in a restaurant, and the men in *Three Men* search frantically for a way to unload "their" baby. The viewer, though, trusts that bonding will occur at some point and that there is no real threat—which would create excess anxiety—to the baby's welfare; what keeps us interested is that we do not know precisely when or how the bonding will occur. Those moments like, for example, when Elizabeth becomes ill or when Peter believes Mary could have been harmed by intruders, unite viewer, novice parent, and new child in a relationship which now ensures the safety of the infant. And for these adult characters— once materialistic and egocentric—the process which leads to their becoming competent, non-biological parents also matures them in other aspects of their lives.

In contrast, Anna in *The Good Mother* has nothing left at the end of the film except the knowledge that she was a good mother. She tells us she is beginning to rebuild her life, but there is little evidence of this. Because the bond between mother and child is taken for granted and therefore cinematically dull, it is the rupture of that bond that provides the basis for plot development. Further, was Anna truly a "good mother"? Where are our sympathies in this film? She is too passive to be a hero, and the concluding scenes of the film suggest that no dramatic personal breakthroughs are on the horizon for Anna as for her adult counterparts in these other films. How can a "good mother" lose her child? Indeed, the title itself is ambiguous and, possibly, ironic. Did Anna love Leo too much to be a "good mother"?

Where are the other biological mothers in films today? At times they are teenagers who become pregnant and give birth like Darcy (Molly Ringwald) in *For Keeps*. Occasionally, as in *Cry in the Dark*, biological mothers are of interest to filmmakers because their children have died. Other films (perhaps following in the wake of the popularity of *Three Men and A Baby*) focus on the masculine view of child-rearing. In *She's Having a Baby*, for example, Jefferson (Jake) Briggs (Kevin Bacon) is a dissatisfied, trapped husband who resents his loss of innocence and blames his wife for it. He narrates the film, which is full of his fantasies and complaints.

The birth of their first child provides the basis for his own rebirth. Though the title tells us that *she's* having a baby, it is *he* who experiences the birth a vehicle for his realization that "what I was looking for was not to be found but to be made."

For the most part, though, recent films which feature mothering (or parenting)—think, for example, of *Raising Arizona, Housekeeping*, and even *Aliens*—work hard to create bonds where there's no biological attachment. In *Aliens*, for example, Newt's own parents could not protect her, whereas Ripley (Sigourney Weaver) remains true to her promise (despite unbelievable obstacles) that she will never abandon the child (who rewards Ripley by calling her "mommy" at their climactic reunion). This phenomenon has been termed by Molly Haskell "motherhood without stretchmarks," and its popularity may result from its difference. Hollywood, as I have argued above, seems to mystify the atypical and the exotic. Today, though most single parents are women and women are the heads of 16% of all households, though more than a third of such households live in poverty, there has been almost no attention to these kinds of living arrangements. If one can truly achieve "motherhood without stretchmarks," then there is nothing that women can do that men cannot. In one scene in *Three Men and A Baby*, Jack stuffs a pillow under his sweater to simulate pregnancy and stands in front of a mirror admiring his new appearance. But he need feel no jealousy of the biological powers of women, since it is ultimately he (and his two companions) who are more suited to raise and nurture Mary.

In reality, women who are mothers actually *lose* power. Unless, like J.C. in *Baby Boom*, they find a man (and her veterinarian happens to be the *only* man in the town "within twenty years of her age"), mothers are likely to be underpaid and overworked. Statistics suggest that even women with husbands continue to put in a "double day" with housework and childcare. In contrast, the men in *Three Men* enhance their social position when they become mothers, never having difficulty meeting women or fulfilling their professional obligations. Women with children, however, encounter a number of obstacles which tend to increase their isolation from the public domain. "Taking care of children, therefore, does not provide women with any real power base. Men can afford to leave childrearing *responsibility* to women, because, given their superior power resources, they are still assured of substantial childrearing authority" (Polatnick 33).

Webster's Dictionary defines mothering as "caring for another with maternal affection or tenderness." Similarly, Sara Ruddick defines a mother as any person who "takes on responsibility for children's lives and from whom providing child care is a significant part of her or his working life" (40). Regardless of whether women are innately better suited to mothering (a question I do not consider here), it seems obvious that a person of either sex is capable of mothering in these senses. Furthermore, most feminists have struggled to reject theories which either explicitly or implicitly entail a biological determinism. Why, then, should we not applaud films which have the potential to subvert traditional norms?

Patriarchy has a knack for incorporating potentially destabilizing modes of behavior and neutralizing their subversive power in the process. Where it might be destabilizing for a woman to be successful *and* be a mother, films like *Baby Boom* trivialize the experience and end by repositioning the mother and child in a nonsubversive nuclear family. A nontraditional arrangement like the one we see in *Three Men and A Baby* has the potential to serve as an alternative to the mainstream family. But this film grounds its appeal precisely in its unreality—we know this model is not one we can seek to emulate. Virtually all these films revolve around upper class families so that nasty issues like making ends meet need never interfere with plot. Films like these exploit the aberrant. What really goes on in everyday domestic life is not of interest to Hollywood moviemakers. This is not to suggest that every Hollywood film ought to provide us with a blueprint for undermining patriarchy. But it is to suggest that these films have failed to provide any vision at all: they remove women from the sphere of mothering by turning children over to men; and they push biological mothers even further back into the privatized (i.e. invisible) domestic world. Unless the mother is pathological like Bette Davis's mother in the classic *Now, Voyager* or Faye Dunaway's portrayal of Joan Crawford in the more recent *Mommie, Dearest*, mothers' lives are not the "stuff of which dreams are made."

There is a pervasive popular ideology that all women want to be mothers and that all women make good mothers. Yet, coexisting with this ideology exist obstacles which prevent truly autonomous forms of mothering from occurring. Whether in the form of single mothering, lesbian mothering, or some other alternative arrangement which might be truly destabilizing— autonomous mothering is neglected, just as is biological mothering. Indeed, women seem entirely secondary to the plot and character development. It is no fluke that J.C. Wyatt finds a "real" man at the end of *Baby Boom* and that not one of the roommates in *Three Men* ends up in a committed relationship.

Further, the ideology of mothering minimizes the drudgery and the monotony of childrearing and magnifies the joys and compensations. The result is an illusion "whereby motherhood will appear to consist of compensations only, and thus come to be desired by those for whom the illusion is intended" (Hollingsworth 27). Most films about mothering make mothering tempting. Few films deal with working class mothers or mothers of color or women who consciously opt out of having children (and don't later regret the decision!). Ironically, films cannot resist this ideology of mothering even when it comes to teen-age mothers like Molly Ringwald in *For Keeps*, who, after great hardship, finds herself, finishes school, and saves her marriage. Abortion is taboo, as are women who choose not to have children.

Finally, I cannot resist a brief discussion of a recent film, *Parenthood*, which suggests that the trend I have been describing here continues with a vengeance. More appropriately titled *Fatherhood*, this film focuses on the experiences of Gil (Steve Martin) and his extended family. This is a fascinating film, in part because of its exploration of intergenerational dynamics. Yet its message suggests that it is fathers not mothers who make the difference to a child's psychological well-being. While one father overprotects, another overachieves, a third ignores, and a fourth abuses, the mothers seem to have little or no influence on the children. They are there to observe the men, possibly to mute their influence (á la women like Edith Bunker in *All in the Family* or Louise Jefferson in *The Jeffersons*); but it is clear that they have no real power, either physical or psychological. Indeed, Gil's own mother is virtually silent throughout the film, in stark contrast to her powerful husband (played by Jason Robards).

One could argue that this approach has merits over the usual tendency in film (inherited, in part, from the psychoanalytic tradition) to blame mothers for any and every familial dysfunction, despite how little real power women have had in the patriarchal family. But this new theme of fathers mothering contrasts sharply with the realities of how few men participate in child care or even pay child support. Further, this potentially destabilizing theme is, once again, neutralized by the film's treatment. The father's reign not only continues, but it continues now with justification; that is, these "family films" help us to understand precisely *why* fathers have had to ignore us or abuse us or push us to excel. At one point in *Parenthood*, for example, a frustrated Gil shouts to his wife: "Everything in my life is a 'have to'!" We end up sympathizing with the needs of patriarchy, and we come to realize that men are well-intentioned after all. The film's conclusion, rather than leave us with the complexities and ambiguities of these troubled characters, opts for a tidy conclusion with *four* pregnancies, one for each of the major female characters. For some inexplicable reason (as in *She's Having a Baby*), we are expected to see that these births represent solutions.

Sara Ruddick has convincingly argued that we cannot "at will transcend a gender division of labor that has shaped our minds and lives" (41). Certainly, given the fact that women have disproportionately cared for children in most societies, we cannot expect an overnight transformation of these entrenched practices. But Ruddick then asks: "Where are the fathers? Where are the caretaking women who are not mothers?" The answer, as this paper has tried to show, is that they are disproportionately present in popular film.

Notes

[1]As a woman and a feminist, I have long eschewed the dualisms of traditional philosophy. In particular, I have sought not to ignore links between the "personal" and the "theoretical." Thus, I want to acknowledge here my debts to two members of my family, my daughter Katherine Raymond and my mother Rose Barsoum, with whom I have learned first-hand about these issues. I thank them here for the lessons they have taught me and for the inspiration for this paper.

[2]More specifically, Dinnerstein argues that asymmetry in parenting arrangements leads to a matriphobia which is rooted in the infant's need to separate from its primary caretaker, i.e. its mother. In separating, the infant/child must devalue the mother (who is also familiar and easily accessible) and attach to the mysterious, powerful father. It is the mother, Dinnerstein maintains, who represents the infant's dependence needs and must hence be rejected; for these same reasons, the mother also represents death itself.

Works Cited

Allen, Jeffner, "Mothering: The Annihilation of Women," in *Trebilcot*, pp. 315-330.

Chodorow, Nancy, *The Reproduction of Mothering*. Berkeley: University of California Press, 1978.

Corea, Gena, "The Reproductive Brothel," in *Man-Made Women*, ed. Gena Corea *et al*. Bloomington: Indiana University Press, 1987, pp. 38-51

Dinnerstein, Dorothy, *The Mermaid and the Minotaur*. NY: Harper and Row, 1976.

Duplessis, Rachel Blau, "Washing Blood." *Feminist Studies* 4,2 (1978)

Gilligan, Carol, *In A Different Voice*. Cambridge: Harvard University Press, 1982.

Gimenez, Martha E., "Feminism, Pronatalism, and Motherhood," in *Trebilcot*, pp. 287-314.

Hanmer, Jalna, "A Womb of One's Own," in *Test-Tube Women*, ed. Rita Arditti, Duelli Klein, and Shelley Minden. Boston: Pandora Press, 1984.

Haskell, Molly, "Hollywood Madonnas." MS. Magazine, May 1988, pp. 84-87.

Held, Virginia, "The Equal Responsibilities of Fathers and Mothers," in *Trebilcot*, pp. 40-56.

Hollingsworth, Leta S., "Social Devices for Impelling Women to Bear and Rear Children." *American Journal of Sociology* 22 (1916), pp. 20-27.

Hoffnung, Michele, "Motherhood: Contemporary Conflict for Women," in Jo Freeman, ed., *Women: A Feminist Perspective*. Mountain View, CA: Mayfield Publishing, 1989, 157-175.

Irigaray, Luce, "And the One Doesn't Stir Without the Other," trans. Helen Vivienne Wenzel. *Signs* 7 (Autumn 1981), pp. 60-67.

Kuykendall, Eleanor H., "Toward an Ethic of Nurturance: Luce Irigaray on Mothering and Power," in *Trebilcot*, pp. 263-274.

Maroney, Heather Jon, "Embracing Motherhood: New Feminist Theory," in *The Politics of Diversity*, ed. Roberta Hamilton and Michele Barrett. London: Verso, 1986, pp. 398-423.

O'Brien, Mary, *The Politics of Reproduction*. London: Routledge and Kegan Paul, 1981.

Polatnick, M. Rivka, "Why Men Don't Rear Children: A Power Analysis," in *Trebilcot*, pp. 21-40.

Rich, Adrienne, *Of Woman Born*. New York: Bantam Books, 1976.

Ruddick, Sara, *Maternal Thinking*. Boston: Beacon Press, 1989.

Trebilcot, Joyce, ed., *Mothering: Essays in Feminist Theory*. Totowa, N.J.: Rowman and Allanheld, 1984.

Sexuality and Images
of Women

The "Strange World" of *Blue Velvet*: Conventions, Subversions and the Representation of Women

Judith Bryant Wittenberg
and
Robert Gooding-Williams

One of the most compelling and unusual films of recent years, David Lynch's 1986 *Blue Velvet*, has engendered a wide array of emotional responses in its viewers. While few intelligent moviegoers have disputed its brilliance or failed to recognize the singularity of the directorial vision that created it, often their reactions have ranged from puzzlement to outrage. Women in particular have tended to be disturbed by the depiction of the psychotic and violent drug dealer played by Dennis Hopper, and his fetishistic, sado-masochistic relationship with a vulnerable nightclub singer whose child and husband he holds hostage. Many regard the film, because of its representation of the central woman character as an almost completely passive participant in her objectification and victimization by controlling males, as fundamentally misogynistic. Although the psychic and physical subjugation of the female is the most obvious problematic, more subtle difficulties are produced by the way in which *Blue Velvet* offers a re-vision of film noir that not only re-casts many of that genre's standard patterns but also undermines the framework from which viewers normally make judgments; it disallows the "normal" moral certainties.

Essential elements of *Blue Velvet* such as narrative structure and character types resemble those in its predecessors of the late 1940s and early 1950s, the hard-boiled American crime movies which the French designated film noir for their relentlessly bleak portrayals of the human capacity for lust, greed, and murder. As do virtually all of its cinematic ancestors, Lynch's 1986 movie portrays a receptive male drawn by a beautiful and sexual woman into a world where corruption is the norm; he investigates the evil and eventually triumphs over it. Nearly all of the characters in *Blue Velvet* are more or less noir types: Jeffrey Beaumont, though younger and more innocent than most of the detectives of the past, is like them in his emotional susceptibility and his unstinting pursuit of the truth; the singer Dorothy Vallens is, in both her coloring and her sexuality, a classic "dark lady;" and she is counterbalanced by the blond and seemingly virginal Sandy

149

Williams from the daylight world of the middle class. Frank Booth and his henchmen are the criminals who must be eradicated. While Hopper's Booth is, with his obscene baby talk, his inhalation of drugs through a surgical mask, and his persistent violence toward women with whom he is obsessed, a more hyperbolic figure than one usually sees in film noir, memorable sadistic criminals such as Richard Widmark's laughing killer in *Kiss of Death* (1947) and Lee Marvin's brutal gangster of *The Big Heat* (1953), who throws scalding coffee in his lover's face, are obvious antecedents.

The earlier film with which *Blue Velvet* seems to have the greatest number of parallels is *Out of the Past* (Jacques Tourneur, 1947), a work regarded by some as the exemplary noir. To be sure, the criminals in Lynch's film are more grotesque than those in Tourneur's, and Lynch omits any use of the retrospective voice-over by which Tourneur's detective reflects on the process whereby he got drawn into the corruption he set out to investigate, but in other respects they are strikingly similar. Both vividly contrast light and dark, not only in the female characters but also in the settings; the daylit middle-class world of intact families and bourgeois employment is juxtaposed with the grimness of the underworld, where illegal gains and aberrant sexual behavior are the norm, even though the lines between the two worlds are sometimes ambiguous. Both also symmetrically compare two romantic triangles, one consisting of the male protagonist and his "good" rival for the "good" woman and another marked by that same male's rivalry with the dominant criminal for the sexual woman. Since the criminal also, in both cases, is older and wiser than the protagonist, he is thus a patriarchal figure who serves implicitly as a sort of surrogate father, so the triangle has some Oedipal overtones. The criminal, is, in addition, a doppelganger, an admonitory figure whose capacity for violent behavior and sexual obsession illuminates that same potential in the protagonist. The presence of Oedipality and the double are far more explicit in *Blue Velvet*, in keeping with its somewhat parodic underscoring of noir conventions.

So many other similarities between the 1947 and 1986 films are evident that it is hard to believe that David Lynch did not intend to call attention to the ways in which *Blue Velvet* self-consciously inserts itself into film history and genre patterns, in a strategy like that employed by other postmodernist artists. The protagonists are named Jeffrey and the trajectory of their initiation into illegality and obsession proceeds along parallel lines, despite telling differences which prevent *Blue Velvet* from appearing simply as a re-make (*Out of the Past* was in fact remade in the 1980s, albeit unsatisfyingly, as *Against All Odds*) and which underscore its contemporaneity.

In each film, a pivotal woman is seen for the first time by the protagonist in a moment where she suddenly appears out of the darkness, though, ironically, in *Blue Velvet* she is the blond Sandy, not the dark and sensual Dorothy; it is a moment that propels the man more deeply into the complexities of corruption and sexuality. The subsequent tale is of course a classic narrative of initiation, like those found in fiction by American writers from Mark Twain to Sherwood Anderson and William Faulkner, but in *Blue Velvet* and *Out of the Past*, as in other film noir, the evil into which the protagonist is initiated is more pervasive and more destructive. In *Out of the Past*, Jeff Markham/Bailey's involvement with the irresistible dark lady leads him down a path marked by betrayal, flight, and eventually, his own death, while Jeffrey Beaumont of *Blue Velvet* finds himself drawn from detection into active participation in sado-masochism and, finally, murder. Although in both movies, the males successfully confront the evil around them, and by implication, in themselves, and manage to eradicate it, they do so at great cost. In each case, the handicapped assistant seen early in the film—in *Out of the Past*, the deaf and dumb young man, in *Blue Velvet*, the blind hardware store worker—is proleptic of the psychic damage which the protagonist will experience. The daylight world of the small-town "good" people is ascendant at the end and the evil-doers have been dispatched, but the triumph is compromised by all that has occurred. Moreover, in *Out of the Past*, Jeff is dead, and whereas in *Blue Velvet*, Jeffrey is restored to his family and his blond girlfriend, the "moral justice" of the moment is undermined by Lynch's artfully campy style.

In *Out of the Past*, puns and overt symbolism—a detective named Fisher and a gambler called Sterling, the fishing nets that surround Jeff as he becomes entangled with his dark lady, or the violent wind that signals their growing passion—call attention to its allegorical qualities and make its artistry somewhat self-conscious. In *Blue Velvet*, these tendencies are increased so markedly that the film becomes playful, despite its bleak story line, and the viewer's emotional identification is subverted; they serve as Brechtian alienating devices. The gangster is named Booth and his tortured victim lives on Lincoln Street; his nemesis masquerades for a time as a pest control man. The plot is set in motion by the finding of a severed ear, and there are subsequent references to Van Gogh, scissors, and getting things "all sewed up," while eavesdropping is a recurrent motif. The ear is also the site of one of the allusions to movies and television shows from an earlier era that make the work self-consciously historical; the moment near the beginning of the film in which the ear, viewed in extreme close-up, becomes a vortex, recalls a comparable instance in Hitchcock's *Psycho*, where the eye is conflated with the dark center of a drain, just as Jeffrey's voyeurism in the closet at Dorothy's apartment seems a direct reference to that same film, though her subsequent assault on him with a knife reverses elements of the comparable scene. The references to a mysterious third man are obvious invocations of another stunningly bleak work, Carroll Reed's great film of 1949.

By the use of these evocative parallels, Lynch underscores our awareness of the way in which his film should be viewed in terms of its links to an earlier genre; other sorts of references, particularly to television shows designed for young children, have an effect that is quite different. Although the use of the surname Beaumont, which is also that of the actor who played the father in *Leave it to Beaver*, is probably too flimsy a connection for us to conclude that *Blue Velvet* is a cynical reworking of that particular sitcom, Lynch's film, with its campy portrayals of small-town life and family dynamics (the voice of the breezy Williams mother, played by Hope Lange, sounds eerily like that of Harriet Nelson), certainly subverts our ability to take that world seriously. Moreover, the frequent references to the neighborhood, and the sadistic Booth's mocking question, "What's your name, neighbor?" have the effect of making us read the film as, at one level, a bizarre send-up of Mr. Rogers, a recreation of his child's program in which a warm welcome becomes a violent threat and the possibility of security is obliterated. Lynch's allusions to family television programs, seeming wildly out of place in one respect, are in other ways quite relevant, serving as part of an overall attack on comforting myths by which popular culture socializes individuals who come to maturity as viewers of its artifacts.

If references to earlier films and television programs reveal *Blue Velvet* as the self-aware inheritor of a popular tradition, some of its symbolism underscores its "message" so emphatically as to make it ludic and thus far from credible. Some, to be sure, is less obvious, like the snake plants in Dorothy Vallens' apartment seen in the background when she and Jeffrey are together, suggesting that he is indeed an American Adam about to bite the apple of sexuality and thus to lose forever the innocence of youth. Other, however, like the camera movement, early in the film, into an extreme close-up of insects battling in the grass near the patch on which Jeffrey's father has suffered a stroke while watering his lawn, heavily stresses the concept that any close examination of seemingly innocent terrain will reveal a dark underside where violence is the norm, a notion clearly borne out by the subsequent action of the film. To see deeply, Jeffrey learns, is also to see evil.

To see, he also discovers, is also, potentially, to participate, and in this respect *Blue Velvet* fully thematizes the implications of spectatorship more explicitly than any film since Michael Powell's brilliant and provocative *Peeping Tom* of 1960. Since in this film—as in *Peeping Tom*—the gaze is overtly male and its recipient female, and its outcome is violent, its adumbration seems in one respect the narrative embodiment of feminist film theory as expounded by Laura Mulvey and Claire Johnston. In one seminal essay of the 1970s, Johnston asserted that within male-dominated mainstream cinema "woman is presented as what she represents for man," functioning simply as a fetishized signifier (410-411); in another, Mulvey explored the way in which a psychoanalytic consideration of the film viewing process, given a spectatorial vantage point that is essentially male, disclosed that the scopophilic drive derived from castration anxiety is essential to the experience of visual pleasure. In cinema this is enacted primarily upon the female body. "The determining male gaze," says Mulvey, "projects its fantasy onto the female figure" (418). The woman becomes an erotic object both for the characters within the screen story and for the spectator within the auditorium (419). This process is particularly evident in the detective film, where the woman literally becomes an object of investigation, as the narrative turns on the male's effort to uncover the truth about her and thus to allay his fears. She is alluring but also dangerous and must be understood and, concomitantly, possessed. Such investigative and demystifying efforts are means by which, asserts Mulvey, the male unconscious reenacts the original trauma of discovering the fact of castration and counterbalances it "by the devaluation, punishment, or saving of the guilty [female] object (an avenue typified by the concerns of the film noir)" (421).

Dorothy Vallens, the helpless "blue lady" of David Lynch's film, proves to be the object of two voyeuristic investigations. The most obviously pernicious of these is perpetrated by Frank Booth, her derangedly violent possessor who has reduced her to a situation of total passivity by imprisoning her husband and child. In perhaps the most memorable scene of the film, one which has also caused the greatest amount of distress for women viewers, Booth comes to Dorothy's apartment and forces her to submit to his degrading procedure. Virtually a parody of the phallic-patriarchal male, he comes dressed in black and leather, brandishes scissors, and demands that she call him "Daddy." Insisting that she spread her legs and "show it to me," he also announces that the gaze is all his, that she had no access to the subjectivity represented by the look; he says "Don't you fucking look at me," and forces her to avert her eyes while he enacts his strange sexual scenario on her submissive body. Were she to look, she would of course be asserting herself as an active agent and thus subverting her status as an object; as Sartre points out, "the explosion of the Other's look in the world of the sadist causes the meaning and goal of sadism to collapse" (526). While there is another scene between Dorothy and Jeffrey where she seems to have control of both the gaze and the sexual power, demanding that he not look at her while she fondles his genitals, holding a knife that she waves as a castrating threat, it is merely a re-enactment of her humiliating dynamic with Frank, with the positions reversed.

Although the sadistic nature of Frank's visual and sexual possession of Dorothy is apparent from the first moment, Jeffrey's is, at the outset, less obvious. The clean-cut young college student initially seems innocent, happening across the severed ear that leads him into the mystery surrounding Frank and Dorothy, but his wide eyes and eagerness to investigate are symptomatic of his potential to be driven by murky impulses from deep in his unconscious. Because he is a sort of Everyman figure and, during the moment he begins as a voyeur trapped in a dark closet, patently a viewer surrogate, his depiction seems a virtual allegory of male spectatorship.

Warned by Sandy that she does not know "if you're a detective or a pervert," Jeffrey proves that he is as much the latter as the former. He enters Dorothy's apartment late at night on the specious pretext that he must do so to begin to clear up the mystery of the ear, and quickly finds himself drawn into the psychological darkness that he sees from the closet where he hides when Frank arrives unexpectedly to perform his brutalizing acts on Dorothy's helpless body. When Jeffrey emerges, he at first resists Dorothy's offer to hit her as they come together sexually, but soon, asserting that he is "seeing something that was always hidden," reveals that part of that "something" in his own capacity to advance from the mild sadism of voyeurism to the full sadism of physical brutality. During his second encounter with Dorothy, he accepts her offer to "do bad things," and strikes her during the sexual act. The roars on the soundtrack and the flames on the screen make obvious the way in which the "beast" in Jeffrey has been aroused, just as it may be for any spectator. Later Frank tells Jeffrey, "You're like me," and kisses him on the lips with a mouth bloodied by Jeffrey's blow. The underscoring of such psychic truths in an uneasily comic way fails to ameliorate their impact; viewers must recognize their own complicity.

The enactment of the dark potential in every human being who may find himself in the same psychic space with a violent secret sharer is not new with *Blue Velvet*—it has memorable cinematic avatars in works like Hitchcock's *Strangers on a Train* (1950), where the suavely psychotic Bruno carries out the illicit wishes of Guy, an obvious Everyman, for his wife's murder—but Lynch's connection of it with the theme of spectatorship makes his movie a particularly self-reflexive artifact. *Blue Velvet* is clearly about voyeurism, about the way in which fascination, itself perhaps a mild pathology, can lead to participation of a more destructive sort.

Even as, at one level, Lynch provides an explicit depiction of the way in which woman is objectified and potentially brutalized in the viewing process, he reveals ways in which that process may be subverted. The scenes in which he shows female spectatorship—Jeffrey's mother watching thrillers on television—are, like Dorothy's investigation of Jeffrey's genitalia, simple inversions in which the female merely assumes a classically "male" position; these reversals, like those in other noirish films of the 1980s that show the woman ascendant, such as *Body Heat*, simply re-present patriarchal cinematic conventions. Nonetheless, other scenes in *Blue Velvet* are more radical in their refusal to construct "normal" visual pleasures. The most striking of these is the sequence, late in the movie, in which Dorothy is found naked by Jeffrey on his porch upon his return from a date with Sandy. Her body is not only so ungainly that it provokes Sandy's friend Mike to ask disgustedly, "Is that your mother?" it is covered with bruises and other marks. Star and director were obviously determined to foreclose the possibility of erotic beauty in this moment; in an interview, Isabella Rossellini spoke of her wish not "to lose weight or be lit in a protective way or do three weeks of intensive exercise. That would have made me so embarrassed, to try to look better, to try to titillate" (Winer). Nor is her unpleasurable nakedness quickly covered; she remains unclothed in Jeffrey's car and for long moments in the brightly lit foyer of the Williams home before someone finally offers her a coat, eliciting discomfort in the other characters and in the viewers (Bundtzen). This unsettling sequence, following as it does upon the careful narrativization of the problematics of spectatorship, serves to bring into conscious view the covert operations of the cinematic apparatus, with their particular implications for women, inside and outside of the diegesis.

Other aspects of the depiction of women in*Blue Velvet* reveal the way in which Lynch manages both to employ and to deconstruct cinematic conventions provocatively. They fall, as mentioned above, into the usual categories of "good"—the young Sandy, the middle-class and uninteresting Mrs. Williams and Mrs. Beaumont—and "bad"—Dorothy, the grotesques in and around "Pussy Heaven"—and Lynch makes use of the standard iconography. Sandy is blond and always wears pink or white, while Dorothy is dressed in black or midnight blue from the skin out and both her wig and her real hair are very dark. Sandy plays the usual redemptive role of the "good" woman, describing dreams in which the "blinding light of love" saves the world from darkness and attempting to keep Jeffrey from straying too far from the path of "normalcy," just as Dorothy is like most other filmic occupants of the demimonde, alluring, sexual, a hazardous companion for a young man; in taking him into her arms in the "Deep River" apartment building, she becomes the catalyst who draws him across the threshold into a world of darkness. His "moral redemption" is signalled by his final alliance with the fair maiden and separation from the dark lady.

Yet Lynch complicates our reactions to these female archetypes by departing from the norm. Dorothy is not the classic female fatale of film noir—most vividly represented by Kathy Moffett of *Out of the Past*, whose crimes range from theft to murder—for she is herself a victim, forced into degraded behavior by the kidnapping of her family. That she seems to enjoy the masochistic activities to which she is forced to submit is only a measure of the extent to which a victim may come to accept and even internalize the forces that humiliate her—a drama repeatedly played out in colonial and racist societies. Even more unusual is the fact that Dorothy is a mother, and, moreover, one who seems to care passionately about her child; devoted maternity has perhaps never before been a characteristic of a noir "dark lady." Nor is her seeming opposite, Sandy, a pure innocent; her first words to Jeffrey, "Are you the one who found the ear?" evince a fascination quite like his, and she appears out of the darkness as if she were the femme fatale rather than the fair maiden. She has already eavesdropped on her father's detecting consulations, so proves a source of information to Jeffrey, and she readily becomes his sidekick on his early forays to Dorothy's apartment. Sandy also reveals a burgeoning worldliness and some equilibrated ideas, serving as the "voice of good sense" when she raises the question of whether Jeffrey is a detective or a pervert and telling him that his determination to enter Dorothy's living quarters "sounds like a good daydream, but doing it is too weird." The fact that Sandy is pictured as often at night as she is in the daytime is emblematic of her larger function, poised between light and darkness, capable of participating in either world.

Dorothy's status as the archetypal "dark lady" of film noir is thus subverted by her victimhood and her explicit role as mere sexual object, no more than a site for the transactions of men, a simple pawn in the male economy of desire; similarly, Sandy, despite her virignal blond looks, has a capacity for insight and a wish to participate in the hermeneutic quest, as well as, perhaps, the potential to explore the darkness within, so that she functions in part as a female counterpart to Jeffrey.

The end of the movie, like the depiction of its central characters, in some ways conforms to the classic pattern and in others forbids its consolations. Sandy, to be sure, is restored to her rightful place within the family, boyfriend at her side, and her vision of the redeeming blinding light of love represented by the robin seems now to dominate, while Dorothy, befitting the fact that she is in no essential way evil, is reunited with her child in a final scene of joyous maternity. Jeffrey, the nemesis of the evildoers, has endured his travails and eradicated the terrible criminal who is also his dark alter ego, psychically ensuring himself of a healthy return to "normalcy." The pastoral scene at the end, with families reunited, Jeffrey dozing in his chaise lounge, and the robin in the window sill, appears as a reassuring moment in which evil has been dispatched and good has triumphed. It is in this like the classic noir, in which the threatening darkness is usually contained and dispelled; corruption may be pervasive, and some innocent people may come to grief, but right is always apparent and ultimately prevails.

Nevertheless, Lynch makes the ending impossible to accept by subverting the conventional structures in disorienting ways. First of all, unlike earlier noir protagonists who were either tragically tainted or redeptively matured by their confrontations with the underworld—either outcome the result of basic moral assumptions common to all the movies—Jeffrey seems utterly untouched by his experiences, without guilt or wisdom. Although his horrifying doppelganger Frank may be dead, there is nothing to suggest that Jeffrey has reached some higher plateau of understanding than the inadequate one from which he was initially drawn in; Lynch refuses to provide a comforting psycho-moral resolution. The final vision of the women is hardly more reassuring. Sandy inanely comments, "It's a strange world," looking at the mechanical robin whose ridiculous message she has previously offered up as though it were some cosmic truth. Even the last shot of Dorothy, maternally enclosing her son in a warm embrace, is undermined by the sound track, where the title song reminds us of the blue velvet she saw "through my tears" and thus of the psychic and physical scars she bears.

More quietly subversive perhaps, but also more disturbing in some ways, is the fact that the ending of the movie simply redeploys the hokey and stylized images from the very beginning of the film. Flowers, fence, and fire engine pass our eyes in mechanical fashion, suggesting that simple repetition is the only truth and mocking any possibility of "moral progress." Moreover, since the end, like the beginning, is so kitschy as to be meaningless, the bourgeois milieu depicted in both is simply something in which we cannot believe. One effect of this non-credible moral framework is the implicit validation of the interior story and its sadistic violence, especially the male brutalization of the female. Our vision of the scarred and victimized Dorothy is not fully subsumed and counterbalanced by the empty visual of the beaming "redeemed" mother, so we are left with the more dominant impression of a horrific female plight. In this respect, the movie offers a vision of women marked less, perhaps, by misogyny than by some bizarre combination of sympathy and prurience.

Lynch's re-vision of classic film noir, because of its lack of the sort of moral intelligibility we expect from this type of narrative, seems very much— and perhaps worrisomely—a fable for our times, implying the bankruptcy of all humanist perspectives. To be sure, its playful allusiveness, its juxtapositions of the comic and the horrific, its uneasy balancing of the feminist and misogynist, and its deconstruction of conventional structures and viewer expectations, all combine to make it a striking, even brilliant artifact. Nevertheless, these postmodernist strategies, however adroitly employed by David Lynch, are somehow more problematic in a popular medium such as detective film than they are, say, in a nouveau roman.

Baudrillard, paraphrasing Bordieu, has written about western society's need for the illusion of morality, for the potential for outrage (27), and Lynch's film denies its viewers either of those consolations. Its "moral" images are defenseless against the forces which undermine them. Walter Benjamin has written of the process by which fascism aestheticized violence and thus rendered it less immediate (241-42); in a comparable way, *Blue Velvet* stylizes morality so that the viewer is irreparably distanced from it, and thus has no value-based armor with which to confront the movie's unnerving violence. Classic films noir, despite their seeming pessimism, always offered vantage points from which clear judgments could be made. Lynch's ludic and stylish film, while admirable in the way it plays with cinematic norms and moral stances, makes it difficult to formulate perspectives. We cannot comfortably navigate its strange world.

Works Cited

Baudrillard, Jean. *Stimulations*. New York: Semiotext(e), 1983.

Benjamin, Walter. *Illuminations*, trans. Harry Zohn. New York: Schocken, 1969.

Bundtzen, Linda. " 'Don't Look at Me!': Woman's Body, Woman's Voice in *Blue Velvet*." Unpublished Essay, 1988.

Johnston, Claire. "Myths of Women in the Cinema." *Women and the Cinema*, ed. Karyn Kay and Gerald Peary. New York: Dutton, 1977.

Mulvey, Laura. "Visual Pleasure and Narrative Cinema." *Women and the Cinema*, ed. Karyn Kay and Gerald Peary. New York: Dutton, 1977.

Sartre, Jean-Paul. *Being and Nothingness*, trans. Hazel E. Barnes. New York: Washington Square Press, 1966.

Winer, Laurie. "Isabella Rossellini Assesses the Role that Haunted Her." *New York Times*, November 23, 1986, Section Two, p. 21.

Women, Danger, and Death:
The Perversion of The Female Principle
In Stephen King's Fiction

Gail E. Burns and Melinda Kanner

Introduction

I hope that this study may lessen the male-centering propensity and shed new light on the psycho-sexual role of woman; that it may indicate how much more that is feminine exists in men than is generally believed, and how greatly woman's influence and strivings have affected social institutions which we still explain on a purely masculine basis. (Bettelheim 58)

With these words, the psychologist Bruno Bettelheim expresses the mission of his cross-cultural inquiry into *rites de passage*. With these words, one might well begin an inquiry into the construction and situation of women in the world of Stephen King's fiction.

In all societies, relations between men and women are expressed, in part, through the symbolic acquisition of the powers and capabilities not normally under the control of one sex or the other. Women seek to capture the social, economic, and political control typically enjoyed and exercised by men; men, on the other hand, symbolically mimic female biological capabilities, most notably menstruation and childbirth, revealing envy of that which they lack.

In a complex, large-scale society such as ours, we turn our attention to the artifacts of popular culture to gain insight into our myths, our irreconcilable conflicts, our symbolic envies. To this end, Stephen King's work provides fertile ground for the anthropologist.

Eric Norden's 1983 *Playboy* interview with Stephen King reveals something of King's attitudes about sex, sexual relations, and women. Asked if he has any "sexual hang-ups," King replies that his only sexual problem is that he is a sufferer of "periodic impotence." Asked why explicit sex is largely absent from his novels and stories, he replies that, first he is uncomfortable with sex, second, he has trouble creating believable romantic relationships which would be necessary to avoid arbitrary or prefunctory sex, and finally, that he has, in fact, included an S & M fantasy in one of his novellas. Norden continues in this line of questioning:

Norden: Along with your difficulty in describing sexual scenes you apparently also
have a problem with women in your books. . .
King: Yes, unfortunately, I think it is probably the most justifiable of all those
[criticisms] leveled at me. . .I recognize the problems but can't yet rectify them.
(Underwood and Miller 45-47)

The women in King's fiction, then, are not carefully crafted, three-dimensional characters. The problem King has with women has nothing
to do with writing women convincingly. Rather the deeply unconscious,
culturally shared understandings of what constitutes Woman that emerge
from the pages of these novels provide the basis for this analysis.

King himself and critics alike have commented that he cannot write
convincing female characters. Our investigation reveals that the construction
of female characters in *Pet Sematary*, as in his other fiction, draws upon
and reinforces widely, if unconsciously, share cultural myths about the female
principle. This paper explores the construction of women in Stephen King
and draws upon his controversial novel, *Pet Sematary*, as exemplary of the
representation of women in King's fiction.

Scholarly Attention and King's Fiction

Precisely because of his immense popularity, Stephen King provides
fertile ground for scholarly analysis. Although critical and academic
audiences for the most part ignore, denigrate, or otherwise declare King's
fiction as unworthy of serious consideration, the vast popularity of this body
of popular culture suggests an area for investigation by the social scientists
as well as the literary critic.

Since the 1974 publication of his best-selling novel, *Carrie*, Stephen
King has received vast popular attention. His novels and collections of stories,
in press continuously from their first publication and frequently converted
into theatrical and made-for-television movies, have generated unprecedented
levels of readership and media attention. Infrequently has this positive and
sustained popular reception been matched with critical enthusiasm. The
schism which traditionally has inhibited serious investigation of popular
culture is dramatically reflected in the lack of academic reactions to Stephen
King. Certain notable exceptions do exist. Two general categories of critical
treatment address the various dimensions on which King exist as a
phenomenon.

First, the predominant approach to King's fiction, written by fans-cum-critics, glorifies King's literary product as unrecognized genius. These authors
have contributed significantly to deepening King's appeal through their
attention to his biography and its connections to his writing, their plot
expositions, and their detailed cataloguing of the corpus of King's work
(see especially Winter, Underwood and Miller). However valuable their
contributions, this treatment has done little to advance our understanding
of the underlying culturally shared symbols which account in large measure
for King's popularity.

A second treatment of King has begun to explore the possibilities of scholarly interpretations by locating King's fiction in the context of theme and genre, of metaphor and archetype.

The recent publication of Hoppenstand and Browne's *The Gothic World of Stephen King* (1987) provides a collection of essays which understands King's fiction and films in the light of the contemporary re-telling of traditional horror myths, the struggle of adolescents in an adult world, the adult re-living of childhood horrors and interpretations of morality (see, for example, Newhouse, Kanfer, and Pharr).

The high-culture low-culture dichotomy which has all but precluded serious literary analysis of King's fiction places the burden of untangling King's signification system on the shoulders of popular culture studies. The literary quality of King's work is not at issue, nor are they myriad explanations for his popular success. The aim here is to understand the women in King's fiction in the larger cultural context, to come to terms with those unconsciously shared and understood ideals, values, and understandings which give his plots and characters meaning, which give his images sustained potency.

Women in Stephen King

In a recent made-for-cable-TV program, *Stephen King's Women of Horror*, horror writers and filmmakers, including Clive Barker, John Carpenter, and Anthony Hickox, comment on the role of women in horror fiction. John Carpenter, a director of horror films, observes:

In society we have a lot of mixed feelings about women, what they should do and what they shouldn't do, and I think you see it reflected in horror movies all the time. It's a kind of anxiety level on the bottom. Women's traditional roles...there's a lot of confusion. The confusion comes from men a lot of the time.

Female reproductive potential, sexuality, and death are forged by King in a manner that invariably locks his female characters into particular, sexually defined roles. Although this analysis focusses on *Pet Sematary*, a cursory examination of the larger context of Stephen King's work reveals that the powerful reproduction/sexuality/death dialectic is present in all his work and provides the symbolic matrix in which all girls and women are embedded. Menstruation, mothering, and female sexual desire function as bad omens, prescient clues that something will soon be badly awry.

Women as mothers are incapable of caring for or protecting their children. In King's world, mothers are pathetically unable to save their offspring: witness Donna and Tad Trenton (*Cujo*), Wendy and Danny Torrance (*The Shining*), Vicky and Charlie McGee (*Firestarter*). Indeed, mothers and maternal figures alike are very often the agents of destruction, as in the cases of Margaret White (*Carrie*), Heidi Halleck (*Thinner*), and Annie Wilkes (*Misery*). King consistently portrays women at the mercy of their hormones, a force of nature that he links with the supernatural and which results in death rather than life.

Women in traditional horror fiction are portrayed as victims, targets of evil, easily terrorized, susceptible to the seductive forces of vampires and murderers. Where women are represented as the agents of horror themselves, they traditionally have appeared as "devourers, vampires, seductresses who can make you crash because you're listening to their song" (John Carpenter, *Stephen King's Women of Horror*). Women in King's fiction are neither vacant, screaming victims nor are they evil incarnate. The ways in which women embody evil and act as conduits for the supernatural are ambiguous and drawn from culturally and socially shared understandings. The evil that women are and the evil women do in King is ambiguous, derived from precisely the forces of life and attraction.

Carrie White (*Carrie*) and Roberta Anderson (*Tommyknockers*) experience some sort of dysmenorrhea which functions as a portent of their personal destruction and, through them, the destruction of their communities. In each case King defines menstruation as the trigger for the paranormal/supernatural events of these novels. Carrie's and Bobbie's reproductive potential cannot result in life; instead it is perverted and becomes the transmitter of mutation and death. This biological conundrum is a hallmark of King's fictional females.

Bobbie Anderson, as she discovers and progressively uncovers the mysterious evil buried beneath the earth, lays open a trench.

She began to unbutton her jeans so she could tuck in her blouse, then paused. The crotch of the faded Levi's was soaked with blood. Jesus. Jesus Christ. This isn't a period. This is Niagara Falls.
(King *Tommmyknockers* 34).

Days later, as she resumes her exploratory digging:

Her period had started again, but that was all right; she had put a pad in the crotch of her panties even before she went out to weed the garden. A Maxi.
(King *Tommyknockers* 67).

Women who do manage to give birth generally fail their children in the most fundamental ways. This failure is linked consistently in King's novels to their sexuality, manifest as excessive or inadequate. Donna Trenton, for example, watches her son die of dehydration and is helpless to act until it is too late. Cujo, the rabid St. Bernard, keeps the mother-child dyad trapped in a disabled Pinto for three days, but it is the mother, Donna, not Cujo, who sets the tragic circumstances in motion and is therefore ultimately responsible for her son's death. The car has not been repaired because her sexual relationship with the local tennis pro, Steve Kemp, estranges her from Vic, her husband, creates havoc in the household, and results in the fatal car break-down.

He [Steve Kemp] had known Donna was cooling it, but she had struck him as a woman who could be manipulated with no great difficulty, at least for a while, by a combination of psychological and sexual factors. By fear, if you wanted to be crude. (King *Cujo* 50)

Wendy Torrance's lack of decision nearly results in her son, Danny's, death. She knows of her husband's recurrent violence; his past alcoholic rages have resulted in child abuse including the broken arm of the infant Danny. Wendy, however, ignores Jack's erratic behavior, his inability to write, and even her growing suspicions that he is drinking again. She takes no measure to end the abuse, to save herself or her son. It is, in fact, Danny's telepathic distress signal to Halloran that results in their rescue from the Overlook.

Why is Billy Halleck (*Thinner*) afflicted with a gypsy curse? Because he killed the old man's daughter. But what caused the fatal automobile accident? Heidi Halleck, who is masturbating her husband Billy as they cruise along a busy city street. The facts that it is female desire, female sexual initiation, and, most importantly perhaps, sexual expression which cannot result in conception all function significantly in the sex/death dialectic.

As Heidi Halleck's desire realizes its expression, this temptation-turned-tragedy results in the death of seven people, including the entire Halleck family.

But he couldn't speak. The pleasure woke again at the touch of her fingers, playful at first then more serious...The pleasure mixed uneasily with a feeling of terrible inevitability...Then: *Thud/thud.* (King *Thinner* 24).

And, when blame is clearly assigned to the granddaughter of the deceased, the underlying cause of the tragedy is made public.

He was getting a jerk-off job from his woman and he ran her down in the street. (King *Thinner* 271)

Heidi unwittingly passes on the gypsy curse to their daughter, through her roles as biological creator and maternal nurturer. They share a strawberry pie, laden with placental, vaginal, and menstrual imagery. The pie, presented to Billy by the old gypsy man, will undo the curse when Billy feeds it to another woman. The imagery of the pie is explicit.

This thing—*purpurfargade ansiket*—you bring into the world like a baby. Only it grows faster than a baby, and you can't kill it because you can't see it—only you can see what it *does*. (King *Thinner* 288)

The pie, with a "darkish slit" under which a blood-like ooze pulsed, would extract the curse from Billy, contain it, and, finally implant it in the eater. As Billy followed the old man's instructions, allowing the blood from his knife wound to spill into the pie, his wound healed, the pie sealed itself, and

He collapsed back against the park bench, feeling wretchedly nauseated, wretchedly *empty*—the way a woman who has just given birth must feel, he imagined (King *Thinner* 289-290)

The conjunction of the expression "the curse" with the bloody mass seeping from a dark slit, the perverse restorative, life-giving powers of the pie, the urgency of oral incorporation of the pie by another, and the ultimate responsibility for the series of devastations aimed at Heidi present an ambiguous exposition of the female to the reader.

In *Firestarter*, another case of an inadequate mother precipitates tragic events. The Shop, a nefarious secret agency, comes after Charlie because of her telepyrotechnic powers. That ability is the result of some genetic mutation caused by drugs used in an experiment for which her parents volunteered. Yet the most rudimentary knowledge of biology assigns the blame to Vicky for that mutant gamete. The evil which pursues them can only be construed as punishment for her flagrant disregard of her future reproductive role.

"I'm Vicky Tomlinson. And a little nervous about this, Andy McGee. What if I go on a bad trip or something?"
He ended up buying her two Cokes, and they spend the afternoon together. That evening they had a few beers at the local hangout. It turned out that she and the boyfriend had come to a parting of ways, and she wasn't sure exactly how to handle it. He was beginning to think they were married, she told Andy; had absolutely forbidden her to take part in the Wanless experiment. For that precise reason she had gone ahead and sighed the release form and was now determined to go through with it even though she was little scared. (King *Firestarter* 14-15)

How do you explain to a seven-year-old girl that Daddy and Mommy had once needed two hundred dollars and the people they had talked to said it was all right, but they had lied? (King *Firestarter* 40)

Her subsequent inability to defend herself and Charlie results in her own grisly death and Charlie's abduction by the evil secret agents.

Carrie's mother, Margaret White, is not, in any conventional sense maternal, but rather a hyperbole of perverted female sexuality and maternity. Her extreme puritanical view of sex—in the best Freudian tradition—produced a very strange girl.

After Carrie's humiliating public first menstruation, she returns home, hoping to find explanation from her mother.

"Why didn't you *tell* me?...Oh, Momma, I was so *scared!*"

Her mother articulates the connection of female sexuality, menstruation, motherhood, and evil:

And Eve was weak and loosed the raven on the world...and the raven was called Sin, and the first Sin was Intercourse. And the Lord visited Eve with a Curse, and the Curse was the Curse of blood. And Adam and Eve were driven out of the Garden and into the World and Eve found that her belly had grown big with child. (King *Carrie* 53-54)

Carrie's menarche somehow endows her with incredible telekinetic powers through which she punishes her classmates, her mother, and the entire town. Specifically, it is her rage at the ignominious outcome of her first date that prompts her to unleash her talents. This date with Tommy, particularly when they are chosen King and Queen of the Prom, is heavy with sexual implication and death imagery. In the recollection of a classmate, Norma Watson, the moment is described.

All at once there was a huge red splash in the air. Some of it hit the mural and ran in long drips. I knew right away, even before it hit them, that it was blood. Stella Horan thought it was paint, but I had a premonition just like the time my brother got hit by a hay truck. Carrie got it the worst. (King *Carrie* 167)

Annie Wilkes (*Misery*), although not biologically a mother, assumes a demented maternal role in Paul Sheldon's life. The fact that she is a killer nurse—notably in a hospital nursery—again punctuates King's death/reproduction theme. She disables and infantilizes Paul with drugs, rendering him dependent on her for all his needs.

Castration imagery figures prominently in Annie's terrorist maternity. First, a hobbling episode, representing both dependence and castration:

Just a little pain. Then this nasty business will be behind us for good, Paul...
She gripped the handle farther up in her left hand and spread her legs like a logger...The axe came whistling down and buried itself in Paul Sheldon's left leg just above the ankle. (King *Misery* 221)

Then later, the surgical removal of another of Paul's appendages in the thumbectomy.

Then he had been still and let her give him the injection and this time the Betadine had gone over his left thumb as well as the blade of the knife...As the humming, vibrating blade sank into the soft web of flesh between the soon-to-be-defunct thumb and his first finger, she assured him again in her this-hurts-Mother-more-than it hurts-Paulie voice that she loved him. (King, *Misery* 253-254)

The contrast between Annie and Misery Chastain, the voluptuous heroine of Paul's best-selling books, might be amusing were it not for Annie's crazed torture of the bedridden novelist. It is Misery's death in childbirth which catalyzes Annie's perverted mothering and underscores both the dangers of women who fail to fulfill their proper roles and the power of the male author over the death and resurrection of his female characters.

Women occupy particularly horrible roles in King's fiction. They are not, typically, wide-eyed, screaming, terror-stricken virgins, nor are they recognizable villains who suck the blood of those who would fall prey to their seductive powers. Rather they are the evil which results from the perversion of convention, the misuse of female sexual desire, the dangers of the empty, or emptying womb, the destruction which is unleashed by a failed mother.

In *Stephen King's Women of Horror*, narrator Strozier notes

It is precisely their essence of femininity, the seductiveness in women that provides a perfect launching point for exploring the taboos of our society, the physical attractions, the compulsions, and attractions...The corruption of one's nature is a prime target for horror writers.

The emotions which surround sex and motherhood are compelling. The manipulation of these feelings serves to disorient, confuse, upset, and attract the reader. King has particular interest in "scaring women to death."

It would be sexist to say that only ladies care about their children—in fact, it would be a downright lie—but there does seem to be such a thing as a "maternal instinct," and I go for it instinctively. (King *Danse Macabre* 173)

Indeed. Quite apart from King's ability to scare women, or men for that matter, his effectiveness depends upon hitting responsive chords, seeking out and bruising cultural sore spots, reflecting and creating images at reflexive and unconscious levels.

Women, Sex, and Death: The Case of Pet Sematary
The soil of a man's heart is stonier, Louis—like the soil up there in the old Micmac burying ground. Bedrock's close. A man grows what he can...and he tends it.
—————Jud Crandall (King *Pet Sematary* 141)

Pet Sematary elaborates the dysfunctionally dangerous, and destructive female principle in the world of Stephen King. The reproductive power of women, distorted in King's novels, becomes the object of envy and perversion. Sex expressed outside the context of procreative intercourse, sex initiated by a female, becomes linked with death rather than life. In this perversion, the power of procreation—of resurrection—becomes the property of men rather than women.

Rachel Creed, the mother in *Pet Sematary*, is a good, if ineffective mother who provides the link between the dangers of life and mysteries of death. Failed by her own possessive, fearful parents and witness to her sister Zelda's agonizing, slow death, Rachel produces Ellen and Gage—children who themselves are doomed. Deserted by his father and protected by his mother, Louis Creed fathers Ellen and Gage in the only distorted ways he can piece together from his skill as a physician and his role as a watchful and compliant "son" to the older neighbor Jud Crandall.

Prompted by Rachel's pathological inability and unwillingness to educate their daughter, Ellie, in matters of death, Louis Creed submits to the tutelage of Jud Crandall, his surrogate father, to learn the secrets of resurrection buried in the man's arcane knowledge.

Rachel's abdication of responsibility is revealed after a visit to the local pet cemetery, a burial ground established by children to honor their dead pets. Ellie's matter-of-fact approach to death is matched by her father's pragmatic, honest responses and contrasted with her mother's paranoid and terrified refusal to expose the child to death in any manifestation. Ellie's next exposure to the possibilities of death held by life comes with the neutering of her male cat, Church. Finally, the accidental death of Church while Rachel, Ellie, and Gage are visiting Rachel's parents set in motion the text of life restored and subtext of sex and death.

This perversion of reproduction is played out in several dimensions. Through two themes King juxtaposes the central elements and resolves the conflicts which inhere: Opposing forces are inverted, transformed and reversed.

Mothers and Fathers, Daughters and Sons

At the center of the mother/father opposition are the dismal, dysfunctional childhoods of Rachel and Louis. Rachel, the daughter of upper middle class, urban parents, is dominated and controlled by her father, Irwin Goldman. Disapproving of Rachel's relationship with Louis from the start, Goldman offers Louis a "scholarship" for his medical school education in exchange for Louis' termination of his relationship with Rachel. The offer rejected, Louis severs himself from the Goldmans in every way possible. Rachel remains, at least partly, under the domination of her parents, succumbing to their pressure and accepting their gifts.

The parent/child mania in this relationship comes from Rachel's childhood. Her older sister, Zelda, had died of spinal meningitis when Rachel had been left by her parents, alone, at age eight, to watch her disabled and dying sister. Rachel was never *told* about death, but rather initiated into its mysteries. Rachel, the product of a politely dysfunctional home, transmits the destruction of ignorance to her own daughter, Ellie. By failing to tell Ellie about death, she leaves her maternal responsibility to Louis.

Louis, a child raised by his mother alone, suffers a different dysfunction. His mother, too, protected him. Where Rachel, as her mother before her, failed to instruct the daughter in the mysteries of death, Louis' mother misled him in matters of birth, about women finding babies in dewy grass when they really wanted one. "Louis had never forgiven his mother for telling it—or himself for believing it" (King 1984:52). Early in his life, Louis is educated about the natural place of death from his undertaker uncle, and by the same mother who had lied to him about sex. In his mind, Jud Crandall's voice and his mother are merged for him as he recalls the death of his first love at age twelve. The mysteries of death, unknown to Rachel, remain mysterious. The secrets of burial are as much a part of Louis' knowledge as his skill as a physician.

Rachel Creed, like the Biblical Rachel, will weep for her children and not be comforted, because they are not.

Sex and Death

The pet cemetery is the site of death and burial and it is the perversely fertile soil, the soil of a man, for rebirth. This is signalled early by Rachel in an argument with Louis about confronting Ellie with the facts of death. Louis argues that Ellie knows the "facts of life," or the mechanics of human reproduction. "Where babies come from has nothing to do with a goddam pet cemetery," Rachel screams at Louis (King 1984:55). Indeed, for the men in *Pet Sematary*, the pet cemetery has everything to do with where "babies" come from. The conversion of death into life, the reversal of natural processes, depends upon a complexly woven code of sex and death, in which all ordering, all processes, all functions become perverted.

Four major manifestations of the conjunction of sex and death form the center of the text: First, the juxtaposition of sexual encounters between Louis and Rachel with a death related episode; second, the metaphorical description of the pet cemetery's attraction and the pull of death as like the power and irresistability of sexual attraction; third, the coincidence of castration actuality, anxiety, and threats with death imagery and death episodes; finally, the specifically sexual nature of the "knowledge" that those who return from the Micmac burial ground articulate in their resurrected state.

Sexual encounters between Louis and Rachel becomes linked with death when they are non-procreative—oral sex, masturbation—or when they occur at Rachel's instigation. On his first day as head of University Medical Services, the same day that Rachel was to schedule the castration of Ellie's cat, Louis Creed presides over the death of a young man fatally injured by an automobile. This man, Victor Pascow, in his dying words, warns Louis about the pet cemetery, speaks the words that Jud would speak ("a man's heart is stonier"). When Louis returns home that evening, Rachel greets him with seduction: a hot bath and a masturbatory sexual encounter. The occurrence of death followed by sex is repeated when Church, the now un-dead cat brings home a Christmas Eve present of a dead crow, which he deposits at the Creed doorstep. Again, as Louis disposes of the crow, Pascow, Jud, Church, and Louis are conjoined in a prelude to sex. When Louis joins Rachel in bed, she greets him again with female-initiated sex, this time fellatio. Sex, when expressed in any way other than one which will result in conception, becomes the link with death. Initiated by Rachel, following Louis' encounters with death, these sexual liaisons confer upon Louis not the powers of female reproductive capabilities, but an inversion of these powers: their accumulation endows him with power of resurrection. The reversal of the sex-conception sequence into the death-sex sequence provides the transforming joint.

A second death/sex conjunction appears in the frequent comparisons between the pull of death and the attraction of the pet cemetery with sex. The necessity of man submitting to the demands of the burial ground is described as something

you do because it gets hold of you. You do it because that burial place is a secret place, and you want to share the secret...you make up reasons...they seem like good reasons...but mostly you do it because you want to. Or because you have to. (King *Pet Sematary* 255).

After Jud calls Louis to deliver the sad news that Church's dead body lies on the road, another victim of the truck route, Louis contemplates how wrong this all seems, how he believed his family would be exempt from such tragedy in another death/sex connection.

He remembered one of the guys he played poker with, Wikes Sullivan, asking him once how he could get horny for his wife and not get horny for the naked women he saw day in and day out. Louis tried to explain to him that it wasn't the way people imagined in their fantasies—a woman coming in to get a Pap smear or to learn how to give herself a breast self-examination didn't suddenly drop a sheet and stand there like Venus on the half-shell. You saw a breast, a vulva, a thigh. The rest was draped in sheet, and there was a nurse in attendance, more to protect the doctor's reputation than anything else. Wicky wasn't buying it. A tit is a tit, was Wicky's thesis, and a twat is a twat. You should either be horny all the time or none of it. All Louis could respond was that your wife's tit was different. *Just like your family's supposed to be different*, he thought now. Church wasn't supposed to get killed...(King *Pet Sematary* 120-121)

Other imagery links male sexuality and the male power of resurrection through the burial ground. Jud describes to Louis some of the secrets he has kept from his wife, Norma.

I used to go up to the whorehouse in Bangor betimes. Nothing many a man hasn't done, although I s'pose there are plenty that walk the straight and narrow. I just would get the urge—the compulsion, maybe—to sink it into strange flesh now and then...Men keep their gardens too, Louis. (King *Pet Sematary* 272)

Castration, first of Church the cat, then Louis's own castration fears are tied to death and the recreation of life. Before their moving to Maine, Louis intervened on behalf of Church and obstructed a scheduled neutering by cancelling the vet appointment. There is the strong suggestion that the cat's virility and Louis' own masculinity are somehow pieces of one puzzle.

In fact there had been some trouble over that back in Chicago. Rachel had wanted to get Church spayed, had even made the appointment with the vet. Louis canceled it. Even now he wasn't really sure why. It wasn't anything simple or as stupid as equating his masculinity with that of his daughter's tom...but most of it had been a vague but strong feeling that it would destroy something in Church that he himself valued...(King *Pet Sematary* 29)

The anticipation of Church's neutering precipitates Ellie's questions about death. The second and successful scheduling of the vet appointment comes immediately before Louis's encounter with the dying Pascow. In a dream, as Louis imagines life had Gage lived, had he not been killed in the same road where Church died, he re-writes the scenario by saving Gage from certain death. In his scenario, his closest contact with himself is genital, as though saving Gage was somehow an act of procreation.

He yanked Gage backward and landed on the ground at the same instant, crashing his face into the rough gravel of the shoulder, giving himself a bloody nose. His balls signalled a much more serious flash of pain—Ohh, if I'd'a known I was gonna be playing football, I woulda worn my jock—but both the pain in his nose and the driving agony in his testes were lost in the swelling relief of hearing Gage's wail of pain and outrage...(King *Pet Sematary* 276)

As Louis embarks on his grave-robbing to recover the body of his son, he encounters the physical obstacles that might block his entrance into the cemetery. As he begins his ascent of the cemetery wall, he comes upon decorative arrow tips at the top of the fence. He realizes that his testicles, not to mention his internal organs, are in peril. As if by protecting his testicles, becoming aware of them, saving Church's sexual potency, unconsciously hurting himself in his fantasy rescue of Gage, Louis invests his testes with the power of resurrection.

Equally important is the nature of the knowledge of sexual intimacies announced by those who return from the dead. Timmy Baterman, a figure from Jud's past, was the only other human re-buried and, importantly, resurrected by his father in the Micmac cemetery. When Timmy returned from the dead, he reveals his secret knowledge.

'Your wife is fucking that man she works with down at the drugstore, Purinton. What do you think of that? She screams when she comes. What do you think of that?' (King *Pet Sematary* 271)

When Gage returns and confronts Jud in prelude to his death at the hands of the un-dead toddler, he reveals the secrets of Norma's sex life, again underscoring the connection of non-procreative sex and the world of death.

Norma's dead and there'll never be no one to mourn you...What a cheap slut she was. She fucked every one of your friends, Jud. She let them put it up her ass... (King *Pet Sematary* 382)

Then, just before the fatal blow is delivered, Gage speaks to Jud in Norma's voice, telling him how she and her lovers laughed at him, how they made love in their bed, how she knew of his whorehouse visits. As

Jud lunges to silence Gage, Gage strikes him with a scalpel from his father's medical bag. The father's instrument of life becomes the son's instrument of death.

Sex provides several vital connections through which Louis acquires the powers to produce a version of life. First as the aftermath of Louis's encounters with death, sex with Rachel allows Louis to gain access to female reproductive powers through this post-mortem contact. Next, the desire to visit the Micmac burial ground to bury first Church then Gage, is presented as like sexual desire. Third, the power to resurrect life is initiated through and invested in male sex organs and male sexuality. Finally, sex becomes the secrets held by the dead who return and share them with the living.

Pet Sematary reveals a slight departure from King's typical treatment of women. Rather than the direct conduit of danger, destruction, and evil, Rachel Creed provides two rather more insidious and vital connections for the horrors of re-birth.

The inadequacies of her own childhood disable her as a mother. Her fatal failure lies in his inability to teach her daughter that which a mother must teach: the mysteries of death. Her pathological inability to deal with death, and thereby save her family, results from the failures of her own parents.

Through her sexual behavior—desire, initiation, preferred forms of expression—she enables Louis to capture that which he lacks as a man, as a father, and as a physician: the ability to give, not simply save, life. Louis's role as a physician-turned father-grave-robber-turned-life-giver is central to the conversion. Louis, who has presided over dozens of deaths, whose life was built upon saving life and relieving suffering, sought not the ultimate goal of his profession but the ultimate, collective male fantasy. A man's heart is stonier, Louis is told by Jud Crandall, and man tends his garden, grows what he can. What is grown in this stonier ground is a rockier life, born of the captured and distorted power of female reproduction.

Conclusion: The Horror of Women

Rather than victims or diabolical villains, women in Stephen King's fiction are the triggers of evil, the literal embodiment of danger. On a complex and subtextual level, women are represented in ways that reveal male fear and envy of female sexuality and reproductive biology. Not unlike the myth and ritual that symbolically play out and, to an extent, resolve male ambivalence toward women, King's women are dangerous figures indeed, to be feared as lovers, wives, and mothers.

Scores of societies known to anthropology play out similar dramas in symbolic and expressive forms. The *couvade*, for example, is a conspicuously ceremonial event in which men symbolically mimic post-partum recovery after their wives give birth. Institutionalized transvestism and clothing exchange, dramatic male rites of passage which entail genital blood-letting, and masquerade cults in which males exaggerate female fertility are, like the underlying drama in *Pet Sematary*, the symbolic working out of male envy and ambivalence. This resolution is derived from and responsible for shaping essential and unconsciously shared images.

Those women who are neither sexually linked to men nor maternally linked to children are not immune from male antagonism. Their failure to fulfill their expected, validated sociobiological functions renders them no less dangerous to their communities. Their sexuality is their vulnerability; the realization of their sexual desire results in destruction and death. Mothers fail their children, witness their abuse, and stand helpless to prevent their deaths. Finally, and most vividly illustrated in *Pet Sematary*, the ultimate perversion of the female principle is illustrated in the male appropriation of the powers of reproduction.

Works Cited

Bettelheim, Bruno, *Symbolic Wounds*. New York: Free Press, 1968.

Gallagher, Bernard J. "Breaking up isn't hard to do: Stephen King, Christopher Lasch, and psychic fragmentation." *Journal of American Culture* 10 (1987):59-67.

Hoppenstand, Gary and Ray B. Browne, *The Gothic World of Stephen King: Landscape of Nightmares*. Bowling Green, Ohio: Bowling Green University Popular Press, 1987.

King, Stephen. *Carrie*. New York: New American Library, Signet, 1975

———. *Cujo*. New York: New American Library, Signet, 1982.

———. *Danse Macabre*. New York, Berkley Books, 1979.

———. *Firestarter*. New York: New American Library, Signet, 1981.

———. "How to scare a woman to death." *Murderess Ink: The Better Half of the Mystery*. Dilys Winn, Ed. New York: Workman Press, 1981.

———. *Misery*. New York: New American Library, Signet, 1988.

———. *Pet Sematary*. New York: New American Library, Signet, 1984.

———. *The Shining*. New York: New American Library, Signet, 1978.

———. *Thinner* (written as Richard Bachman). New York: New American Library, Signet, 1988.

———. *The Tommyknockers*. New American Library, Signet, 1988.

King, Tabitha. "Living with the bogeyman." *Murderess Ink*. Dilys Winn, ed. New York: Workman Press, 1981.

Magistrale, Tony. "Stephen King's *Pet Sematary*: Hawthorne's Woods Revisited." *The Gothic World of Stephen King*, Hoppenstand and Browne, eds. Bowling Green, Ohio: Bowling Green State University Popular Press, 1987.

Pharr, Mary Ferguson. "A dream of new life: Stephen King's *Pet Sematary* as a variant of *Frankenstein*." *The Gothic World of Stephen King*, Hoppenstand and Browne, eds. Bowling Green, Ohio: Bowling Green State University Popular Press, 1987.

Reino, Joseph. *Stephen King: The First Decade,*Carrie *to* Pet Sematary. Boston: Hall, 1988.

Schroeder, Natilie. "Oz the Gweat and Tewwible" and "The Other Side." The theme of death in *Pet Sematary* and *Jitterbug Perfume*. *The Gothic World of Stephen King*, Hoppenstand and Browne, eds. Bowling Green, Ohio: Bowling Green State University Popular Press, 1987.

Schuman, Samule. "Taking Stephen King seriously: Reflections on a decade of best-sellers." *The Gothic World of Stephen King*, Hoppenstand and Browne, eds. Bowling Green, Ohio: Bowling Green State University Popular Press, 1987.

Simmons, John (director). *Stephen King's World of Horror: Stephen King's Women of Horror*. Made for Cable T.V., USA Network. Simmons/Fortune Productions. Written by John Simmons. Narrated by Henry Strozier, 1989.

Underwood, Tim and Chuck Miller, Eds. *Fear Itself: The Horror Fiction of Stephen King*. New York: New American Library, 1982.

_____ *Kingdom of Fear: The World of Stephen King*. San Francisco: Underwood Miller, 1986.

_____ *Bare Bones: Conversations on Terror with Stephen King*. New York: McGraw Hill, 1988.

Winter, Douglas. *The Art of Darkness*. New York: New American Library, 1984.

Humor and Gender
in Feminist Music Videos

Robin Roberts

Humor is the oldest form of deconstruction; it breaks down barriers, shatters polarities, and conducts subversive, or even liberatory, attacks upon the reigning order. B. Ruby Rich (559)

Feminist humor is, as Nancy Walker explains in the subtitle of her book on the subject, "A Very Serious Thing," especially when it appears in popular culture. Humor can be used to make trenchant criticisms of patriarchal society. Through humor, an audience can be manipulated into seeing or at least laughing at gender stereotypes or patriarchal conventions. Laughter can rupture the illusion of patriarchal authority and imperviousness. Most importantly, using humor can make a feminist message appealing to a wide audience. Feminist humor is aggressive, disturbing, disruptive. As Regina Barreca explains in her introduction to *Last Laughs: Perspectives on Women and Comedy*, " 'women's comedy is marginal, liminal, concerned with and defined by its very exclusion from convention, by its aspects of refusal and its alliance with subversive female symbols. The difference of women is viewed as risk to culture. So it should be' " (15). Humor deserves to be singled out for its liberatory power, as Rich argues in the epigraph to this article. As Walker explains, for an oppressed group, humor can be used as a way of bonding: "women have used humor to talk to each other about their human condition, to survive and frequently to protest their condition" (x). Her identification of the humorist as someone who is "at odds with the publicly espoused values of the culture" (9) allows her to explain the appeal of humor for American women in particular, for they are "members of a subordinate group in a culture that prides itself on equality" (x). Because humor is aggressive, "the humorist adopts at least a *stance* of superiority...a position of privileged insight" (25). Perhaps the most useful contribution that Walker makes is her distinction between feminist and female humor. She cites Gloria Kaufman distinguishing between feminist hopefulness and female hopelessness, a definition that allows the viewer to appreciate the feminism of humorous music videos, which are marked by their sense of hopefulness. In part because of their optimism, these feminist music videos suggest that humor can be a particularly effective tool in the arena of popular culture.

A popular form of the music video genre, humorous music videos draw attention to the use of sex as a promotional device and to the commercial aspects of the star system of American corporate rock and roll. Video performances by artists like Pat Benatar, Julie Brown, Cyndi Lauper, Tina Turner, Annie Lennox, David Bowie, Billy Idol and Weird Al Yankovic demonstrate the ways in which performers and directors can use humor in a self-reflexive fashion to expose the commercialism of music videos and to address issues of gender formation. These videos suggest that the genre is more complex than some of its critics acknowledge. The participation of performers in self-deprecating parodies suggest that humor is a persuasive way of criticizing a popular genre from the inside. While not all humorous music videos are feminist, humorous videos performed by women show that a feminist message can be conveyed in a popular genre through an inviting sense of humor. Feminist critics need to examine humor as a strategy because of the possibilities it offers for criticizing patriarchal institutions: music videos present a promising case study of humor and gender.

Julie Brown's *The Homecoming Queen's Got a Gun* and Tina Turner's *Typical Male*[1] deserve particular attention as humorous feminist appropriations of the video form. Despite formal differences in their visual and musical styles, both videos promulgate a feminist message through humor. Both artists use self-reflexiveness, pastiche, exaggeration and parody to expose the ridiculousness of stereotypical gender roles and the serious effect such rigid stereotypes have on relationships between men and women. *The Homecoming Queen's Got a Gun* is, as its title suggests, more directly and simply humorous than many other feminist videos. The incompatibility of a sweetly attired and excessively feminist homecoming queen and the American symbol of machismo, a gun, reveals the blatant nature of Brown's attack upon sex stereotyping. Turner's tongue-in-cheek title similarly suggests that gender roles will be the object of her humor, which is played out within the conventions of postmodern sensibility. Both videos use the self-reflexive humorous frame characteristic of postmodern art forms to make their feminist points. In music videos, self-reflexiveness appears in the numerous references to the filmic nature of a video, such as the television camera filming the homecoming queen's rampage, or the television set in Turner's video. To understand the range and complexity of their humor requires some appreciation of postmodern art, for postmodern qualities lend themselves to humor production. Postmodern art is defined variously, but its core qualities include: fragmentation; a breakdown between the fine arts, the avant garde and the mass media; an emphasis on pastiche; repeated self-reflexiveness. In general, postmodern art stresses paradox, contradiction and self-awareness. By calling aesthetic and cultural assumptions into question, these elements lend themselves to the deconstruction of gender through humor. As the music video viewer watches these critiques, she begins to realize the myriad absurdities forced on us by gender roles. The ludicrousness of the role of the homecoming (or prom) queen is illuminated by the violence of this particular young woman, but also by the chagrined glances of the runner-up, clearly distraught at losing out to Debbie and by the panoply of pseudo-regal activities that surround the "queen." *The Homecoming Queen's Got a Gun* and *Typical Male* contain deconstructive and subversive possibilities created by their use of videos as a postmodern art form, possibilities emphasized by the controversy surrounding the airing of Brown's video on Music Television.

The response of MTV to Julie Brown's music video attests to the power of feminist humor; the station initially refused to air *The Homecoming Queen's Got a Gun*. After the refusal was assailed in *The New York Times*, however, the song received brief but heavy airplay and it was later released in a anthology of comedy music videos. Her song and video parody conventional gender roles, allowing the viewer to see the humor in sex-stereotyped high school role models for young women. This depiction of high school stereotypes such as the beautiful, blond, smiling homecoming queen, the peppy cheerleaders, the burly football player, the geek, and the school mascot reveals how ludicrous the heavy-handed and sexist customs of high schools are. Like many other feminist music videos, this video follows the detailed story lyrics closely. The narrator, a narcissistic Valley girl, describes the shooting spree of her best friend, Debbie, the Homecoming Queen. The first verse depicts the narrator's elation at her friend's promenade as Homecoming Queen and includes details about her dress and the sentimental song the band is playing. The narrator breathlessly compares the scene to the Cinderella ride in Disneyland, a comparison that reveals how passive and unrealistic this cultural myth is and how it is embedded in high school ritual. The pleasant scene is punctured by someone screaming "the Homecoming Queen's got a gun" and immediately thereafter, Debbie begins shooting. Perplexed by Debbie's actions, the narrator asks "How could you do what you just did? Are you having a really bad period?" The police arrive and Debbie is killed by a shot in the ear. Before she dies, however, she manages to gasp out (in response to the narrator's insistent questions) "I did it for Johnny," an enigmatic response that the narrator identifies with the movie *Citizen Kane*. Over Debbie's body, the narrator meets the eyes of a handsome police officer and walks off into the crowd with him. The humor of the song is stressed by Julie Brown's playing both the role of Homecoming Queen and her Valley Girl friend.*

Even though *The Homecoming Queen's Got a Gun* employs a traditional narrative plot structure, Julie Brown uses a postmodern sensibility to create the humor. Playing the role of both the Homecoming Queen and her girlfriend emphasizes the artificiality of each as a role, as a representation. In this sense, Julie Brown stresses the performance qualities of femininity, just as contemporary artist Cindy Sherman does with her photographs of herself in various feminine guises. Throughout the video, humor is generated

*A Valley Girl is identified by a distinctive slang, narcissism and materialism. The name comes from the San Fernando Valley, an upper class part of Southern California.

through a postmodern sensibility that relies on pastiche, self-reflexiveness and breakdown of distinctions between genres and forms. For example, the mass murder committed by the Homecoming Queen is depicted in terms of cartoon graphics. No actual or believable violence occurs, even when Debbie herself dies. She leaps off her float with a perfect backward somersault, in an amusing and performative demise. Her death reminds the viewers that they are watching a video, a film. This type of representation allows the viewer to laugh rather than cry as Debbie kills off her schoolmates, who represent caricatures of sex stereotypes. Secondly, humor is generated by the contrast between the narrator's attitude and the activities that she is describing. Debbie's friend is more concerned about her reputation and her friend's dress than she is about the carnage. Her blasé attitude is reflected in the actions of other characters—for example, the police officer who sells t-shirts as Debbie continues to shoot more victims or the television reporter who seems more concerned with combing her hair than with the violence around her. The commodification of the event through the sale of t-shirts reminds viewers that they themselves are watching a promotional video. Needless to say, the television reporter, the camera and the microphone that Debbie appropriates evoke the self-reflexiveness characteristic of postmodernism. Such incidents continually remind viewers of the artificiality of representation. Throughout the video, humor is produced by the basic role reversal of not only a woman, but a prim and proper homecoming queen, a cultural icon, behaving murderously. The role reversal is stressed by the huge gun that Debbie totes, presumably hidden in the bosom of her dress. The camp outfits, mixtures of nineteen-sixties scarves, bright colors, mini-skirts, and the diverse mixture of fashion styles throughout the video enhance the sense of bizarre and amusing inappropriateness. Pastiche dominates, again reminding us that femininity is a construction. For example, Debbie's forced beauty queen smile contrasts with her murderous actions, and she puts her compact to an unusual use when she peers into it to shoot the math teacher in a balcony behind her.

The source of the humor, then, lies in the representation of femininity. The humor in the video stems from what Walker identifies as "the myriad absurdities that women have been forced to endure in this culture" (xii), in particular, having to act and look like Cinderella, being brainwashed into a search for romantic love, being a cheerleader, and so on. While stereotypical representations of femininity are exposed through humor, Brown also legitimates feminism. Both Brown and the viewer share a position of superiority in relation to the characters in the video. As Nancy Walker explains, "Because the humorist adopts at least the *stance* of superiority by claiming the freedom to point out incongruity or absurdity in a world that others are accustomed to accepting on its own terms, he or she works from a position of privileged insight" (25). Watching this video, the viewer is forced into a feminist gaze. Whatever their particular ideologies, when viewers watch this video and laugh, they create a feminist community, if only temporarily, if only unconsciously. As this community is created, so is a feminist critique.

Although Brown's song is humorous, her message is serious—sexist roles breed violence and rage in women. Through the striking contrast between the prim and proper Homecoming Queen's appearance and her murderous rage, Brown exposes the hollowness of this feminine success story. Her friend the narrator is delighted with Debbie's new role, but the Homecoming Queen has something else on her mind. The narrator's description of Debbie looking like Cinderella, particularly Walt Disney's Cinderella, suggests the superficiality of this role for women. Although Debbie looks like Cinderella, in Brown's feminist revision of this fairy tale, Cinderella is the aggressor rather than the victim she is in the original fairy tale. *The Homecoming Queen's Got a Gun* resembles feminist fairy tales written by contemporary women authors like Tanith Lee, Robin Morgan, Angela Carter. Like other feminist revisions of fairy tales, Brown's parodic song serves as a warning of the suppressed anger of women trapped in traditional roles. Her Homecoming Queen functions as Sandra Gilbert and Susan Gubar suggest the Queen does in *Snow White*, as a symbol of how "conventional female arts *kill*" (40). Like the Queen in *Snow White*, Brown's Homecoming Queen is "mad," but her madness illuminates the oppressive nature of the only power available to women in a patriarchal culture.

The absence of a clear motive suggests that the role of Homecoming Queen itself produces Debbie's rage. Brown stresses the pervasiveness of shallow roles for women through the Valley Girl narrator and other female voices. The anonymous narrator inadvertently reinforces the reasons for Debbie's shooting spree as she describes the scene. The narrator admires Debbie's appearance, without appreciating its artificiality. A chorus of female voices reiterates the importance of appearance with "Stop it Debbie you're making a mess/ Powder burns all over your dress." When Debbie gasps out her last words, the narrator tries to discover who Johnny is, dismissing the one guy she knows because he was a "geek." Her blindness to any other interpretation of Debbie's actions is demonstrated in the final shot, when the narrator walks off into the crowd with the cop she met over Debbie's body. Her action stresses the folly of romantic love, exemplified by a romance that takes primacy over her best friend's death.

Encoded as popular culture, this video is consumed as part of a package—that is, the record packaging can be read alongside the video. Brown connects the two through parody. Her feminist message is emphasized by the album jacket that contains a mock newspaper account of the Homecoming Queen's shooting spree. The quite plausibly sensational headline on the album cover—"Sugar and Spice and Everyone's Dead"—stresses the importance of gender stereotypes in Debbie's shooting spree. Significantly, Debbie's first targets are the cheerleaders, girls who—like her—typify the secondary status of girls. On the album cover, Brown stresses the importance of sexism to Debbie's outbreak. In a fake "article" about the shootings on the album cover, the football coach complains, " 'I've always said a woman's got no place in the football field. Was I right or wasn't I?' " In a year when young women are beginning to find a place on the football field as players, the coach's comments emphasize the hostility that young women face if they challenge the construction of the feminine as passive. Debbie's violent response to her sex-stereotypical role belies the purported passivity and weakness of girls.

The heart that surrounds the narrator and her new boyfriend at the video's end evokes *Love American Style*, which concluded each episode in the same fashion. This and many other allusions to other representations of femininity in popular culture suggest that popular culture provides its own referent system and that perhaps the best response to sexism in a genre occurs *within* that genre. For example, Brown raises the spectre of another popular depiction of apparent resistance to traditional feminine roles— Stephen King's *Carrie*. In contrast to King's Carrie, however, Brown's murderous Homecoming Queen packs a gun, instead of the mysterious witchlike powers Carrie depends on. More importantly, Debbie is a "success" in traditional terms; she does not strike out at her classmates as revenge for humiliation or ridicule. Brown's Homecoming Queen singles out representatives of the culture who are part of the structure that oppresses women—the cheerleaders, the football player, the math teacher. By eliminating them, she exposes the sexism they typify.

In *The Homecoming Queen's Got a Gun*, Brown not only criticizes feminine roles, but shows how little they have changed over time. The pastiche of music and costuming emphasizes this sense of history. The music begins with the sounds of nineteen-fifties rock 'n' roll, moves through the early sixties and songs like "Johnny Angel" and "The Leader of the Pack" to the hard rock guitar solos of the nineteen-seventies. In Brown's updated version of rock 'n' roll rebellion, however, it is the woman who is the rebel/ victim, rather than a young man. Debbie's last words about "Johnny" draw attention to those well-known songs and highlight Brown's role-reversal. Ironically, Brown uses the same narrative and musical style to criticize the romantic and sexist roles promulgated by the popular songs of the early nineteen-sixties. The costumes also strengthen this parallel; Debbie's dress, the narrator's and those of the other actors combine elements of both the nineteen-sixties and eighties.

Brown suggests, however, that popular culture can also provide channels for resistance and that nineteen-eighties retro presents subversive possibilities. (That the music in the nineteen-eighties that allows this attack on the construction of femininity is stressed by the "article" on the album cover, in which Debbie's mother confesses "Lately [my daughter] had been listening to a lot of that new-wave type music. . .") Like Aimee Mann, another feminist performer, Julie Brown depicts new wave music as liberating for women. Also like Aimee Mann, Julie Brown drew on personal experience to create her feminist heroine, for she too "was a homecoming princess and rode a float similar to Debbie's in the video." (Kort, 60) Where Brown differs from Mann and other feminist performers is in her clever use of humor to make a didactic message appealing and engaging.

Through her humor, Brown's ironic presentation of femininity reaches a far wider audience than a straightforward critique could. And the entertaining presentation of the song may keep the viewer's attention longer as well. For the space of a few minutes at least, the viewer is invited to laugh at a cherished icon, a representation of American femininity at its finest. It may not be Hélène Cixous' "The Laugh of the Medusa," but it is a laughter that challenges conventional notions of gendered behavior and foregrounds the artificiality of this representation of American womanhood.

While Tina Turner is not known primarily as a comedian (unlike Brown, who has her own comedy show on MTV), she has made a spectacular career comeback by drawing on the same tropes used by Brown. Her tremendous popularity attests to the success of an assertive and positive feminist depiction of female humor as a commercial strategy. This video is the second feminist video for Turner; the first was the even more popular "What's Love Got To Do With It?" a clever and straightforward assertion of female sexual desire. While that video certainly has humorous moments, it is in "Typical Male" that Turner is most explicitly and directly feminist, under the aegis of humor. While Brown focuses on gender stereotypes but only briefly alludes to their effect on male-female relationship, Turner emphasizes this aspect. Her video relies less on lyrics and more on image to produce the humor, but the dynamic is the same as that in Brown's video: through self-reflexiveness, pastiche, and stylized parodic violence, Turner criticizes gender stereotypes. While Brown focuses on femininity, however, Turner directs her attention to masculinity and to racism.

The patriarchal is represented in this video through the figure of a spectacled white male. On a superficial level, the video's plot focusses on Turner's attempt to captivate this man. He represents more than a character, however, as the symbols that surround him demonstrate. The video opens with Turner pirouetting around a gigantic male shoe and leg, pantomiming her desire and inability to attract and retain the attention of a typical male. Images suggest that gender roles and sexuality are games—puzzles, toys, a chess game, a plastic bat, are all employed to evoke the idea of pleasure and competition, in its most extreme and ridiculous aspects. She tries again and again to captivate this spectacled male and finally at the end of the video, she succeeds. She walks away hand-in-hand with the man, as the camera pans the giant shoe and leg, finally toppled. The end of the video answer questions the viewer might have about the point of Turner's desire to captivate the male character. It is a conversion rather than a scopophilic relationship because Turner succeeds in breaking the viewer/viewed relationship when she grasps the man's hand and leads him out of the video. At the end the white male consents to be lead by her; he leaves behind the symbols of patriarchy. Significantly, the edifice of a male shoe is depicted as spats, an old-fashioned and out-of-date piece of men's wear. Its demise is timely and promising. The camera angle throughout stresses the end of framing and fragmentation of woman. At no point in the video is any one part of Turner's body highlighted in the stereotypical fragmentation of a woman's body into fetishized parts. Again, this emphasis on the wholeness of Turner's affect contrasts strikingly with the stress laid in sexist music videos (like David Lee Roth's *California Girls*) that focus on female breasts, a conventional objectification of a female part. Furthermore, Turner's articulation of desire occurs in the context of a setting that continually calls patriarchal articulations into question through exaggeration and reference to toys.

Unlike Brown's video, which focuses on an unenlightened narrator, Turner plays herself and exudes an air of confidence and delight that emphasizes that she is conscious of and directing the humor in the video. She continually plays for the camera with a variety of smiles and knowing grins. She laughs in delight at her performance and at the humor of her attempts to distract the man and at the ridiculous nature of his masculine obsessions—baseball, calculations, chess. Through her laughter, she undermines and challenges the authority of patriarchy. Wrapping herself around the giant male shoe (itself a humorous rendering of patriarchy) does not evoke debasement but rather her sense of fun or challenge—with her facial expressions, she lets the viewer know from the beginning that she is determined to topple that symbol of male authority and the viewer has no doubt of her eventual success.

Because she is the singer, and because she manipulates the camera so skillfully, Turner defies the conventional depiction of woman as object for a male gaze; it is her own gaze that determines the action of the video, her own sense of humor that she gratifies. This shift in emphasis is made clear when Turner gyrates, not directly into the camera, but to her own reflection in a series of mirrors, laughing and smiling all the while. In her video, Turner asserts the right of the woman to develop and mature through the identification of her sexual selves in the mirror. Like the other videos, this one also explicitly evokes the idea of self-reflexiveness. Turner dances for her own pleasure as well as that of the viewer and the male character. Her subversion of the music video form draws on the assumption of her character that women feel and have a right to assert sexual desire. Again humor is used to make this message explicit but non-threatening; the camera plays with phallic symbols like the baseball bat which Turner handles lightly; there can be no doubt that the violence is stylized because of the bat's ludicrous size and bright red color; it is a toy, as is the phone and the other items with which she bombards the man. Most appealing perhaps is the implicit idea of equality in sexual relationship. The scales seen early on in the video evoke this idea, but the final image of the toppled male shoe and leg combined with Turner's walking off hand-in-hand with the white male character suggests a healthy female sexuality concerned with equality rather than with replacing male dominance with female dominance. Turner does not want to erect her shoe and leg, but asks for and implies sexual and racial parity. In this sense, the casting of a blond white male is particularly significant. This casting choice forces the viewer to look at the video's larger symbolic frame which criticizes racism and to appreciate the cooperative nature of Turner's actions. She does not attempt to reverse the relation of power, but to replace it with a relationship that signals equality.

Significantly, she does so in a video marked by a prevailing tone of humor. The self-reflexive nature of music videos appears in the frame of a television screen that Turner enters in order to grasp a plastic bat from a ballplayer. She then uses the bat in a stylized act of violence to attack the "typical male." Here Turner criticizes a whole system that separates men and women—the institution and televising of sports. The mirrors that she dances in front of stress the film aspects of video, for they stress reflected images. These images emphasize the breakdown of women into separate and alienated selves. At the same time, the mirrors stress fragmentation, for there are six of them in a row, creating a number of images, first of Turner, but then also of the saxophone, a phallic image that echoes the spats and like them, represents conventional masculinity. Fragmentation also occurs in the confusing array of images that dominate each frame— there are a plethora of graphics, actors, and large over size props, like the gigantic red telephone receiver on which both Turner and the male actor sit on. The postmodern world is dominated by signs of everyday life exaggerated as in the work of Claus Oldenberg. The emphasis in the video reminds its viewers that even everyday objects are subject to interpretation and that these objects can become alienating, particularly if they alienate women from men. The evocation of high art and cartoon-like graphics creates a pastiche similar to the effect produced in "The Homecoming Queen's Got a Gun," but in a more overtly stylistically humorous context.

If, as many critics have argued, humor is socially constructed, feminist critics must more carefully examine the site of its construction, and be ready to look for humor in unexpected places. Music videos display the sense of doubleness, of play and diversity recognized in popular culture by critics like Iain Chambers, who suggests that critics of popular culture need to look for resistance to as well as domination by hegemonic forces (123). The emphasis in feminist criticism on the ways in which popular culture abuses and degrades women has demonstrated the harm in the dominant representation of women in popular culture, especially in the world of rock and roll; however, through humor this world also offers moments of resistance to such abusive stereotyping. The "image" of woman is more complex than the picture of woman as sex object so familiar to us. To reduce popular culture to 'its worst stereotype and to dismiss it as a site of feminist inquiry is to deny any possibility of a feminist presence or voice; more importantly, to neglect popular culture is to ignore the moments of resistance and instances of feminist triumph such as these humorous music videos in an arena that reaches a far wider audience than the most popular feminist criticism.

Note

[1]Please see "Sex as a Weapon: Feminist Rock Music Videos" in *National Women's Studies Association Journal* 2 (1990): 1-15 for my discussion of this video in context with other feminist music videos.

Works Cited

Barreca, Regina, ed., *Last Laughs: Perspectives on Women and Comedy*. New York: Gordon and Breach, 1988.

Carter, Angela, *Fireworks: Nine Profane Pieces*. New York: Penguin, 1987.

Chambers, Iain, *Popular Culture: The Metropolitan Experience*. New York: Methuen, 1986.

Gilbert, Sandra M. and Susan Gubar, *The Madwoman in the Attic*. New Haven: Yale University Press, 1979.

Cixons, Hèlerìe, "The Laugh of the Medusa." *New French Feminisms*, ed. Elaine Marks and Isabelle de Courtlvron, New York: Schocken, 1981, pp. 245-264.

Kort, Michelle, "Homecoming Queen Number One with a Bullet." *Ms.* 13 (October 1985), p. 60.

Lee, Tanith, *Red as Blood or Tales from the Sisters Grimmer*. New York: DAW, 1983.

Morgan, Robin, *Dry Your Smile*. New York: Doubleday, 1987.

Rich, B. Ruby, "Review Essay: Feminism and Sexuality in the 1980s." *Feminist Studies* 12 (1986).

Walker, Nancy, *A Very Serious Thing: Women's Humor and American Culture*. Minneapolis: University of Minnesota Press, 1988.

That's Why the Lady Is a Drunk:
Women, Alcoholism, and Popular Culture

Melinda Kanner

Introduction

Clinical experience shows that alcoholism in women is much less frequent than it is in men...what alcoholic women seem to lack in quantity, they certainly do make up in quality. By clinical observation, alcoholic women are much more abnormal than alcoholic men; in common parlance, when an alcoholic woman goes on a tear, 'it is terrific.' The reason for the difference probably lies in the fact that even in this sophisticated age women are still subject to more repressions then men...When, therefore, the pressure becomes so great as to make it beyond control...it may break out in the form of alcoholism. (Karpman vii)

Although American popular culture has long and widely dealt with alcoholism, relatively few films specifically treat women and alcoholism as their central problem. Fewer than twenty feature films present alcoholic women explicitly, largely due to the long-standing and persistent stigma associated with women and drinking. In the past fifteen years, television has introduced a proliferation and wider dissemination of images of alcoholic women. Variously depicted as morally decayed, sexually promiscuous, tragically inadequate mothers and wives, or, more recently, as women seemingly in control of their own lives and their own recovery, these representations of alcoholic women have in common several critical elements.

In terms of explanation of origins, consequent destruction and degradation, and motivation for recovery, popular culture representations situate alcoholic women first and foremost in the context of their relationships with men: as fathers, lovers, and husbands. In addition to this contextual, sex role stereotyping, women's alcoholism itself is not an expression of self or autonomy. Women who are alcoholic in television and movies become alcoholic because of men, through an implication of genetic or social inheritance, through failed relationships, and through their unbridled and misused sexuality. Alcoholic women are social obscenities, more humiliated, somehow harder to watch than alcoholic men. Women who are alcoholic devastate themselves and their families. Men who are alcoholic are typically represented as amusing, engaging, as raconteurs, as tragically flawed artists, and as autonomous agents guided by free will. Indeed the "light drunk" as perfected by actors such as Gig Young and Tony Randall is a man's, not a woman's role. Men drink because they want to drink; women drink because they have no choice. Since 1935, across media of cinema, television, theater, and advertising, representations of alcoholic women have been thus constructed. Both as reflections of their social contexts and as mechanisms of socialization these media representations have diverged from the social discourse over these decades. Where medical and popular notions of alcoholism have changed, popular culture representations of alcoholic women have remained largely uniform. Irrespective of the socioeconomic, professional, and temporal situation of the alcoholic woman in an individual text, the alcoholic woman's identity depends upon her relationship to a man. Although the changing nature of explanatory models of alcoholism is often visible throughout the history of these filmic representations, the static nature of the alcoholic woman persists even within this changing framework.

This paper investigates these popular culture images of alcoholic women as they have remained constant over time even as social and medical conceptions of alcoholism have changed. Part one surveys a number of filmic representations of women and alcoholism from the 1930s through the 1970s. In establishing this historical context, popular culture representations of alcoholic women are explored in the light of three central issues: first, as the alcoholic woman exists in a broader cinematic and sociocultural context; second, as the text constructs the alcoholic woman; and, finally, as the alcoholic woman compares to the alcoholic men who surround her in the text. Part two examines several recent texts, including *Clean and Sober, Ironweed, Bar Fly,* and *The Morning After.* These contemporary examples will be shown as strikingly similar to films over the past fifty five years in their constructions of the female alcoholic and their contrasts of alcoholic men and women. Finally, the television dramatic series *Cagney and Lacey* will be reviewed as a modestly but significantly divergent case.

The Movement Through Time: An Historical Survey
There is no counterbalancing gift to redeem the female alcoholic and, repeatedly, female alcoholism is shown to embody a cluster of entirely negative attributes. Perhaps the reason for this is that the fatal flaw of the woman alcoholic is that she is a woman, and can therefore never transcend herself. (Harwin and Otto 40)

Dangerous (1935) won Bette Davis an Academy Award for her interpretations of a successful star, Joyce Heath, who "hits the skids," bottoms outs, and finally is rescued and rehabilitated by Franchot Tone. This earliest of the films which have as their primary themes an alcoholic woman outlines the contours which shape images of alcoholic women for more than fifty years to come. Early films about alcoholic women provided three possible roles: the celebrated and successful woman who suffers a fall (*Dangerous* [1935], *I'll Cry Tomorrow* [1955], *Too Much, Too Soon* [1958]); the house-bound, relationship-fettered woman who drinks because her man drinks (*Smash-Up* [1947], *Days of Wine and Roses* [1962]); and the sluttish bad girl who stays bad (*Key Largo* [1948]),*Farewell, My Lovely* [1975]). In *Dangerous*, Tone tells Davis that she tells the truth "like a gentleman." Davis, as the jinxed Heath, replies that, "Perhaps I'm not lady enough to lie" (Haskell 244), thus suggesting one of the central structures of these films: Women who drink too much are not ladies. Ladies employ female strategies for coping, which involve lying, deceit, and sexual manipulation. Women who drink enter a man's game, into which they descend because of men and from which they are delivered by men.

Hollywood films from the thirties and forties marked a movement from lack of faith in American way to restoration of faith which was, in part, grounded in an ability to confront problems. Whereas the films of the thirties treated social problems in terms of severe social crises, the films of the forties interpreted social problems, including alcoholism, as "pockets of distress in an otherwise sound society" (Roffman and Purdy 228). In the post-War climate of thousands of returning men, women in the 1940s cinema were either faithful partners to men or their betrayers. They were good wives or tough dames. In this context, the popular culture alcoholic woman of the 1940s is constructed.

Key Largo (1948), is director John Huston's story of a returning soldier, Maj. Frank McCloud (Humphrey Bogart) who triumphs over gangster Johnny Rocco (Edward G. Robinson), befriends the wheelchair-bound father of his dead war buddy, and wins the heart of widowed Nora Temple (Lauren Bacall). Held captive by Rocco on the island, this group illustrates the major archetypes of 1940s film women. Through its internal contrasts of the faithful and decent Nora and Gaye Dawn (Claire Trevor), a faded singing star, the nature of one type of alcoholic cinema woman becomes clear. Dawn, as mobster Rocco's mistress is an ex-singer with a once bright career, whose most ambitious goal now is her next drink. She is a dame, a questionable woman who has lived a questionable life, and now denigrated by even the amoral Robinson. In what Molly Haskell has called "one of the most degrading scenes in cinema," Rocco makes Gaye sing to the captive-captor group (Haskell 1974:206). He will grant her a drink when she shows the assembled company some of her old stuff. She shakingly forces herself through the song and is told by Rocco, "It wasn't good enough." Maj. McCloud rescues her, and grabbing the bottle, presents it to her. Finally, as McCloud stages a daring rescue attempt, Gaye Dawn steals Rocco's gun and slips it into McCloud's hands, in a gesture which matches and recalls McCloud handing her a drink. This alcoholic woman is sluttish, the gangster's moll whose chief talent was entertaining and who crushed even that with whiskey. Ultimately she betrays Rocco, and in the last ditch heroics of the unstable alcoholic, she redeems herself by setting in motion McCloud's successful escape. Perhaps this resolution, in part, anticipates Dawn's recovery: As McCloud handed her the bottle which was the link to Rocco's subjugation of her, so Dawn engineers Rocco's undoing with his other weapon—his gun, thus suggesting her liberation. Although she takes the initial risk of transferring the gun, McCloud, a man, must be seen as the active agent of her potential freedom.

Alcoholism was not easily brought to the screen, especially in the post-prohibition era. The production of Billy Wilder's *The Lost Weekend* (1945) confronted massive obstacles which mitigated against bringing alcoholism into an entertainment medium. The forces came from backers who believed that a film based on Charles Jackson's best-selling novel would be unmarketable because of its depressing subject, and from powerful and vocal alcohol lobbies who believed the film would be injurious to the reputation of the alcohol industry (Roffman and Purdy 1981:257-259, Zolotow 1987:125-133). Prevailing against such odds, the film was made, won several Academy Awards, and established a precedent for the production of films about alcoholics.

A brief examination of this film and the "woman's version" (Roffman and Purdy 1981:259) which closely follows it illustrates the gender dependence of filmic constructions of alcoholism. *The Lost Weekend* stars Ray Milland as Don Birnam, a terminally blocked writer who finds himself crashed against the waves of a weekend alcoholic binge. In *The Lost Weekend*, Birnam suffers from an existential dilemma which is articulated in his profession. He cannot write and, therefore, his life amounts to nothing: "I've never done anything...Zero, zero, zero." As he desperately tries to find money to continue his binge, he tries to hock his typewriter only to discover the pawnshops closed on Sunday. On the verge of suicide, Birnam is confronted with a reason to recover and live: a bartender returns his beloved typewriter that he has left behind in some forgotten bar. Expressed through the person and words of his ever-faithful fiancee, Helen, (Jane Wyman), the resolution is clear. "Someone, somewhere, sent this typewriter back. Why? Because you're to stay alive! Because he wants you to write."

Smash-Up: The Story of a Woman (1947), starring Susan Hayward, recounts the story Angie Conway, a nightclub singer who foresakes her career to become a devoted wife and mother. As her husband's singing career flourishes her frustration and boredom grow, dulled only by her continuing and accelerating consumption of alcohol. Ultimately Conway recognizes her bottoming out when she accidentally burns down their house and nearly kills their baby. As she becomes reconciled to her life as a housewife and mother she becomes able to discard her independence upon alcohol.

In contrast to Don Birnam, Angie Conway suffers from a different, graver, socially devastating affliction: She has rejected her appropriate role as wife and mother. Although she drank throughout her successful singing career, she clearly became alcoholic in response to her domestic dissatisfaction. Her acknowledgment and recovery result only from her acceptance of her life. Where the return of Don's typewriter signals his recovery, the near loss of her baby triggers Angie's road to sobriety.

In the 1950s, films such as *Something to Live For* (1952), *I'll Cry Tomorrow* (1955), and *Too Much, Too Soon* (1958) provide clear examples of both the filmic construction of the female alcoholic and the variance between conceptions of alcoholism and the representations of alcoholic women. Medical and popular explanations of alcoholism in the 1950s began to shift from a moralist to a medical interpretation. Psychological and medical explanatory models gradually replaced moral discourse. Alcoholism became recognized widely as a treatable problem rather than a corruption of spiritual convention. Although not fully embraced for more than a decade, the notion of the connection between personality and alcoholism began to dawn in cinema consciousness. Concentration on early childhood experience, complex sociocultural variables, and personality are woven into the fabric of the cinema alcoholic woman.

In *Something to Live For,* Joan Fontaine suffers from a dual torture of alcoholism and love for a married man, played by Ray Milland in a reversal of his earlier role. Perhaps this casting depends upon the continuity of the audience's understanding that Milland (earlier as Don Birnam) is no longer the practicing alcoholic he was in *The Lost Weekend.* Her love for Milland is her reason for living and her reason for drinking. Similarly, Dorothy Malone's portrayal of Diana Barrymore's alcoholic decline and Susan Hayward as Lillian Roth reveal components central to the construction of the alcoholic film woman. Their drinking commences because of men (lovers and fathers), revolves around men, and their recovery is both inspired by and dependent upon men. In the cases of *I'll Cry Tomorrow* and *Too Much, Too Soon,* extraordinary, celebrated, successful women whose lives otherwise might be enviable provide illustrations of what it means to be an alcoholic woman. In each of these, alcoholic male characters supply contrasts which demonstrate the gender-dependent cinema construction of alcoholic women.

Too Much, Too Soon presents the case of the beautiful, talented, rich, famous, and drunk Diana Barrymore. Her father, John Barrymore (Errol Flynn), also alcoholic and advantaged, provides her model for alcoholism. Malone as Diana is destructive, miserable, and irretrievable. Flynn as John is charming, entertaining, and detached. Diana's alcoholism is not only linked to her father and his alcoholism, but results in her destruction of her father and the man she intends to marry. When both men leave her, she enters a period of sexual and emotional promiscuity. Her drinking has explicit and immediate consequences for her sexuality.

I'll Cry Tomorrow, based on Lillian Roth's autobiography, shows another successful woman with adoring fans and a dismal family and romantic life. Susan Hayward as Lillian Roth is a singer with a disrupted childhood. Where Diana Barrymore had a weak, absent, self-absorbed father, Lillian Roth is burdened with a totally absent father and domineering mother. Rather than destroy the men around her, she is totally shaped by her relationships with men. Her drinking career begins in desperation over the sudden death of her fiancee and continues throughout a succession of dysfunctional and sexually promiscuous relationships with alcoholic men until she is rescued by Alcoholics Anonymous, embodied in the person of Burt McGuire (Eddie Albert).

I'll Cry Tomorrow presents itself as the story of the triumph of a woman over alcoholism, a positive female image. Indeed, Susan Hayward's performance is compelling and the closing shot of the film shows the sober Lillian walking to the stage of the television program *This Is Your Life* to share her experience, strength, and hope. However, the ways in which the text constructs Roth's alcoholism weld strong bars of a gender prison. Not only is the female protagonist an alcoholic, the women in her life are sources of distress rather than support, thus suggesting that Roth's drinking is the result of her relationship with men and, in insidious ways, facilitated by women.

Katie, her controlling and domineering mother, dictates Roth's every move and guides her professional career from her childhood through the beginning of her drinking career. Constantly in search of her mother's approval, constantly under mother's control, Lillian's earnest pursuit of alcohol to her represents an escape from these maternal clutches. After the death of David, the man she intends to marry, Lillian is despondent. A private nurse, Helen, is engaged to attend her. A resolution to her insomnia is literally at hand. Helen pours Lillian a drink of water to steady her; then, thinking better, she pours a stiff drink. In an extreme close-up, Helen profers this first drink. Lillian begins to binge, dating a soldier whom she had earlier rejected, and finding herself married with no memory of the event. One drunken relationship follows another; physical, emotional, and sexual abuse follow after drinking. In every relationship she drinks because she is sucked into the alcoholic vortex of the alcoholic man. Even her attempt to live dry is thwarted by the sadistic Tony (Richard Conte). Later, as she begins her downward spiral toward bottoming out, she enters a bar. A waitress (who, not coincidentally bears a striking resemblance to Helen) sympathizes with the shakes she observes in Lillian, and in a camera shot which matches her first drink, she hands Lillian a drink. After her unsuccessful suicide attempt, she realizes that she wants to live and live sober, and finds her way to an AA meeting. There she meets Burt, who becomes her sponsor (in violation of the AA practice of same sex sponsorship). On one level, her recovery appears to be the result of her own courage and her AA program. A careful examination of the text, however, reveals that Burt is responsible for her self-discovery and identity. Through Burt she literally finds her voice, first through piano and voice duets at meetings and later through her declaration of love for him.

The representations of alcoholic women in the 1950s, then, reveal a greater crystalization of the alcoholic woman. For her, even professional success is never enough to fill her emptiness and satisfy her longings. She is incomplete without a relationship with a man. Her drinking is, in part, the search for an identity she never had, and her eventual success in bonding with a man signals both her recovery and the realization of her identity.

Alcoholic women in the films of the 1960s move to the logical extension of the characters who have come before them. Where *Dangerous, Too Much, Too Soon,* and *I'll Cry Tomorrow* have as their central stories women and their struggles with alcoholism, the films of the 1960s, with the exception of *The Days of Wine and Roses,* do not distinctively treat alcoholism as their central problem. Instead, their alcoholism is one defect among many in these women's catalogues of psychosexual distresses. These women are grotesques, harridans, villains in every sense, consonant with filmic representations of women as sexually-defined, neurotic, fragmented women during this period.

But even these, the great women's parts of the decade, what are they for the most part? Whores, quasi-whores, jilted mistresses, emotional cripples, drunks. Daffy ingenues, Lolitas, sex-starved spinsters, psychotics. Icebergs, zombies, and ballbreakers. That's what little girls of the sixties and seventies are made of. (Haskell 327-28)

Like *Too Much, Too Soon, The Days of Wine and Roses* illustrates the sexual stratification of alcoholism in film with the pairing of both male and female alcoholics in a single text. *The Days of Wine and Roses* is the story of Joe and Kristie Clay, a young urban couple marching up the ladder to archetypal 1960s success. Joe is an upwardly moving advertising executive whose success depends upon his ability to entertain clients; this entertainment increasingly becomes a matter of abusive drinking. Kristie, beautiful, beloved, wholesome, at first has no part of Joe's drinking. As their relationship becomes enmeshed in Joe's drinking, Kristie finally succumbs, abandoning her earlier choice to abstain from alcohol. She is pulled into her alcoholic world by the force of Joe's career demands, by his will, by his choice, by his dysfunction. Both bottom out after devastating themselves and their relationship. Joe, after a series of false starts, finds his recovery through Alcoholics Anonymous. In contrast, Kristie, for a short time following the birth of their child, attempts to give up drinking but slips back into her alcoholic haze, leaving Joe alone to care for their child. Joe's recovery is successful; the still-drunk Kristie is lost at the conclusion of the film.

Anne Bancroft's Mrs. Robinson in *The Graduate* (1967) is the lecherous and alcoholic older woman who seduces Benjamin (Dustin Hoffman) and emotionally savages her daughter. Her drinking and reckless sexuality are intertwined, both self-destructive and destructive to all those who populate her life. Likewise, Elizabeth Taylor's Martha in the 1966 *Who's Afraid of Virginia Woolf?* presents a sluttish, gruesome package of sterility and madness wrapped in unremitting alcoholism. Centered around the psychotic fantasy life and mutual torture George (Richard Burton) and Martha create for themselves, this film's two central characters again juxtapose male and female alcoholic behavior and render clear pictures of the gender-bound definition of female alcoholism. Once again, female alcoholism both results in and is identified by female maternal and sexual dysfunction. George's personal inadequacies involve his lack of professional ambition and success; his fatal error was committed when he married Martha. Martha's flaws would not be erased by abstinence; rather they are defined by sex and irremediable. She has failed to bear children and has, throughout their marriage, engaged in a series of casual sexual affairs. Where male alcoholics are individuals who, apart from their alcoholism, might be otherwise sympathetic characters, alcoholic women are uniformly hopeless, unsympathetic individuals whose alcoholism is yet another character defect among their emotional and sexual deficiencies and excesses.

The 1970s and 1980s witnessed an acute and growing public awareness of alcoholism. Jellineck's disease concept of alcoholism had penetrated the social medical consciousness for over a decade (Jellineck). Neither a moral failing nor a psychological disorder alcoholism was recognized as a treatable disease. Prominent persons pronounced their alcoholism and recovery stories publicly. Alcoholics Anonymous ceased to be viewed as a bastion of skid row bums and instead assumed its place in the American mind as the most widely recognized, if not the most effective recovery resort for members of all segments of society. Women were becoming not so much "invisible alcoholics" as alcoholics who also happen to be women (Sandmaier). Social and medical discourse on alcoholism moved forward. To a certain, limited extent, alcoholism was thus reflected in popular culture. The limitation is gender.

Few feature films of the 1970s treat women and alcoholism, and then alcoholism is secondary to the plot. These include *Red Sky at Morning* (1970), *Farewell, My Lovely* (1975), and *Opening Night* (1978). The alcoholic women of the seventies continue the tradition established thirty-five years earlier. Based on Raymond Chandler's novel, *Farewell, My Lovely* is a period piece set in Los Angeles in the 1940s. Jessie Florian (Sylvia Miles) is a former nightclub singer and dancer, who represents the slatternly, slovenly, broken-down tramp female drunk and the key to the betrayal of one of the central male characters. In *Opening Night* Gena Rowlands is a fading, drunk actress facing a midlife crisis precipitated by the death of an adoring fan. These representations, like those which came before

seem informed by some archetype in which the drunken woman is sluttishly dressed, or undressed to be more correct...usually having gone to fat and facially older than her years. The overtones usually indicate sexual degradation of a kind that comes about when a woman has lost her self-respect and knows that she has lost everyone else's. (Harwin and Otto 48)

Contemporary Cases: Retrospect and Prospect

The last decade has brought with it a proliferation of popular culture representations of alcoholism across the media. Day-time serials, most notably *All My Children, General Hospital, Santa Barbara,* and *Generations,* have, in some cases for nearly fifteen years, had alcoholism as an intermittent part of major story lines. Prime-time dramas, including *Dallas, Hill Street Blues,* L.A. Law, and *Cagney and Lacey* have focussed on alcoholism and alcoholic characters, both male and female. A number of made-for-TV movies dealing with women and alcoholism have had as their primary plots recovery rather than degradation, including *The Betty Ford Story, Sarah T., Life of the Party,* and *Between Friends.* Since 1987, four feature films have been produced which variously represent alcoholism and the female alcoholic: *The Morning After* (1987), *Barfly* (1987), *Ironweed* (1988), and *Clean and Sober* (1988). The last decade has not, however, ushered in a new popular culture representation of the alcoholic woman; these women are still configured in terms of their sexuality and their sexual and romantic relationships to men. Most of them cannot recover, and those who can and do recover do so because their love gives them a reason to stop drinking.

The Morning After, presents Alex Sternberger (Jane Fonda), an actress with a failed marriage, a decaying career, and meaningless sexual relationships in her future. Her present is composed of little more than extended periods of drunkenness and hangovers. As the film opens, Alex finds herself in bed with an unknown dead man and no memory of the events of the night before. The mystery is unraveled by Turner Kendall (Jeff Bridges) who provides Alex's identity by naming her and her behavior: "You're a drunk," Kendall tells her, who has "pissed half your life away." Kendall himself had been "a drunk for ten years" as a police officer, and has now straightened out his life. The denouement finds Alex in Kendall's hospital room as he recovers from near-fatal injuries sustained in rescuing her. At this point, as they negotiate their potential for a relationship, she is able to identify herself as a "lush" and announces that she has not had a drink in two days. With this offering she finds hope for recovery and life with Kendall.

Clean and Sober is the story of Daryl Poynter (Michael Keaton), a successful and affluent cocaine and alcohol cross-addict. Three women figure significantly in this story; each is unable to recover as Poynter finally does. In the film's opening shot the camera lingers in a close-up pan shot of a woman's naked body. She has died of an overdose from earlier activities with Poynter. Desperate to avoid the dead woman's family, police inquiry, and his company's realization that he has embezzled huge sums of money to support his habits, Poynter hides out in a treatment center. There he encounters, among others, Charlie (Kathy Baker) and Iris. Iris, it is revealed in a group session, has violated the program's rules and has continued to take drugs and drink. She is asked to leave the center. Charlie, on the other hand, becomes involved with Daryl. When the two complete their treatment periods, they continue their relationship; for Charlie this relationship is an escape from her abusive husband who continues to drink and use drugs. Daryl's recovery moves forward under the guidance of his sponsor. Charlie again becomes caught in her former life with her husband, and, as Daryl discovers after they make love, she is using cocaine. She has failed in her attempt to recover, whether through her twisted attachment to her husband or her own weakness, and she has betrayed Daryl and his recovery. Torn between her attachment to her husband and her interest in Daryl she drives wildly into the night, snorting cocaine behind the wheel and fatally crashes. Though ancillary characters, the dead woman, Iris, and Charlie each represent the inability of the female to recover and her fundamental inability to define her own identity independent of men. Men recover in *Clean and Sober*; women die.

William Kennedy's novel *Ironweed* was adapted in 1988 for the screen. Set in the late 1930s, *Ironweed* follows the lives of Francis Phelan (Jack Nicholson) and Helen Archer (Meryl Streep). Each has had moments in the sun, he as a major league baseball player and she as a radio singer and they now live in the streets, eat at the mission, and sleep where they can. Again a comparison of a male and female alcoholic in a single text provides insight into the sexual specifications of the female alcoholic. In an opening sequence, Francis inquires of Rudy, a fellow street dweller, as to whether he has seen Helen that day. Rudy asks Francis, "What's Helen's name?" "Helen." "What's her other name?" "She's only got one name." Later, when Sandra, another drunk, is found unconscious in the street, these questions and answers are echoed. Sandra has been a bum—a drunk and whore—all her life, and in a similar inquiry, her last name is unrevealed, unknown, unimportant. The female alcoholics in *Ironweed* whore for their drinking money; the men work at day labor jobs. When Helen is too cold to spend the night in the street with Francis, he delivers her to an abandoned car occupied by several street men. In the morning, she must masturbate one of the men in exchange for the warmth of the car the night before. Francis determines that he will visit the home and family he abandoned twenty-two years earlier; in intercut shots Helen is seen rescuing their few possessions and reclaiming their room in a rooming house. As Francis attempts to make some peace with his family he buys a turkey for them with his day's wages. At the same time Helen attempts to bring to her life with Francis some order, cleanliness, comfort. In matching shots, Francis soaks in a hot tub in his former home and Helen washes her hair and dresses in a silk gown. Francis is invited by his wife to "come home for good" because he remains part of the family. Helen, alone, overcome with the ravages of alcoholism, sinks to the floor and dies. Francis is no less alcoholic than Helen, no less despairing, but he has a family. Finally, after Helen's death, Francis hurls a full pint of whiskey from a moving train, suggesting hope for his future. Helen's universe revolved around Francis. As Francis tells his wife about her nine-year relationship with Helen, she tells him, "She needs you. What do you need, Fran?" Francis replies: "I need a shoelace." Again, the alcoholic woman die and the alcoholic man lives, perhaps to recover.

Perhaps the most vivid recent treatment of a female alcoholic is seen in the 1987 *Barfly*. In his description of characters, screenwriter Charles Bukowski articulates the differing natures of the two central alcoholic characters, Henry Chinaski (Mickey Rourke) and Wanda Wilcox (Faye Dunaway):

If he [Henry] is mad, then it is the madness of the disowned who lack interest in the standard way of life. Rather than enter the treadmill of society he has chosen the bottle and the bars...Drinking seems a way to hide...[Wanda] has an intelligence born of disillusion. She is even more alcoholic than Chinaski. But unlike Chinaski who drinks because there is nothing else to do, Wanda drinks because it is the only thing to do. (Bukowski 7)

The physical descriptions of this pair reveal even more about sexuality-based construction of the female alcoholic:

He moves slowly for a young man, rather stiff-shouldered, but at times his movements show a sudden swiftness and grace. It is as if he were saving himself for some magic moment, some magic time...Wanda was once quite beautiful but the drinking is beginning to have its effect: the face is fattening a bit, the slightest bit of belly is beginning to show, and pouches are forming under her eyes...Her drunkness and the madness in her eyes would seem to suggest that she would be great in bed. (Bukowski 7)

Henry's alcoholism is somehow noble, somehow romantic, and clearly a matter of personal choice. Even in comparison to the dirty, pugnacious, offensive Henry, Wanda is "even more alcoholic" than he. Wanda survives by having affairs with men, with a particular man, Wilbur, who accomodates her habit by allowing her to run tabs at liquor stores. Henry is a writer whose fiction has interested a magazine publisher. Although Wanda's primary interest is drinking, not sex, she would go anywhere, do anything with a man who offered her a bottle. The three male characters, Henry and the two bartenders Jim and Eddie, are constructed as good-hearted, quick-fighting individuals who, in spite of their drinking, retain essential goodness. Two female characters in addition to Wanda depend upon their sexuality for definition and are, again, "more alcoholic" than their male counterparts. Lilly is "a thin lesbian, dry-stick, ugly, horrible, like a witch without character" (Bukowski 8). She is worse than death. Grandma Moses, another of the barflies, is an aged drunk whose sole activity outside of drinking is performing oral copulation for all takers. There is no recovery, no escape for anyone in *Barfly*. The closing scene has Henry walking to the alley to engage in another of his endless fistfights with Eddie, and Wanda following him. Even in this tedious, endless world of drunken misery with no escape at the conclusion, it is clear that female alcoholics fare far worse than males in their representations in *Barfly*. Defined by their sexuality, their physical attractiveness, and their sexual behavior, the text renders these women as less desirable, less understandable, more alcoholic than the men who also inhabit this textual universe.

Cagney and Lacey: A Lone Exception

When alcoholic women move from the big screen to television, very little changes. Even when a woman successfully achieves sobriety, she continues to be bound by an alcoholic label and victimized by men, for example in the case of Sue Ellen Ewing (Linda Gray) on *Dallas*. Women on daytime serials fare no better, as in the cases of Devon Sheppard (*All My Children*) or Susan Moore (*General Hospital*). Over the past decade, a period during which alcoholic women increasingly became part of television programs, only one such representation presents a character who transcends much of the gender baggage of the last fifty-five years: the CBS drama *Cagney and Lacey*. The medium of television provides a set of possibilities and limitations quite different from those of film. Perhaps most significant is the fact that television allows for a longitudinal development of character and audience identification. The potential for progress in images of alcoholic women is enormous, and the impact of regression is felt widely. Hence, a woman like Sue Ellen Ewing is victimized over many episodes and in many situations. A woman who is confused and searching and beings abusing alcohol as part of this confusion, such as Grace Van Own on *L.A. Law* is developed more fully than most feature films permit.

Chris Cagney, of the dramatic series *Cagney and Lacey*, is a New York city detective sergeant. In the early years of the series, Cagney is shown as a moderate to heavy drinker in social situations. Cagney drank frequently with her father, Charlie, a retired police officer. Charlie's drinking is legendary in the Department. At Charlie's death, Chris discovers that she has followed in her father's footsteps in this way as well. Through the help and encouragement of her partner, Mary Beth Lacey (Tyne Daly), Chris is able to identify herself as an alcoholic. Still burdened by the suggestion of paternal inheritance, this stands alone as the definition of Chris' alcoholism and recovery in terms of her relationships with men. Mary Beth forms the nucleus of her support system, and it is Mary Beth who accompanies her to her first AA meeting. Although she has had both serious and casual relationships with men, and, after some length of sobriety begins a new relationship, men play a well-delimited role in her life. Her drinking is self-determined, her identification as an alcoholic is hers to assume, and her recovery is an act of autonomy and self-direction.

Consonant with the character established over some four television seasons, Christine Cagney's alcoholic bottoming out more than anything represents her liberation from her father's shadow and his image of her. Though in mourning over the loss of her father, she is freed by his death—freed of her quest for his approval and freed of her own alcohol dependence.

Conclusions

This review of the treatment of women and alcoholism in films and television over the past fifty-five years has introduced an important and complex area of for further research. Largely suggestive, it asks as many questions as it answers. However, several conclusions can be drawn from the evidence presented. Perhaps most striking is the inescapable observation that where popular, social, and medical discourse on alcoholism has changed over five decades, popular culture representations of alcoholic women have not reflected prevailing understanding. In contrast, representations of alcoholic men have changed slightly in response to changing attitudes and explanatory and interpretive structures. Recent representations have become aligned with contemporary thinking. Importantly, alcoholic men traditionally appear in popular culture as the bon vivant, the tortured artist, the troubled soul. They possess redeeming qualities which frequently salvage their image in a text and trigger their recovery. Their drinking results from cosmic struggles; either their recovery or their textual salvation is certain and complete. Alcoholic men wrestle with *human* struggles that relate to themselves and to the universe. Alcoholic women's struggles do not extend beyond their own universe as it is conscribed by men. Even in the most apparently hopeless cases (for example *Barfly*) the male alcoholic—a man who drinks as a statement about the human condition—is constructed as better than the female alcoholic.

The self of alcoholic women in popular culture is defined by men. Unchanged over time, the alcoholic woman is represented as somehow far worse than alcoholic man, recalling the words of Bejamin Karpman written in 1948. She is incapable as a wife, negligent as a mother, under- or over-sexed as a lover. She drinks because she is disappointed in love, because she cannot adequately adjust to her prescribed role, because alcoholism is simply a part of a package of female neuroses and defects. Her prospects for recovery are dim. Where and when she recovers, her recovery depends upon men for its inspiration and realization.

The popular culture representation of alcoholic women presents yet another illustration of a classic gender-based double bind. The social stigma attached to women and drinking has resulted in a scarcity of film and television presentations. When such presentations are available, the reasons for a woman's alcoholism, the tragedy which ensues from her drinking, and her very nature are conscribed by damaging sex role stereotyping. When she recovers, her recovery is likely to be incomplete. When she continues in her alcoholism, the tragedy is centered around her failings as a woman.

Several questions remain, and pursuit of the answers suggests a lengthy and comprehensive study. The central problem involves determining the origins of these representations. If they diverge fundamentally from the movement and direction of attitudes and understandings of alcoholic women, what is their basis? Clearly these images are derived from a deeper level of unconscious, shared ideas about women and, consequently, alcoholic women. The prison of alcoholism in an individual text might be surmountable; the prison of gender is not.

To what extent and in what ways are these representations accurate, that is, do these popular culture representations of alcoholic women resemble women's actual experiences with alcoholism and recovery? This is a vital and complex question, and one which potentially reveals the nature of popular culture as a mechanism of socialization. Television and movies provide models for behavior, they shape our expectations, and they supply an interpretive system for life experiences (see, for example, Wallack, Breed, and Cruz; Macdonald, and DeFoe, Breed, and Breed). It is likely, therefore, that some congruence might exist between the broad lines of popular culture alcoholic women and active and recovering alcoholic women. This is perhaps the most disturbing conclusion, for such images will perpetuate the second class self-concept and culturally shared image of alcoholic women as particularly vulnerable, defined by sex, and limited by gender. Representations that do not reflect responsible information and ideologies serve only as impediments to recovery.

To what extent do popular culture media represent a kind of public trust which explicitly acknowledges their role in shaping behavior and expectations, if not concepts of self? By what data and perspectives should these media images be informed?

Finally, some hope is warranted. The popular and critical success of *Cagney and Lacey,* particularly the series of episodes which concentrate on Chris' alcoholism, suggests that realistic, strong, self-possessed and recovering alcoholic women can exist within an entertainment medium. The specific and individually felt effects of this representation are unknown. However, *Cagney and Lacey* has demonstrated that popular culture representations can transcend the limitations of gender conventions and can re-shape images of alcoholic women to validate the self-awareness and autonomy which are central to the experiences and recovery of real-life women.

Works Cited

Bukowski, Charles. *The Movie "Barfly."* Santa Rosa: Black Sparrow Press, 1987.

Cook, Jim and Mike Lewington. *Images of Alcoholism.* London: BFI, 1979.

DeFoe, James, W. Breed, and L.A. Breed. "Drinking on television: A five-year study." *Journal of Drug Education* 13(1) (1988):25-38.

Ettorre, Betsy. "Women and drunken sociology: Developing a feminist analysis." *Women's Studies International Forum* 9(5) (1986): 515-520.

Dyer, Richard. *Stars.* London: BFI, 1979.

Halliwell, Leslie. *The Filmgoer's Companion.* New York: Avon, 1974.

Harwin, Judith and Shirley Otto. "Women, alcohol and the screen."*Images of Alcoholism.* Eds. Cook and Lewington, London: BFd, 1979., 37-50.

Haskell, Molly. *From Reverence to Rape: The Treatment of Women in the Movie.* New York: Holt, Rinehart, and Winston, 1974.

Jellinek, E.M. *The Disease Concept of Alcoholism.* New Haven, CT: Hillhouse, 1960.

Karpman, Benjamin. *The Alcoholic Woman.* Washington, D.C.: Linacre Press, 1948.

de Lauretis, Teresa. *Alice Doesn't: Feminism, Semiotics, Cinema.* Bloomington, IN: Indiana University Press, 1984.

Lowery, Shearon Anne. *Soap and Booze in the Afternoon: An Analysis of the Portrayal of Alcohol Use in the Daytime Serial.* Unpublished Ph.D. Dissertation. Washington State University, 1979.

Macdonald, Patrick. "The 'dope' on soaps." *Journal of Drug Education* 13(4) (1983): 359-369.

Matlin, Leonard. *T.V. and Movie Guide.* New York: New American Library, Signet, 1989.

O'Hara, Shirley. "Review of *Smash-Up.*" *The New Republic* 24 (1947) Feb:39.

Rivera, Geraldo. host. "Housewife addicts." Transcript of the *Geraldo Show* 19 Jan 89. New York: Journal Graphics, 1989.

Roffman, Peter and Jim Purdy. *The Hollywood Social Problem Film: Madness, Despair, and Politics from the Depression to the Fifties*. Bloomington, IN: Indiana University Press, 1981.

Sandmaier, Marian. *The Invisible Alcoholics: Women and Alcohol Abuse in America*. New York:McGraw-Hill, 1980.

Wallack, Lawrence, W. Breed, and J. Cruz. "Alcohol on prime-time television." *Journal of Studies in Alcohol* 48(1) (1987):33-38.

Watts, Thomas D., Ed. *Social Thought on Alcoholism*. Malabar, FL: Krieger, 1988.

Winfrey, Oprah, host. "Controversy about alcoholism." Transcript of *The Oprah Winfrey Show* 08 Mar 89. New York: Journal Graphics, 1989.

Zolotow, Maurice. *Billy Wilder in Hollywood*. New York: Limelight, 1987.

Videography

FEATURE FILMS

Barfly 1987 (d. Babet Schroeder), screenplay Charles Bukowski, Mickey Rourke, Faye Dunaway, Wanda Wilcox, Alice Krige

Clean and Sober 1988 (d. Glenn Gordon Caron), Michael Keaton, Kathy Baker, Morgan Freeman

Dangerous 1935 (d. Alfred Green), Bette Davis, Franchot Tone

Days of Wine and Roses 1962 (d. Blake Edwards), Jack Lemon, Lee Remick, Jack Klugman

Farewell, My Lovely 1975 (d. Dick Richards), Robert Mitchum, Charlotte Rampling

From the Terrace 1960 (d. Mark Robson), Paul Newman, Joanne Woodward, Myrna Loy, Leon Ames

The Graduate 1967 (d. Mike Nichols), Dustin Hoffman, Anne Bancroft

I'll Cry Tomorrow 1955 (d. Daniel Mann), Susan Hayward, Richard Conte, Jo Van Fleet, Eddie Albert

Ironweed 1988 (d. Hector Babenco), Jack Nicholson, Meryl Streep

Key Largo 1948 (d. John Huston), Humphrey Bogart, Lauren Bacall, Claire Trevor, Edward G. Robinson

The Morning After, 1987 (d. Sidney Lumet), Jane Fonda, Jeff Bridges

Opening Night 1978 (d. John Cassavetes), Gena Rowlands, Joan Blondell, John Cassavetes

Red Sky at Morning 1970 (d. James Goldstone), Richard Thomas, Catherine Burns, Richard Crenna, Claire Bloom

Smash-Up: The Story of a Woman 1947 (d. Stuart Heisler), Susan Hayward, Marsha Hunt, Eddie Albert

Something to Live For 1952 (d. George Stevens), Joan Fontaine, Ray Milland

Too Much, Too Soon 1958 (d. Art Napoleon), Dorothy Malone, Errol Flynn

Under Capricorn 1949 (d. Alfred Hitchcock), Ingrid Bergman, Joseph Cotten, Michael Wilding

Who's Afraid of Virginia Woolf 1966 (d. Mike Nichols), Elizabeth Taylor, Richard Burton, Sandy Dennis, George Segal

MADE-FOR-T.V.-MOVIES

The Betty Ford Story 1987 (d. David Greene), Gena Rowlands, Josef Sommer

Between Friends 1983 (d. Lou Antonio), Carol Burnett, Elizabeth Taylor

Life of the Party: Beatrice 1982 (d. Lamont Johnson), Carol Burnett, Lloyd Bridges
Sarah T.—Portrait of a Teenage Alcoholic 1975 (d. Richard Donner), Linda Blair,
    Mark Hamill, Verna Bloom, Larry Hagman

PRIME TIME DRAMAS
CBS *Cagney and Lacey* 1982-1988
CBS *Dallas* 1978-ongoing
NBC *L.A. Law* 1986-ongoing

DAYTIME SERIALS
ABC *All My Children*
ABC *General Hospital*
NBC *Generations*
NBC *Santa Barbara*

Return of the Planet of the Apes, or What is a Woman?: Science and Gender in *Probe*

Kerry Shea

In her recent study *Science and Gender: A Critique of Biology and its Theories on Women*, Ruth Bleier argues that "We [women] have been led to believe that the discourse on woman and her nature, a discourse, like all others, from which women have been absent and excluded, has been an objective investigation because it was conducted by science. But in fact, science itself, the tool for the investigation of such natural objects as women, has always been defined as *the* expression of the male mind: dispassionate, objective, impersonal, transcendent" (Bleier 196). Concerned with what she regards as a tendency among some scientists to work from a set of assumptions based on cultural expectation, Bleier seeks to undermine this presumed objectivity, to expose the cultural beliefs which drive scientific investigation and to chart the effect of Western science not just in an academic sphere but as its conclusions are disseminated in popular form. She points out that the white male bias in science has made it easy for nonscientific and religious organizations to garner large followings because they can claim the backing of "science" and thus gain intellectual credibility for their social positions.

With the upsurge in Creationism and Sociobiology, "sciences" which lend support to the agenda of the New Right, particularly in the late '70s and early '80s, the always problematic relationship between woman and technology has become exceedingly popular and perhaps even more disturbing.

Television, that mine sweeper of public consciousness, has been quick to capitalize on renewed interest in the place of woman in society from a scientific perspective. For example during the winter season (1988/89) many PBS stations broadcast a documentary science program, *The Sexual Brain*, as part of a series on the body and science. The show featured the research of a number of scientists (several of them women), who, having already decided that differences in behavior between men and women are biologically based, searched for brain variations to explain such ill-defined traits as "aggressivity," "coyness" and "shyness." No mention was made at any time of the influence of environment, of cultural expectations, stereotyping, or political inequalities. At one point the show argues for the brain's ability to override "biological instinct" in women, while the camera pans across a women's self-defense class. The voice-over (white male) suggests that women are able in some instances to overcome their natural, nonaggressive (i.e. feminine) biology and learn more masculine modes of behavior in order to defend themselves against rape. The claim that fighting in self-defense is not natural, not feminine, leaves unstated but readily apparent the position that masculine aggressive behaviors which include rape and wife battering are in fact "natural" and acceptable. The male perpetrator is simply a victim of his biology. Although such assumptions do unfortunately exist in our society, they become far more dangerous, far more "true" when linked with scientific research which in this century has set the parameters of the knowable.

Primetime commercial TV has also recently been dabbling in the problem of science and gender. In a 1988 ABC replacement series co-created by Issac Asimov, and the subject of this paper, *Probe*, "good" science as a generic category functions as the morally responsible element in Western society, pitting a super genius scientist with a computer-like mind and his female side-kick against various forces of evil and corruption in American life. Since the scientist-humanitarian, played by ex-*Hardy Boy* Parker Stevenson, uses his vast computer network to solve mysteries and foil the plots of would-be criminals, one might argue that this show maintains that super computer technology, no longer a part of that excessive sci-fi world but the driving force behind reality, is also, or at least can be, the mechanism for the impulse towards "goodness," and, that a society which uses science and technology correctly, as our hero will no doubt do, displays both its superior intelligence and humanity and consequently maintains its position as world leader.

The episode which I will discuss even attempts some social criticism directed primarily at pertinent and controversial scientific concerns such as violence against animals through inhumane scientific research, the overuse and effectiveness of the death penalty and experimentation with fetal brain tissue. The "science as salvation" theme has always been at the core of science fiction, but despite the collaboration of sci-fi author Asimov, the show remains firmly rooted in the technology of the present, blurring lines between real issues in the scientific community and fictive displacement into the safer improbable. What we are confronted with here is TV for the late eighties from which a new American hero emerges—the individual scientist with a social conscience who uses his superior knowledge to fight against greed, ignorance, inefficiency and injustice. In this era of conspicuous consumption, tacit government support for a widening gap between haves and have-nots, and numerous financial scandals in Washington and on Wall Street, the show nominally upholds ethical as opposed to economic values as the spiritual core of both society and the individual. But for all its attempts to elicit support for socially progressive concerns and its stabs at trendy issues, this episode, anyway, contains a disturbing subtext. Despite the hi-tech paraphernalia and the humanitarian influences, the working out of gender relations suggests standard differentiation dependent on traditional binary oppositions which relegate woman to the emotional, irrational, and excessively sexual and place her in a position hierarchically inferior to that of the "super" man who possesses "right reason," defined not in religious but scientific terms. The plot of *Probe* rigidly conforms to the traditional structure of adventure/drama: the hero solves the mystery, saves the pretty girl, outclasses the authorities and rights the chaos and confusion wrought by the female characters. The superior scientific knowledge of this late twentieth century Sherlock Holmes allows him to investigate the crime successfully, but as Bleier maintains in her critique of science, the object of the investigation and thus the source of moral degeneracy is "woman."

As the episode opens our super scientist with female side-kick in tow is accosted by a nerdy-looking female grad student who claims to have disproved the hero's data on some incomprehensible problem in astrophysics. Although the side kick attempts to remove the presumptuous woman, the scientist is intrigued and allows her into the warehouse where he lives platonically with the woman but in a rather kinky relationship with the computer. At the same time the scientist is also accosted by a female animal behaviorist with a female orangutan (shades of Edgar Allan Poe) in tow, who claims to have taught the ape sign language and thus to have verified that apes possess a kind of human intelligence defined as the ability to understand and produce human speech. She badgers the hero, the "greatest scientific mind of the century" (Jarvis 9), until he agrees to test the ape which is then moved into his warehouse in a special cage. When the scientist and his side-kick decide to leave, the grad student, in a major move into predictability, slips a piece of paper over the lock, thereby bypassing with child-like ease what must be a multi-million dollar security system. After the others have gone, the student reenters the building and begins to rifle through the scientist's files, much to the displeasure of the ape who knows stealing and plagiarism when she sees it. The camera then cuts to the outside. We are suddenly peering at the warehouse through binoculars. The viewer, well versed in recent red-baiting on TV, immediately assumes Soviet spies, but in the only surprise in this two hour episode, we discover that the sinister figures lurking behind the rock formations are the crack commandoes of an animal rights organization bent on rescuing the much-abused ape. As it grows darker a figure in black approaches the building and begins to scale the wall. We hear a shot. The camera cuts to the interior. The ape is in her cage; the grad student is dead on the floor. The remaining hour or so is devoted, as one might expect, to discovering the killer. With no imagination and no scientific data, the police arrest the ape. After she is convicted, in a state where the penalty for murder is death, the characters think of ways to free the doomed animal. Aided by the animal rights activists and by the orangutan herself, who types her story in her own language on a PC, the scientist investigates and unravels the mystery. The ape's human intelligence did not occur naturally but was induced by the behaviorist who had fetal brain tissue secretly grafted onto the brain of her specimen. Motivated by sexual jealousy, the ape did in fact commit the murder. Having fallen hopelessly in love with the scientist, the ape shot the grad student whom she perceived as a sexual rival and in the final moments of the show makes a second attempt on the side-kick for the same reason. The hero saves his lady, absolves the ape of responsibility and discredits the female scientist for her inhumane and unethical conduct.

As we work towards the highly climactic solution to the mystery, it seems to me that several socially progressive positions are emphasized superficially by this program in order to displace other, perhaps more controversial, issues. First, the animal rights activists, all of whom are male, not only did not kill the woman, they did not even make it into the building which is guarded by a sophisticated alarm system designed and installed by the hero (which was deviously and easily overridden first by the female grad student then by the female primate). Later, when they attempt to rescue the ape from prison, they are again foiled so that they do not actually break any laws—at least not technically. Although their cause is obviously just and probably cheered by members of PETA, the show cannot condone crimes against property even in a worthwhile cause. The warehouse remains inviolate; the group does not steal the animal. The justice of their claim is in fact legitimized by their bumbling inability to pull off the caper, and audience sympathy for them increases throughout the program without the unacceptable complication of real crime. So we are never asked to judge whether crime is acceptable if the options are limited.

Second, while all property remains inviolate, some murders can be explained. The audience has no chance to feel sympathy for the victim, who, unlike the animal rights activists, would have stolen or copied the scientist's research. Her foray into real crime (plagiarism and theft) results in apparently justifiable homicide: we blame the victim. Moreover, the judge who condemns the ape to death is so callous that the controversial, emotional stigma of the death penalty evaporates into near parody. The audience thinks only of the ape and not of the dead woman who quickly disappears without a mention.

Third, despite the fact that the ape has murdered once and makes a second attempt for a remarkably sexist and silly reason, blame falls on the female behaviorist who has acted unethically by performing experimental surgery on the primate. The controversial use of fetal tissue, although clearly depicted as unacceptable given the consequences (murder), is never confronted directly; rather the entire issue is displaced onto the less antagonistic question of animal rights. From these three examples we can elucidate that the morality which governs this show actually remains carefully entrenched in a kind of fuzzy conservatism, willing to give prime time support for animal rights as long as the rights of property owners, fetuses and men are upheld. But the superficially progressive stance advocated by *Probe* assumes an association with scientific ojectivity which it implies can solve (or at least side-step) moral dilemmas through knowledge. That the scientist succeeds in tracking not only the murderer but the real culprit even as the law enforcement agencies fail further champions the supremacy of reason.

But while science, epitomized by the thoroughly rational, impossibly unemotional super scientist, uncovers the "truth," this episode also suggests that science is a strictly male domain which takes woman as the object of its investigation, that woman is easily reproducible in a lab, and that gendered behaviors are not the result of cultural expectation and indoctrination but are genetically motivated and thus inescapable. While the show makes no specific references to the doctrine of sociobiology, the subtext of this episode is replete with its influence. Proponents of biological determinist philosophies use the guise of science to argue that traditional white western social patterns are in fact based not in political and social inequities but in biology, notably genetics. Thus, rationalism, aggressivity, and desire to work outside the home are seen as genetically encoded male behaviors, while jealousy, coyness, fidelity and desire to remain in the home are encoded female behaviors: "It is perfectly good biology that business and profession taste sweeter to them [men] while home and child taste sweeter to women" (Barash 114). This is a form of science which many feminist scientists, including Bleier and Evelyn Fox Keller, find most objectionable. Based on traditional definitions of gender, it offers no challenge to these notions; rather it confirms them as real through a sleight of hand—through circular logic.

In *Probe* the male characters arrange themselves hierarchically with knowledge as the key to this macho pecking order. The scientist has no male competition. The inept animal rights activists and the bungling law enforcement officials, while all male, are secondary characters with bit parts who quickly assume submissive postures with regard to the dominant male. But despite the major difference in their intellectual capacities, the scientist, the police and the activists remain united throughout the show. Mental incapacity within this social grouping does not override the primacy of gender.

All of the women in the show, in contrast, are defined by their adherence to traditional definitions of femininity. Although they are all also connected with science in some way, their claims to elevated knowledge remain inappropriate and illegitimate. Only the male scientist understands all branches of science, refusing to specialize but nevertheless unrealistically mastering all fields simultaneously. The two female scientists naturally cannot compete on this level (they are not super heroes), but they are not shown diligently laboring within their own specialties; rather we discover that they cannot cope with the rigors, both moral and intellectual, of their profession. To survive they cheat, steal and ignore ethical standards. The behaviorist grafts brain tissue onto a monkey then lies about it so that her work, teaching sign-language to primates, will be recognized and compensated. The grad student attempts to steal the true scientist's work which she will no doubt pass off as her own. They have not chosen to take the "sweeter tasting" route of home and hearth and, as the ideology of the show makes clear, can find no place for themselves in their chosen fields. In fact the two are guilty precisely because they are women and have dared to challenge the hero (the grad student claims his data was incorrect; the behaviorist attempts to disprove his claim that apes cannot understand human language). Ruth Bleier notes that "science as it is currently constituted is by its very nature inherently masculine, that woman can apprehend it only by extreme effort of overcoming their own nature which is inherently contradictory to science" (Bleier 196). If science has founded itself on a principle of domination, the triumph of the investigating male mind over the passive female object, then women can never achieve objectivity within the scientific community, because they are by definition "objects"—that which is being investigated—and cannot therefore attain the rank of scientist without denying their own subjectivity as the program illustrates. It is no coincidence that the male scientist has access to all knowledge, all science. He is the male mind, the paradigm of patriarchal society in this century, whose claim of higher intelligence, of an understanding of the workings of the natural world, allows him to analyze, quantify and rectify woman (the quintessential natural phenomenon) while abdicating all responsibility for the conclusions because science is objective.

Not only do the female scientists trespass beyond their biologically determined capacity professionally, worse, both are portrayed as intensely unattractive, intensely, that is, unfeminine. In a world and in a medium (TV) which judges women through the look of the empowered male gaze, neither character has any erotic appeal. The middle-aged behaviorist is overweight, dressed in a lumpy bush jacket, khaki fatigue pants, rumpled and unkempt. The grad student, although probably only in her twenties, wears thick cat's eye glasses which distort the shape of face and eyes, making her look much older, has a hair style which has been out of fashion for at least thirty years, wears an ill-fitting skirt and frumpy socks, and with books constantly clutched in front of her chest, lacks breasts. Although it is obvious that both are attracted to the scientist (the highest ranking male), whom they erroneously assume they can win through intellectual competition, they both seem to have on-going casual relationships with down and out men who are their intellectual inferiors and whom they dominate both verbally and physically. The behaviorist appears to be having an affair with her balding, alcoholic assistant who actually propositions the female grad student, thereby insinuating that he is unfulfilled and she is "loose." The grad student orders around a similarly dressed young man who appears to be her male counterpart. The audience infers that the unpalatability of the men results from the emasculating tendencies of these women. The two female scientists are obviously presented as having discarded their femininity for professions in which, we have seen, they can have no part. This lack of traditional femininity when coupled with dishonesty, ambition and a serious absence of nurturing qualities makes these two women truly villainous.

In contrast, the side-kick played by Kristen Allanzo of both day and night soap opera fame, who lives platonically with our hero in the warehouse, is stunningly beautiful with unbound, but impeccably coiffed, waist-length hair, a lithe, graceful figure which she sheaths in costly, and therefore fashionable, dresses flowing down to a demure mid-calf. She is a Disneyland Cinderella among the step-sisters. We are astonished that the hero doesn't even seem to notice her. But a kind of sacred sexual purity hovers about the science in this show. Sexually aggressive, sexually active, women do not fare well. The side-kick, we are not surprised to discover, has little formal scientific training, but her role does not involve preparing experiments or collecting data. Instead, she nurtures the scientist, preparing his meals not his petri dishes, making certain he wakes up on time, acting as a secretary— in short fulfilling her genetically assigned role as mother. The two female scientists do not share this nurturing capacity, which must be the proper role for women since it is the dominant quality of the prettiest girl. They are portrayed as having traded away their investment in their genetic heritage through sexual promiscuity. They are not mother figures; they do not take care of their men. Neither particularly cares for the ape who becomes the focus of the sympathetic "mom's" attentions. And perhaps most importantly, the behaviorist has no hesitation about implanting human fetal tissues into the orangutan, demonstrating her extreme anti-maternal tendencies.

The striking opposition between the female scientists and the beautiful mother, both in appearance and values, underscores the sociobiological argument that appears to be at the core of this text. Not only does *Probe* argue that science is male territory and that women do not possess the capacity to engage in scientific inquiry, but it makes clear that concepts of gender are immutable. The female scientists cannot succeed because they are women; they are unattractive to men because they have betrayed immutable genetic impulses and attempted to compete with their betters. Only the mother figure survives physically and morally. Having remained within the prescribed boundaries of femininity, she triumphs not as scientist but as victim—an object to be rescued by the hero.

If the argument that the categories "male" and "female" are not social constructs, taking their meaning from the culture that imposes them, but instead universal and genetically based, has not been made sufficiently clear to the audience through the polarization of the female characters, the altered ape finally dismisses all questions. When the ape has fetal brain tissue grafted onto her brain, she no longer behaves or thinks as an ape but as a woman. She falls in love with the most eligible man around—the scientist—who no doubt possesses superior genes, and then sets out to win him. When he enters her cage, strokes her and talks to her, treating her more or less the way he treats his female companion, she gently flirts with him and attempts to convince him to remain in her cell with her. His failure to respond to her sexual cues leaves her despondent, and leads her, naturally, to perceive other women as a threat to her necessary sexual conquest. The scientist explains to the audience as well as to police that the ape murdered the grad student because she sensed her attraction to himself and, fearing a rival, eliminated her. When she later perceived the side-kick as an additional rival, she surreptitiously returned to the warehouse and violently attacked her. This explanation solves the mystery. Left unarticulated, however, are two unfortunate but inescapable readings suggested by the centrality of the female ape. The implication that female fetal brain tissue already has certain "female" behaviors genetically encoded, that this "female" tissue can account for the transformed ape's sexual jealousy, duplicity, and desire for the highest ranking available male, finally locates guilt in female sexuality, confirming scientifically what misogynistic literature has maintained for centuries: woman is simply Other. A second, even more disturbing reading of the criminal orangutan argues that woman is actually sub-human, can be constructed by science—just a paste-up combination of primate body and fetal brain tissue, both animal and infantile. In this reading woman is not only the object of science but the creation of science, not born but made. Having established this definition of woman, science, the male mind, then relinquishes all culpability: a woman perpetrated this monstrosity on another female body. The female scientist's artificial, "bad" mothering is ultimately responsible for the creation of the psychotic woman/ape and for murder, the murder of other women. As Judith Spector points out, male science fiction writers who followed the "mother" of the genre, Mary Shelly, "were quick to appropriate 'mental motherhood' as their rightful and logical domain. They were to fight for the privilege of cultural sublimation and to repudiate not just Mary Shelly as the mother of science fiction, but all mothers and women as well" (Spector 164). By locating murderous psychosis in female sexuality and then adducing it to anti-maternal (unfeminine) behavior, *Probe* situates social degeneracy and violent crime in a lack of adherence to traditional "female" values. Meanwhile, male agencies—science, the law, paramilitary organizations—wait innocuously on the margins, ready to intervene after the women have finished killing each other off.

Woman's otherness, her non-human status, also finds confirmation in the show's denial of female access to language. The super scientist, correct, of course, in his assertion that apes/women cannot learn or imitate human speech, must "translate" the orangutan's story which she types in a language bearing no resemblance to any known language family. Able to communicate only through the mediation of the Father—the master of the science of linguistics—the woman/ape offers up her story, her voice to his reconfiguration, acquiescing to his reading, his analysis, finally acknowledging herself as victim of the monstrous mother. As the show ends, the nonmaternal woman who has attempted to steal knowledge and has victimized "women" stands silent under a barrage of accusations by the hero. However, her silence only mirrors the silence of the other female characters. The ape, the scientist and even the motherly side-kick end up in essentially the same position as the dead graduate student—a mild disturbance but easily removed and ignored at the end of two hours.

While television may celebrate new technology and new knowledge, the disturbing subtext of this episode resorts to old clichés and old stereotyping, reinforcing traditional and clearly marked gender definitions. By the end of an evening woman has been defined as unmistakably subordinate, morally suspect—a species wholly different from the male and in need of investigation and exposure. Under the borrowed guise of scientific objectivity and moral responsibility, *Probe* not only perpetuates long standing anxieties about women in science but recuperates on a prime time scale pseudoscientific, biological determinist views on gender and behavior which argue for the genetic otherness of woman.

Fortunately, after a six month run ABC cancelled this "sci-fi snoozer," having set it up in the "death slot" opposite *The Cosby Show* (Jarvis 9). But if the show's untimely demise was merely the result of bad timing (*Cosby* has apparently sent many a show down the tube), then we can probably expect more programming to follow in *Probe's* direction, especially if Hollywood makes an attempt to justify its programming for the 12-18 year old set by playing on the American math/science deficit anxiety of parents. If *Probe* is any indication of science shows to come, the anti-feminist backlash of the 80s is bound to continue into the next decade.

Works Cited

Barash, D.P. *Sociobiology and Behavior, 2nd ed.* New York: Elsevier, 1982.

Bleier, Ruth. *Science and Gender: A Critique of Biology and its Theories on Women.* New York: Pergamon, 1984.

Jarvis, Jeff. "Picks and Pans." *People Magazine* 29 (March 7, 1988): 9.

Keller, Evelyn Fox. *Reflection on Science and Gender.* New Haven: Yale University Press, 1985.

Spector, Judith. "Science Fiction and the Sex War: A Womb of One's Own." *Gender Studies: New Directions in Feminist Criticism.* Ed. Judith Spector. Bowling Green: Bowling Green Popular Press, 1986: 163-176.

Sexuality and Politics

Platoon and the Failure of War[1]

Bat-Ami Bar On

At face value *Platoon*[2] tells its viewers a rather simple story about a soldier's experience of an unpopular war the worth of which was doubted by soldiers too. The story is Taylor's, a young man who dropped out of college and volunteered to serve in the military in order to do for his country in Vietnam what his grandfather did in the first world war and his father in the second and because he believed that the burdens of war should be shared by men who like him are from privileged families.

When looking at *Platoon* in the ordinary forward fashion of the first time viewer, the chronological progression of Taylor's stay in Vietnam provides the only structure to Taylor's story. He is seen during his first few minutes in Vietnam, just after landing, during his first week in the field, at a fire base at the beginning of his second month, and in the field again in his fourth month and later. Tied to each recognizable piece of time is an episode or a cluster of episodes that capture some aspect of the American Vietnam combatant's war experience.

Immediately after landing, Taylor, dressed in a well-pressed uniform and looking fresh, still engulfed in the dust stirred by the troop carrier from which he descends, sees the bagged bodies of dead soldiers and a squad of old-timers, experienced "grunts," looking neglected and haunted. He hears the same squad taunting the squad of new men—the "fresh meat"—to which he belongs. During his first week he is in the jungle, he does not know nor is he instructed about what to do and like in the airport, he is taunted by the old-timers, his supposedly but not-yet-comrades in arms. He sees his first rotten body and vomits in response. He is afflicted by ants and faints from dehydration. He is on patrol or ambush, eats C-rations, and digs fox-holes. He is drenched by the rain and sleeps and sits in mud. He writes home. He is in his first fire-fight and feels the fear that precedes combat for the first time. He sees his first death. He is wounded and feels the fear of death for the first time.

At the beginning of his second month he makes friends with some of the old-timers in his platoon so that he finally has comrades in arms. In his fourth month and later, he is back in the jungle on more patrols and in more fire-fights. He sees more death. He experiences rage at and fear of the Vietnamese at a new level of unexpected intensity. He witnesses murder, rape and destruction in a Vietnamese village and the internal moral struggles

211

in his platoon that accompany such destruction. He is in battle. He kills his sergeant avenging the killing of another. He is mentally, emotionally and physically fatigued and is finally—at the film's end—evacuated.

Each episode in Taylor's chronologically structures story is presented so vividly and seems so authentic that for anyone familiar with war, the only thing lacking is the smell. The missing smells, however, do not detract from the sense one has at the end of the film, of having lived, or of having gotten as close as possible to living, even if only for a few hours, the experience of war of the American Vietnam combatant, "the grunt." Following from this is the sense of acquiring a special understanding of the horrors of war as they are experienced by the soldiers who fight them.

Because the special understanding in question is of the horrors of war as they are experienced by the soldiers who fight them and because it comes out of watching a film that consists of a realistic presentation of the combatant's life, it is tempting to think of *Platoon* as using the forms of the combat film subversively to protest rather than to valorize and edify war. But, I shall argue that *Platoon* nonetheless valorizes and edifies war, even if very subtly.

* * *

Taylor's chronologically structured story is not Taylor's only story. His other story is a death and rebirth story, a story of the radical transformations of a man through his soldiering. To see this story one needs to look at *Platoon* from the perspective established by Taylor's retrospective thoughts about the war. They are presented at the end of the film.

The death-rebirth story starts with Taylor's doubts which begin during his first week in Vietnam and are deep enough to shake his conventional values. It ends with Taylor's realization that the lost values were replaced with an acute awareness of an internal conflict between ruthlessness, a relentless drive to use any means to an end one is able to justify to oneself, and a sincere worry about justice which principally screens both ends and means. According to Taylor, this conflict is the microcosmic manifestation of the war fought in Vietnam, a war that Taylor comes to see as a war that Americans fought with themselves.

Taylor's initial doubts concern his ability to live the values he has upon arrival in Vietnam, the values he relied on to come voluntarily to Vietnam as a ordinary combatant. These doubts are grounded in his day-to-day life during the first week. It is a life that is always in danger and the danger is not exhilarating but exhausting with endless jungle patrols, fox-hole digging, night ambush, guard duty, and never enough time to rest or sleep. It is also a life void of comradery because the unwritten rules are that new inexperienced men, "the fresh meat," are not befriended by old-timers, the experienced "grunts" since they are likelier casualties and have yet to earn the special friendship of a comrade in arms. The constant exhaustion and the lack of comradery makes this life, according to Taylor, a life where reason is impossible, hence, a hell, and he wonders whether he made a terrible mistake and whether he is capable of the effort needed to complete a year long tour of duty.

Taylor next doubts his values and concludes that he no longer knows what is right and what is wrong because conventional rights and wrongs seem irrelevant to his combatant's life. His confusion, the product of the experience of war, of a life under a constant threat of death, of intense fears and rage, unearths a capacity for cruelty which he encounters when he briefly psychologically torments a young crippled Vietnamese man after the platoon enters a Vietnamese village that could reasonably be suspected of cooperation with the Viet Cong, an entry that followed a fire-fight and the discovery of a comrade's dead body hung for display by the Viet Cong. But Taylor is not only capable of cruelty, he is also capable of controlling it and he finally does not hurt his captive. Moreover, he also manages to exert some control over the cruel acts of members of his platoon, stopping, for example, their rape of helpless Vietnamese girls.

Eventually, Taylor kills a helpless man, yet not cruelly. The man Taylor kills is not a Vietnamese but an American, Sergeant Barnes, a man ruthlessly committed to the war ends, who believes that war suspends the demands of justice and acts accordingly. Barnes who is placed in opposition to another American, Sergeant Elias, a good leader principled in his treatment of his subordinates as well as of the Vietnamese, and an outspoken defender of his principles. Taylor kills Barnes because Barnes killed Elias. Elias's killing by Barnes cannot be avenged through the use of the military judicial system because there is no evidence other than circumstantial evidence that could be used to substantiate the accusation. So, Taylor, using the devastation of battle for his cover, instead of aiding Barnes who was wounded in the battle, kills him.

Killing Barnes as he did, Taylor behaves like Barnes, ruthlessly suspending procedural justice to achieve his end. Were Taylor not to kill Barnes, he would have been like Elias, which is what Taylor seems to evolve to be through his friendship with and admiration for him. But he cannot be just like Elias because in retrospect, years after the war, Taylor sees himself as both Elias's and Barne's son. Barne's killing, then, is also a form of patricide, a patricide necessary because through it Taylor is able to be both Elias's and Barne's son. In doing so, Taylor becomes a man whose being is constituted by the unresolved continued fight between Elias and Barnes, between a principled and ruthless pursuit of an end, rather than a man who resolved the conflict in favor of one or the other parties and the positions each represents.

Taylor's killing of Barnes ends his rebirth process. After it he is evacuated from the battle field and the film ends. The rebirth process begins when he returns to his platoon after treatment in the hospital for wounds received in his first fire-fight. Even though he is only wounded, he symbolically dies during this first fire-fight, a point made upon his return to his platoon by an old-timer who jokingly introduces him to others as Chris, saying that he was a new man who could not be Taylor because Taylor died in the fire-fight that ended his first week as a combatant in Vietnam, the week that leads to his grave doubts and the loss of his conventional values.

* * *

It is through Taylor's death-rebirth story that *Platoon* valorizes and edifies war. This is because through this story war is presented as a generative setting in which men born to women die and are then reborn as the sons of men. The presentation of war as such a setting is not only uncritical of war but romanticizes it and undercuts the criticism implied by its presentation as a cluster of shakingly horrifying episodes that no one could survive unscarred.

The romantization of war in *Platoon* resembles the romantization of violence even by Sartre who in the preface to Fanon's *The Wretched of the Earth* wrote about the colonized that:

> ...by this mad fury, by this bitterness of spleen, by their ever-present desire to kill us, by the permanent testing of powerful muscles which are afraid to relax, they have become men...their petty thefts mark the beginning of a resistance which is still unorganized...there are those among them who assert themselves by throwing themselves barehanded against the guns...others make men of themselves by murdering Europeans. (pp 17-18)

What typifies the romantization of violence is the expectation that violence be generative, that it bring into being a new reality and do so while destroying another reality whose destruction is necessary for the formation of this new reality. This expectation is not extended to all forms of violence but only to violent acts that lead to something of value. Nonetheless, the expectation romanticizes violence because, as Hannah Arendt notes in *On Violence*, it does not constitute violence merely as an instrument, and specifically as an instrument of coercion and destruction, but attributes to it a unique positive transformative power. Thus, Sartre *sees* more than coercion and destruction by the colonized. He expects the destruction of European property or the murder of Europeans by the colonized to be generative because, even if perverse, the destruction of property and the murders are, according to him, at the same time acts of self-assertion in resistance to colonization and, therefore, constitutive of a self that is not colonized.

In *Platoon* the expectation that violence be generative is an expectation from war and it is present in the film because of the death-rebirth story it tells. Like Sartre's colonized acts of violence, Taylor's presence in Vietnam as a combatant may be perverse. Still, again like Sartre's colonized, he is fundamentally changed by his acts and what he becomes is deep and complex. He leaves the war not the naive young man that he was when he came but a mature man who understands the tension between good and evil as a lived experience and chooses to go on living it.

There is another way in which *Platoon* presents violence as generative and it too is a function of its telling Taylor's death-rebirth story. The telling of this story is the retelling of a myth and the telling of this particular myth, especially its ritual telling, is, according to Rene Girard, designed both to remind a community of the terrors of unchecked violence and, at least momentarily to serve as a mechanism of its control by uniting the community torn by dissension and strife through a cathartic experience. Through the telling of the death-rebirth myth, then, violence generates communal unity.

And, this is just what Oliver Stone claimed that *Platoon* accomplished when he accepted the 1987 Academy Award. According to Stone, *Platoon* generated a sense of healing, a sense of communal unity that glosses over the strife and dissension generated in the US by the very war it portrays, the Vietnam War.

* * *

Platoon's presentation of war as generative and its attribution of a generative power to war is actually a presentation of men as generative and an attribution of a generative power to men. The world of *Platoon*, the world of war, is a men's world, a world without mothers in which men father each other. When Taylor is reborn, he is reborn as the son of two men.

War, of course, is not a men's world because war is not a world unto itself but one that touches deeply on the lives of many who may not be combatants, including women who may be related to combatants or be combatants themselves; who may be doctors or nurses in the field or in the veterans' hospitals, who may be entertainers or prostitutes; who may be the victims of war or of soldiers at war; who may protest war in general or some particular war. Insofar as *Platoon* presents war as a men's world, it is because Stone, like many film makers, focuses on the battlefield, hence on men as warriors. He thus exhibits a tendency that others have noted as common to military historians since the nineteenth century, the age of the militarization of support services and, therefore, the exclusion of women from the military camps. (See, e.g., Hacker)

It is not that women are totally outside of the world of *Platoon*. The men of *Platoon* do have some relationships with women. Thus, Taylor's mother and grandmother are mentioned, as are another soldier's girl-friend and American nurses. We see occasional Vietnamese women. But when Taylor comes to Vietnam, he is already estranged from his mother. Though he is in touch with his grandmother, by his fourth month in the war after Elias is killed, he loses his ability to continue his correspondence with her. The man whose girl-friend is mentioned is killed in the first fire-fight during his first week in Vietnam. When the American nurses are mentioned, it is there mastrubatory services to the wounded men that are anticipated. Of the Vietnamese women on screen, two are pointed out as mothers and are killed by American soldiers. The Vietnamese girls who appear are taken to be raped by American soldiers.

Men's relationships with women in the world of *Platoon* differ from men's relationships with women in the world created by most pre-Vietnam war films. In films about the first and second world wars, for example, men's relationships with women are essential to the preservation of their civility and humanity, hence for their ability to trust each other. A film that makes this point in the most poignant way is *Paths of Glory*.[3]

Paths of Glory is critical of high-ranking officers who treat war as a means to augment their power and as a vehicle for their political ambitions, independently of the consequences this may have for the rank and file soldiers. In *Paths of Glory*, these rank and file soldiers are sacrificed in a strategically unsound operation, accused of treason, tried in a mock trial and executed in order to cover up the incompetence of generals.

The setting of *Paths of Glory* is the French army during the first world war. There is only one time in the film that a woman is seen and this appearance lasts only a few minutes. She is a young German woman, thus a member of the French soldier's enemy's society. She is supposed to entertain the soldiers who have just witnessed the execution of their comrades in arms. The soldiers look at her and treat her as a sex object until she begins to sing a German folk love song. This at first silences them. Then they join her and as they do, they begin to cry.

This scene is the last in the film. It has another aspect. Listening first to the yelling of obscenities and later to the singing is the one officer who has not made war a self-serving means and who attempted to defend the soldiers. When he hears the soldiers yelling obscenities, he experiences for a moment doubt in his own judgement, wondering whether the elitist claims of his superiors that the soldiers he commands are no more than unruly beasts are true. His faith in his men is renewed as he hears them sing and feels the emotion in their singing.

In a film like *Paths of Glory* woman is the soldier's other and she is powerful enough to make it possible for him to leave war behind, even if momentarily. In *Platoon* woman is victimized by war, she is killed or reduced to a sex object, and she is powerless. She does not have the power to remove men from war. On the contrary, she loses her son or lover to it.

The powerlessness of women empowers men. The men of *Platoon* do not need women to rehumanize them in the context of the trauma of war which is strong enough to dehumanize them. They are self-sufficient because the group contains within itself a permanent tension and struggle between the power to dehumanize and the power to rehumanize. If they survive the war, they become self-sufficient individuals who contain these elements in permanent tension and struggle within themselves. At the end of the war, Taylor becomes self-sufficient in this way. Barnes and Elias, possessing only one of these elements, do not survive the war. But Taylor is the son of two men and he does not need women to rehumanize him because he contains the power to dehumanize—the Barnes power—and to rehumanize—the Elias power—within himself.

* * *

Little could valorize and edify war today, when thinking about it is so conflicted, more than a presentation which produces men like Taylor. Taylor, the experienced Vietnam war combatant, the "grunt," seems to embody an ideal that Jean Bethke Elshtain outlines as an alternative to both the masculine ideal of the "just warrior" and the feminine ideal of "beautiful soul" which she believes constrain Western thinking about war. The ideal is that of "maternal thinker" and she writes:

Maternal thinking as an alternative to Beautiful Souls and Just Warriors can do the following for us: it can answer the realist recognition that the world is tough and we must no be naive about it in a way Beautiful Souls cannot. For against Beautiful Souls the maternal thinker knows we cannot opt out of the world, nor remain pure within it... . With the Beautiful Soul, however, maternal thinkers recognize that human reality is about matters of the spirit, not just about power or material conditions. (348)

But Elshtain's concept of 'maternal thinking' is different from that of Sara Ruddick who coined the phrase. For Ruddick, war is anything but generative. According to Ruddick, maternal thinking is a capacity of women and not men which makes women into socio-culturally constructed yet nonetheless deeply moved pacifists. It is a capacity that soldiering erodes.

For Ruddick *Platoon*'s hidden claims about soldiering would be unbelievable as they should be. War may mature some men, but even the combatants who survive it are its casualties as the statistics on post traumatic stress syndrome for Vietnam veterans only begin to reveal.

Notes

[1]A version of this paper was presented at the meeting of the American Society for Value Inquiry with the American Philosophical Association, December 1988.
[2]*Platoon* was produced and directed by Oliver Stone, who also wrote the script. It was released in 1987.
[3]*Paths of Glory* was directed by Stanley Kubrick. It was released in 1957. It is based on Humphrey Cobb's novel by this name.

Works Cited

Arendt, Hannah, *On Violence*. New York: Harcourt, Brace and World, 1969.
Elshtain, Jean Bethke, "On Beautiful Souls, Just Warriors and Feminist Consciousness." *Women's Studies International Forum* 5 (1982): 341-348.
Girard, Rene, *Violence and the Sacred* (French, 1972). Baltimore: Johns Hopkins University Press, 1977.
Hacker, Barton C., "Women and Military Institutions in Early Modern Europe: A Reconnaissance." *Signs: Journal of Women in Culture and Society* 6 (1981): 643-671.

Ruddick, Sara, *Maternal Thinking*. 1989.

———. "Pacifying the Forces: Drafting Women in the Interests of Peace." *Signs: Journal of Women in Culture and Society* 8 (1983): 471-489.

Sartre, Jean-Paul, preface to Fanon, Frantz, *The Wretched of the Earth*. (French, 1961), New York: Grove Press, 1968: 7-31.

Xmas Ideology:
Unwrapping the American Welfare State
Under the Christmas Tree

Timothy W. Luke

Scores of films either about Christmas or with a Christmas element have been spun out of Hollywood's fascination with the holiday season. Yet, after their initial release, most of these works fall into almost complete obscurity, rarely being seen in theater release or on televised broadcast. A small handful, however, have acquired virtual cult status in being closely identified with the rituals of Christmas itself. These films, which this analysis directly addresses, are *Holiday Inn* (1942), *It's A Wonderful Life* (1947), *Miracle on 34th Street* (1947), and *White Christmas* (1954).* With the spread of television, these movies also have acquired intense followings in their perennial rebroadcast and re-release. They have become fixtures of the Christmas season as much as decorating the Christmas tree, braving the holiday shopping crush, and sipping eggnog by the fire. Repeated every holiday season, often numerous times on different broadcast channels or cable, viewing these films is becoming part of the Christmas ritual itself.

This analysis suggests that many of the central ideological discourses about the economy, the state, and society of the modern American welfare state are woven through the "classic" Christmas movies of the 1940s and 1950s. In decoding these films more critically, it seems fairly apparent that the outline for a special "Xmas ideology" is generated by the images of *Miracle on 34th Street* and *It's A Wonderful Life*. In turn, the representations of this ideology reveal the key codings, central symbols and basic signs of the larger post-1945 regime of colonizing the everyday lifeworld of ordinary Americans by corporate capitalism and the welfare state. As the focus of a significant ritual behavior, the cultural cues, and codes embedded in these films can have tremendous impact on a diverse nation-wide audience on a continuing basis year after year. On the one hand, these films continue to grow in popularity because they express the wishes and desires of many people in postwar America. On the other hand, however, they also may mediate a decentered mode of power cinematically by constituting critical

*This chapter is excerpted from a longer study dealing with all four of these films. The discussion here only considers *It's A Wonderful Life* and *Miracle on 34th Street*.

icons of identity, meaning and purpose in a setting where the forms of life often seem indistinct or wholly void of direction in the machinations of modern society.

Most importantly, they seem to embody and express the outlines of the fusion of civil society and the state through bureaucratic design during the New Deal era as it was managed in the partnership of corporate capital and the national state (see Braverman, Chandler, Ewen, and, Wolfe). The mobilization of traditional American cultural rituals and values during WWII to conquer the Axis continued after the war to organize the body politic in the mass consumption society. These films articulate some of the discourses of cultural meaning and direction that made such direction possible. By reexamining and rereading how these films seem to communicate such cultural values, we might understand more about the symbolic function they play in society, the basis of their enduring appeal, and the importance of various political actors, institutions and values in the organization of the current social regime. These texts, of course, are open to multiple interpretations. The partial, limited readings presented here of their economic, political and social implications simply call attention to some of their contextual connections to the modern American welfare state. Some of these meanings may have been intentional, others are incidental, still others are perhaps wholly unintended. Yet, given the origins and grounding of these films, they are, at least on some level, carriers of potent messages about the entire post-WWII order.

The Picture as Panopticon: Power Through Normalization

How does the individual subject come to self-knowledge and by what means does inner consciousness and individual conscience develop? What mediations might these kinds of self-knowledge work through? Foucault claims that one must reexamine people "in relation to other kinds of things which are customs, habits, ways of doing and thinking" (1979b: 11) to answer these questions. This analysis looks at individual subjectivity in relation to these two Christmas movies to examine how customs, habits, ways of doing and thinking may be acquired in part by watching and rewatching movies that are densely encoded with important political, economic, and cultural messages about the structure and process of everyday life in contemporary American society. As one kind of special disciplinary structure, films both reinforce and recreate a mythic structure of idealized subjectivity suitable to the reproduction of a particular constellation of personal, corporate and state powers in the era after 1945.

Film here is treated as a disciplinary practice fully capable of exerting a normalizing effect upon those who accept a role as its audience. Motion pictures, in a sense, serve as panoptical devices of normalization by casting particular behaviors and meanings as "truthful" expressions that can guide the behavior of individuals along particular tracks (see Foucault, 1980a; 1980b; and, 1979a). As Foucault asserts, "whenever one is dealing with a multiplicity of individuals on whom a particular form of behavior must be imposed,

the panoptic schema may be used" (Foucault, 1979a: 205). Film organizes
time, space and meaning along particular tracks of interpretation, while,
at the same time, denominating the individual's personal response in equally
tight fields of reception. In watching, decoding and interpreting meanings
from film, individuals enter complex discursive grids that frame and reframe,
define and redefine, articulate and rearticulate the demands of subjectivity
in the prevailing order of power. Knowing how to act, what to be, where
to go, when to speak, why to believe all are discursive directions implicitly
and explicitly inscribed in film. Consequently, it makes an immense amount
of sense to reexamine these Christmas films, which have a uniquely ritualized
position in contemporary American society, in terms of their special
disciplinary potential as ideological texts that construct certain kinds of
personal knowledge and social truth.

Meaning, of course, remains an essentially contested terrain of ideas
and interpretations where it individually is produced and consumed. Each
of these film texts, and the various political meanings they embody or elicit,
are also contested and contestable fields of interpretations. The particular
interpretive outcome of this examination of Christmas movies may be wrong.
But, the Christmas films' images carry complex meanings about the welfare
state in modern America which are no accident. Hence, we must look into
their possible political grounding. And, how well these interpretive narratives
theoretically fit the actual workings of the welfare state regime itself remains
to be determined in further reflection. Yet, this analysis presents one way
that films enable audiences to coproduce such psychosocial meanings as
they decode and receive the "truthful" messages of the diverse images
presented in films. The symbolic territory that each of these Christmas films
cover is not identical, but when taken together they do cast light upon several
different aspects of the contemporary system of power and knowledge.

It's A Wonderful Life and *Miracle on 34th Street*
The essential structure of Frank Capra's *It's A Wonderful Life* recounts—
in a flashback narrated by two angels from Heaven—the life of George Bailey
of Bedford falls as he struggles with the normalizing demands of personal
responsibility embedded in the everyday life of smalltown America. Always
wanting to leave town for a career elsewhere, George continually is forced
to remain by family, personal, and civic responsibilities. Brought to the
brink of complete dissolution by the pressures of his role as the head of
the town's building and loan society, George prepares to attempt suicide.
Yet, he is "rescued" in his attempt by a guardian angel, Clarence, who
allows him to see how Bedford Falls might have been without his continuing
presence in the life of the town. In this "Dreamland" vision of what might
have been, George recognizes that all he is and has been indeed is "important."
Seeing that life is worth living, he returns to his life in Bedford Falls on
Christmas Eve, recognizing that despite his continual disciplinary subjection
in the prevailing order still "it's a wonderful life." However, freedom denied

and repressed is exactly the real nature of this wonderful life rather than any liberation from the demands of everyday life.

Bedford Falls in many respects is presented as a microcosm of contemporary America. In it, a reactionary plutocratic capitalist, Mr. Henry F. Potter of the Bedford Falls Trust and Savings Bank, constantly maneuvers to own and control more of Bedford Falls through his financial power. Opposing him are the Bailey brothers of the Building and Loan, Peter and Billy, who struggle to pool together the resources of the town's common people to build a better and more progressive life for everyone. George's father, Peter, and his somewhat incompetent brother Billy, represent the limited powers but good intentions of local progressive elites as they constantly struggle against the oppressive powers of predatory local capitalists. As George's father tells George at the dinner table scene, he has spent his life at the Building and Loan believing that "in a small way we are doing something important. Satisfying a fundamental urge. It's deep in the race for a man to want his own roof and walls and fireplace, and we're helping him get those things in our shabby little office." When George's father dies, George is drawn into his place, forced against his will by the Building and Loan's Board (but for the good of all) to continue resisting Potter's power.

George wanted to become a world traveller, a major architect, and master builder in the big time away from his little hometown. However, he is trapped by circumstances into remaining in Bedford Falls for his entire life. Thus, the would-be Horatio Alger of nineteenth century small-town America is normalized into the George Bailey myth of twentieth century small-town America under the welfare state. Within this context, he continually struggles to fend off Potter and his exploitative aspirations. And, in the process, he uses his individual talents to keep the Building and Loan essentially solvent and doggedly committed to helping "little people" build small comfortable homes in Bailey Heights, the new Building and Loan Housing subdivision. In George's life, then, one sees the contradictory dynamics of normalization working out an individual text of subjectivity from his earliest boyhood through his adult maturation. The disciplinary codes of loyal son, responsible employee, civic leader, devoted husband, caring father, and local leader all form a particular subject in a grid of unrelenting control and limited freedom. While George's friends and brother are able to live out the dreams that he believes he has been denied, he is trapped within the demands of his obligations and chooses to live a life that is much less than he dreamed of but just enough to sustain hopes.

Henry F. Potter represents capitalism in two different modes, as puritanical and as hedonic. Working within Bedford Falls with George Bailey, George's father, and the other progressive leaders of the community, Potter is limited in how far his greed can take him. Given the progressive popular opposition, he only lives as a rentier on his existing assets while picking and choosing a few targets of opportunity to expand his smalltown capitalist empire. But, at the same time, the Building and Loan provides a democratic and accessible alternative as the little people bank together to oppose plutocratic powers like Potter. Thus, Potter plays the puritanical capitalist scrooge, hoarding his money and decrying the small saving and spending programs of ordinary people who use the Building and Loan rather than his bank. He owns a great deal of rental housing and controls a lot of the town's jobs, but he still is not totally hegemonic. As George decries during the depositor's run on the Building and Loan, Potter wants to dominate everyone in Bedford Falls:

If Potter gets hold of this Building and Loan there'll never be another decent house built in this town. He's already got charge of the bank. He's got the bus line. He's got the department stores. And now he's after us. Why? Well, it's very simple. Because we're cutting in on his business, that's why. And because he wants to keep you living in his slums and paying the kind of rent he decides.

Only collective action, led first by Peter Bailey and now by George, can stop him as George assures everyone that, "Now, we can get through this thing all right. We've got to stick together, though. We've got to have faith in each other."

Potter tries to buy George off at the point where Bailey Park was beginning to become a very successful alternative to Potter's slums, but George rebukes him as being "nothing but a scurvy little spider." Potter's greed and power lust also cause George's final crisis on the eve of his brother's return from the war when Uncle Billy misplaces $8,000 of Building and Loan money in Potter's bank and Potter finds and hides it. George begs Potter, as a Building and Loan board member, for a loan to straighten out his accounts. Potters tells him, "Why don't you go to the riff-raff you love so much and ask them to let you have eight thousand dollars. You know why? Because they'd run you out of town on a rail....But I'll tell you what I'm going to do for you, George. Since the State Bank examiner is still here, as a stockholder of the Building and Loan, I'm going to swear out a warrant for your arrest. Misappropriation of funds-manipulation-malfeasance." Because of Uncle Billy's bumbling of the Building and Loan deposit and Potter's mendacious exploitation of Billy's mistake, the Building and Loan is thrown into a crisis in the government auditor's discovery of the lost money. As the Building and Loan's head, George sees himself as betraying the people's trust. He finally snaps, goes on a bender, and then comes to jump off a bridge into an icy river to commit suicide and thereby raise the lost money from his life insurance. At that moment, Clarence jumps into the river first, and George follows to "rescue" him, which, in fact, begins Clarence's rescue of George by taking him into the "Pottersville" that Bedford Falls would have been without him.

With Mary's help during George's dreamland sequence with Clarence, Potter is proved absolutely wrong as George's good works over the years move virtually everyone in town to chip in and help George replace the $8,000 that Uncle Billy lost. Thus, again on Christmas Eve, the importance of family, community, and collective action all are reaffirmed as vital values to be embraced and followed in everyday life. Yet, as Clarence's vision of Bedford Falls without George shows, Potter also is represented as capitalism run amok without the countervailing forces of the Bailey brothers and their Building and Loan. Bedford Falls completely falls under the greed-driven domination of Potter, turning into Pottersville. Potter's power, in turn, now is shown as exceeding that of the smalltown rentier capitalist as he transforms every human need and any personal fantasy into a commodified good or service. The quaint Norman Rockwell vision of smalltown mainstreet America is reconstituted in Potter's unchecked hedonic capitalism into a flashy tenderloin district of sleazy dance joints, bars, bowling alleys, burlesques, all night grills, and bordellos. Without the progressive opposition of George Bailey and his coalition of "little people," capitalism turns every impulse and any dream into a marketable commodity. The result is a complete corruption of individual identity and the public sphere. The common good slips away into a totally individualized pursuit of personal pleasures and private vices made easily available by Potter's mobilization of desire to advance his own capital formation even more effectively than his previous puritanical mode of accumulation.

With Potter, Capra anticipates the cultural contradictions of capitalism in the twentieth century. Sensing that growth can proceed only so far under one set of cultural constraints grounded in sacrifice, frugality, and constant saving, the promise for greater growth lies in eliminating or lessening these cultural constraints by basing capitalist exchange on self-gratification, prodigality, and unchecked spending. While the Bailey brothers clearly are in favor of mass consumption, their progressive intent is to guarantee a decent life with all the essentials for everyone. The puritanical Potter would deny basic decency to the masses to control them and the hedonistic Potter would sell them total indecency to dominate them even more closely. In either event, George's influence or lack thereof is presented as a critical intervening variable in balancing this social equation. At the same time, the film represents in a microcosm the same class conflicts and forces at play in FDR's New Deal Welfare State. Just as in Bedford Falls, progressive political elites were struggling with reactionary elements of corporate capital who sought to oppress rather than emancipate the little people of America from their troubles. Without the welfare state system organizing everyone against predatory capitalist greed, all of America might become a Pottersville. And, just like America, these progressive elites all over the nation occasionally need a boost from an omniscient and omnipotent outside force, like Heaven or Washington, D.C., to put everything on the right track.

Miracle on 34th Street is perhaps the most explicit text on Xmas ideology. It begins with Kris Kringle (Edmund Gwenn) walking the streets of New York *in cognito* as Kris Kringle, an elderly but gentlemanly resident of a Long Island nursing home, on Thanksgiving. Nearby Doris Walker (Maureen O'Hara), a junior management type at Macy's, is organizing the line-up of the annual Christmas parade, but also is having tremendous trouble with a drunken fake Santa Claus on the Christmas float. It is Kris Kringle who first discovers the drunken Santa Claus, and then volunteers to stand-in for the drunk posing as him by riding on Santa Claus' sleigh in the float. Here, the stage is set as the riotously positive crowd reaction to Kris moves Maureen O'Hara to hire him as Macy's Santa for the season. At home, her daughter, Susan (Natalie Wood), of course, does not believe in Santa, even though she saw Kris Kringle in the parade imitating himself and thought he was the best ever. The rest of the film focuses upon overcoming the mother's and daughter's ardent disbelief in fantasy and Santa Claus by showing them the important power of fantasy and faith in coping with everyday life. Doris' doubt over Kris Kringle actually being Santa Claus leads her to have him visit Mr. Sawyer, Macy's own neurotic personnel psychologist, who exclaims Kris is a lunatic and plots to have him committed to the city's psychiatric hospital. Believing Doris set him up, Kris accepts his commitment until Fred Gailey (John Payne), who also has been wooing Doris, explains to him that it all was Sawyer's work. A lawyer by training, Fred accepts Kris' request to spring him from the hospital, but this necessitates Fred proving in court that Kris "is" Santa Claus. Mr. Macy and Kris' other friends willingly testify that they think Kris is Santa Claus, but Fred ultimately mobilizes the U.S. Post Office to deliver all of New York City's Christmas-time "letters to the North Pole" to Kris. Arguing that it is illegal to misdirect mail, Fred wins his case by proving that since the U.S. Government believes Kris *is* Santa Claus, then he must be. Judge Henry X. Harper, fearing the wrath of his family and the voters, concurs, and Kris is freed. Thus, corporate capital, the State of New York, the legal profession, and the Federal Government all coalign to certify that Santa Claus exists and this Kris Kringle is Santa. And, in the process, Kris Kringle successfully mobilizes the myths of Xmas and its consumerist fantasy for all who will give up on traditional practicality and puritanical realism to accept its liberating rewards.

Doris Walker, and her daughter Susan, are presented as the ultimate traditional capitalist personalities—realist, self-sacrificing, ascetic disbelievers in "make believe"—waiting to be won over to the new system of fantasy-driven capitalism. Kris Kringle sees them as his "test case," representing "in miniature" everything that has gone wrong in Christmas. Instead of understanding Christmas as a special "frame of mind," Doris and Susan have reduced it, as practical realists, to just "another day." Since Doris wants to raise Susan "realistically" and to be "completely truthful" with her, she does not allow her to believe in "fairy tales," "giants," or "Santa Claus" to avoid "a harmful mental conflict" with the real rat race of life. Yet, Kris Kringle pushes them both into believing in their fondest dreams; and, in their slowly accepting the vital importance of fantasy, he also works to have them realized in bringing the atomized individual lives Fred, Doris and Susan in midtown Manhattan together as a family unit in Susan's suburban dream house out on Long Island.

Miracle on 34th Street completely disconnects Christmas from its original Christian meanings and significance. From the opening scenes, Christmas is presented as an almost purely commercial spectacle and secular family ritual, driven by individuals' willingness to share in the fantasy of Christmas giving, Santa Claus, and personal dreams come true. Taking place in New York, the global capital of the emerging post-WWII transitional economy, Christmas and its rituals are designed, staged and managed by corporate capital (Macy's) and the state (New York City and State) to sustain and/ or increase consumer spending. The Thanksgiving Parade is an elaborate consumer spectacle, in part dedicated to commemorate Thanksgiving; but, to a larger degree, it is aimed at launching the Christmas shopping season. Warmed up with images of Santa and his reindeer, big business invokes consumers to spend the next two days after Thanksgiving and few weeks up to Christmas mobbing the department stores in a media-managed frenzy of personal consumption. The fantasy of satisfying basic needs in consumption and sharing within the family is embodied in the sign of Santa Claus, who decries the crass commercialization of Christmas, but who, at the same time, mobilizes his spirit of commercialized caring to fulfill the fantasy of consumerist society in Christmas exchange.

Miracle presents a double-edged but positive image of corporate capital using kindness and concern to move products. Once Kris Kringle as Macy's department store Santa starts the ball rolling by directly telling Macy's customers to shop at Gimbel's for products that Macy's does not have, Mr Macy sees the advantages of putting "public service ahead of profits." In doing so, he aims to cast Macy's as "the helpful store," "the caring store," "the store with a heart." Yet, this policy is implemented not as Kris Kringle argues, "to get 'the commercialism' out of Christmas," but rather "to make more profits than ever before." Thus, expanding this policy throughout the whole network of stores will equally expand results in building sales. Here, corporate capital is shown as losing its old "high pressure" entrepreneurial capitalist sales tactics of "selling the customer something he doesn't want," and acquiring a caring face of facilitating the customer's construction of his or her own merchandise fantasy. Likewise, once Macy's moves to this strategy, Gimbel's, Stern's and Bloomingdale's also jump on the band wagon of "helpful, caring salesmanship." Once the head of Macy's toy department saw Kris as a "born salesman," who will easily sell more toys than ever, Macy's signs on to the Santa Claus myth to the point of Mr. Macy himself swearing in open court that he believes Kris is Santa Claus.

Maureen O'Hara and Natalie Wood as hard-nosed realists and would-be iconoclasts, who say Santa Claus "is not real," represent all who doubt the powers of this Xmas ideology. And, in doubting, the film not only mobilizes their own personal experience to sway their beliefs, but also corporate capital and the state to prove that Santa Claus does indeed exist. While it all is done with a light tongue in cheek tone, it is clear that the film ends with the message that one should not *doubt* Santa Claus exists but rather that one should not doubt that he does *not* exist. His hand, on one level, is at work in reconciling personal doubts, individual anxieties, and wayward individuals needing the unity of the family. On another level, his hand checks the unconstrained greed of corporate capital in cut-throat competition within its own ranks (Macy's versus Gimbel's) by providing a caring conscience to serve the customer over getting the sale. And, on another level, he wins official sanction from the State of New York and the Federal government, "licensing" him as it were to continue providing these valuable ideo-political services within the secularized workings of post-1945 America. Therefore, the myths of secularized Christmas rituals are made legitimate beyond personal belief by becoming embedded in the accumulation interest of capital (Macy's would not deny Santa Claus' existence because it would kill sales), the legal careerism of the Supreme Court Judge (Judge Henry X. Harper would not deny Santa Claus' existence because it would destroy his reelection), and administrative agenda of the state (Post Office endorses his existence to clean out its dead letter files and open space for other uses.)

Once again, film provides a rationalization grid for anchoring and steering behavior through entertainment. Left as a movie, these tendencies have "maximum plausible deniability." Yet, when repeated over and over, these films can have significant ideological impact on their viewers by constructing "the truth" about Christmas as well as creating "knowledge" about how big business, the state, and contemporary society work. These outlooks and roles are there to be decoded and practiced, and in the right context, easily might be. *Miracle* anticipates and thematically resolves the increasingly common crisis of broken families coping with the myths and psychic demands of Christmas ritual. Its central thematic blends the family, the firm, and the state into a seamless whole, affirming the integrity of family life, the benevolence of corporate capital, and the wise guidance of the state. Legitimacy of myth is provided by capital (Macy's) and the state (U.S. Government and the State of New York courts), making Santa Claus an ideologically approved icon of happy suburban consumption and family unity.

Miracle actually is a close study of the entire post-WWII regime of social control shifting from dour, puritanical, individual labor to fantasy-driven, suburban consumerism. The benevolence and public-spiritedness of corporate capital brought into collusion with state power to affirm mass fantasies of consumer satisfaction via judicial litigation also takes flight here. It is the central fragment of the complex code of control. The regime of total administration via mass media myths, such as Santa Claus, breaks down ethnic, class and income barriers to create a single but polyvalent symbol representing the promise of giving, sharing, unselfish service, and faith in goodness.

Xmas Ideology: Unwrapping the American Welfare State

Christmas movies may seem an unlikely or far out place to find images of the American welfare state and its ideologies of power at work. Yet, they clearly are there. The class conflicts, political myths, and collective purposes of post-1945 America are strung directly through both of these films, particularly the increasingly significant role of the state, big business, and the military in mass society and the individual's life. In view of their salient position within many Americans' cultural enactment of their Christmas holidays, what messages and meaning do these films possibly present that keeps them in the center of the mass audience's attention. Apart from the splendid personal performances, entertaining stories or directorial virtuosity that might account for much of their enduring popularity, what broader cultural messages or deeper social significance can be found in all of these enduring film classics that tells us something about contemporary America and its celebration of Christmas?

The substance and style of popular culture are continually in the process of being reimagined and reinvented. Over time, however, certain expressions of popular culture—like the Christmas movies being appraised in this study— become fixtures in the self-understanding and practice of holiday rituals by ordinary individuals. In turn, their messages continue to reveal much about the popular imagination of the state, civil society, and everyday life in the present era. While these issues are multidimensional, it seems apparent that a more general and complex "Xmas ideology" emerges with the welfare state regime modern American society. In turn, the disciplinary norms of this ideology significantly direct the behavior and thinking of many throughout some aspects of their everyday activity.

It's A Wonderful Life, and *Miracle on 34th Street* cannot be dismissed as being "mere" movies. They are important ideological texts. In large part, "what we know" and "how we know it" are increasingly imparted through constant exposure to and learning from such cultural texts. Even more so that most other movies, these films have an almost permanent presence in recurrently showing up every year on or before Christmas. They are the cultural icons of a commercial Christmas that have helped to generate a Christmas culture driven on and by commercial icons. As hyperreal image packages, they have molded what is taken for being "the real" for four decades as the holiday has come to embody the promise of fantasies of personal reward, group solidarity, and cultural fulfillment realized for all at least once a year. They are among the primary mediations of the Xmas ideology. Specifically, there is embedded within this Xmas ideology an entire range of beliefs about personal life, fantasy, everyday happiness, individual obligation, material satisfaction, and personal belief that reveals much about the structure of the post-war modern American welfare state. The film discourses expressing this Xmas ideology are much more than symbolic interplays. They are, at the same time, the primary mediations of power, which deploy images of truth, codes of knowledge and systems of practice, to affirm specific constructions of power-ridden disciplines in the larger political order. They organize reality, they make possibilities of individual action available or unavailable, and they also frame the legitimacy and illegitimacy of institutions based on these discourses' truths.

On a material level, the Christmas shopping season is the centerpiece of the consumer-based economy of post-1945 America. Nearly two-thirds of the GNP is directly related to consumer spending, and often one-half to two-thirds of many businesses total receipts are dependent on holiday spending. The strength of consumer spending and consumers' willingness to spend more than "last year" are monitored weekly in the news media throughout the season. Not surprisingly, anything that accelerates these impulses, like continual viewing and belief in these Christmas films myths, is essential. They are among the most reliable and familiar of the season's mobilization orders to individual subjects as shoppers to express and fulfill their subjectivity as shoppers.

On a personal level, Xmas ideology presents consumption as the focus of meaning, purpose and identity in the current regime of power. Denied many rewards during the rest of the year, lacking identity and unity in everyday life, burned out by the pressures of career and vocation in the weekly grind, Christmas is a special time and space to fulfill, if only for a while once a year, all that is lacking otherwise and elsewhere—as Fred Gailey, George Bailey, Bob Wallace, Phil Davis, and Jim Hardy realize. Moreover, it is done with the full support of the state and capital, who recognize that the psychosocial charge of the Xmas ideology simultaneously might legitimize other power-driven state agendas and capital-accumulative corporate plans.

Xmas ideology, then, appears to be a basic code for practicing some kind of personal subjectivity and realizing some limited collective meaning in a social context that continually destroys the basis of subjective significance. To not accept its outlook, as "the realist" Doris Walker, "the suspicious" Judy Haynes, or "the confused" George Bailey learn, one lacks any center of existence. The modern dynamics of capitalism are driven by continual alienation and commodification, robbing individuals of their life force, personal meaning, and collective identity in the upheaval of the marketplace. To sustain these psychosocial tendencies, it appears useful to generate ideologies of self-gratification and fulfillment as in the cult of Christmas, which rather than being cast as a Christian celebration of Christ's birth, is instead turned into a fantasy of self-fulfillment and collective solidarity as part of a celebration of materialistic giving (and receiving). Consequently, like the modern secular welfare state, everyone of any faith or non-faith can participate in its workings. These possibilities serve tremendous social purposes, bolstering the ideological instruments of corporate hegemony, and driving the legitimation of consumer-based capitalism.

On the political level, the Xmas ideology is one framework of normalization enabling a decentered mode of power to insinuate its influences into the everyday life of individuals. It both expresses and effects these influences on the lives of those who attend their play and coproduce these meanings in these ways. The individual characters that it depicts are normalizing spaces/places of identification, comparison, justification for those who check out the film and television screens during the movies' perpetual reruns from year to year. Xmas ideology, then, is one of the key ingredients for understanding the politics of everyday life in post-1945 America. The mythos of home, hearth and family that was so potent in the song "White Christmas" during WWII, which surfaced first in *Holiday Inn*, and then became the focus of an entire presentation in *White Christmas* and *It's A Wonderful Life*. Xmas ideology represents a fusion of the personal and social, private and public, corporate and state, individual and collective that defines and legitimates what America is about since the New Deal: the fantasy of self-fulfillment in family unity and personal consumption in *Miracle on 34th Street*. The centrality of military power and experience are prominent in three of the films; the role of the state in fighting entrenched professional, business and private interests; the power of the media as mass mobilizing forces all surface in these films.

The Christian rituals of Christmas, then, have been transformed by capital and the state into one of the central myths of unity and meaning for the welfare state's consumerist family. Without it, the rituals of life in consumer society might disintegrate even more than they have already; hence, it has become an essential aspect of exchange in contemporary consumer society. It mediates the forms of personal subjectivity in the intimate sphere of caring with the corporate agendas of spending and having. Christmas as "Xmas" becomes in film an essential simulation of settled social traditions, family unity, and collective purpose in societies that otherwise largely lack them. The social disintegration and cultural fragmentation so endemic to everyday existence in society are suspended, postponed or bracketed in the normalizing utopian images of white Christmases, the pleasant escape to a Holiday Inn, Bedford Falls as America, and the bustling shoppers on 34th Street that frame the screen-driven construction of this holiday.

Works Cited

Braverman, Harry. (1974) *Labor and Monopoly Capital: The Degradation of Labor in the Twentieth Century*. New York: Monthly Review Press.

Chandler, Alfred D., Jr. (1977). *The Visible Hand: The Managerial Revolution in American Business*. Cambridge, MA: Belknap Press.

Ewen, Stuart. (1976). *Captains of Consciousness: Advertising and the Social Roots of the Consumer Culture*. New York: McGraw-Hill.

Foucault, Michel. (1980a). "The Eye of Power," *Power/Knowledge: Selected Interviews & Other Writings, 1972-1977*, ed. Colin Gordon. New York: Pantheon. 146-165.

——— (1980b). "Truth and Power", *Power/Knowledge: Selected Interviews & Other Writings, 1972-1977*, ed. Colin Gordon. New York: Pantheon. 109-133.

——— (1979a). *Discipline and Punish: The Birth of the Prison*. New York: Vintage.

——— (1979b). "On Governmentality." *Ideology and Consciousness*, 6 (Autumn). 3-19.

Wolfe, Alan. (1977). *The Limits of Legitimacy: Political Contradictions of Contemporary Capitalism*. New York: Free Press.

Sexual Politics in the 1980s:
Terms of Endearment and *Independence Day*

Douglas Kellner

With the eruption of the woman's movement in the 1960s, sexual politics became an especially charged terrain of Hollywood films.[1] During the late 1960s, Hollywood barely reacted to feminism and the woman's movement. While Hollywood attempted to capitalize upon the excitement generated by the student movement and counterculture with a series of films depicting the rebellions then going on in U.S. society, no comparable wave of woman's movement films appeared.[2] Few films of the era even attempted to depict individual woman struggling for liberation and a better life; no films have appeared to date which focus on the dynamics and experiences of the woman's movement: clearly one of the great scandals of exclusion in the sorry history of Hollywood film (consider the amount of films now re-negotiating Vietnam to grasp the magnitude of the complete exclusion of the woman's movement from Hollywood culture).

Some films of the late '60s and early 1970s did depict individual woman carrying through revolts against social restrictions and male domination. *Rachel, Rachel* (1968), a film produced by Paul Newman and Joanne Woodward, starring Woodward as an unmarried woman struggling for more dignity and a better life, projected an all-too-rare focus on a woman struggling alone to better herself. A film produced by Frank and Eleanor Perry, *Diary of Mad Housewife* (1970), depicted an upper middle-class woman rebelling against a mediocre marriage and highly constricted life. But probably the most interesting film of the era depicting woman's oppression is Barbara Loden's *Wanda* (1971). The film stars Loden as a poor woman from Appalachia, rebelling against a wretched life. Wanda leaves her husband and sets out on a failed quest for a better existence. Her encounters with men are uniformly oppressive and she is stuck at the end of the film, without money or prospects, in the midst of a crowd of people at a bar. Jerky camera movement and garish, expressive lighting highlights her desperation and alienation, alone in a crowd.

Most "women's films" of the first era of feminism were in fact anti-woman, punishing women who "destroyed" marriages and left their families (i.e. *The Rain People, The Godfather* and *Such Good Friends*). Another cycle of films dealt with mentally disturbed women (i.e. *Images, Play it as it Lays, A Safe Place, A Woman Under the Influence*, etc.), while blatantly

231

sexist films like Sam Peckinpah's *Straw Dogs* punished sexually provocative women with rape and abuse.

Thus with few exceptions Hollywood's initial response to the woman's movement was hostility. It seems that while the male-dominated Hollywood film industry could make concessions to '60s social movements in the sphere of civil rights, the anti-war movement, and counterculture, feminism was beyond the boundaries of what could be depicted and circulated in popular culture. As a version of liberal feminism, however, was institutionalized in U.S. society and culture, during the 1970s a cycle of liberal woman's films appeared depicting women's friendships and relationships (i.e. *The Turning Point, Julia,* and *Girlfriends*) and women struggling for independence and a better life (i.e. *Alice Doesn't Live Here Anymore, An Unmarried Woman,* etc.). In addition, Fonda and Jill Clayburgh starred in a cycle of liberal films that depicted woman struggling to define themselves, to succeed in jobs and to establish equalitarian relationships with men.[3]

As part of the "Right Turn" in U.S. culture in the late 1970s and into the Reagan era, however, conservative films attacking women and feminism appeared.[4] Male heroes returned to popularity and dominance and a cycle of films villianized women for destroying marriage and the family.[5] *Kramer vs. Kramer* (1979) showed a woman unhappy with her marriage and life leaving her husband and family; this popular film clearly sympathized with the male and never really explained the woman's need to break away from the marriage. *Ordinary People* (1980), the most important family film of the following year, showed a cold mother causing emotional distress for her teen age son and focused sympathy on the male members of the family. A cycle of films showed a woman leaving the family, or dying, and sympathetically portrayed males as nurturers while in most cases villifying women (i.e. *Author! Author!, The Champ, Hide in Plain Sight, Dinner for Eight,* etc.).[6]

Yet, within certain boundaries, sexual politics within Hollywood film is a contested terrain. Even during the conservative 1980s liberal women's films contested the conservative ones and, as women gained more power in Hollywood and U.S. culture, for the first time more radical feminist statements began appearing in films by Susan Seidelman (*Desperately Seeking Susan*), Donna Deitch (*Desert Hearts*), and Lizzie Borden (*Born In Flames, Working Girls*). Other women and some male filmmakers also had occasional feminist moments in their films, so that some liberal and even radical feminist positions countered the dominant conservative ethos of the popular culture of the 1980s.

In this paper, I shall depict a typical contest between liberal and conservative sexual politics in 1980s film by contrasting *Terms of Endearment* with *Independence Day*. Both films deal with contemporary issues in sexual politics and both focus on women, offering opposing models of womanhood. Both deal with cancer and how to cope with the death of loved ones. Both intensely focus on familial relationships, although they offer quite different models of the family and familial relationships. Both, I shall argue, are responses to feminism typical of the highly conflictual 1980s struggles over sexual politics and the films show some of the ways that popular culture of the era processed feminism. My argument is that *Terms* is typical of a conservative backlash to feminism while *Independence Day* presents a positive feminist perspective. While *Terms* is often seen as a "liberal" film, I shall argue that comparison with the thematically similar *Independence Day* shows that it is really closer to the conservative discourses of the era. That *Terms* was extremely popular while *Independence Day* was rather marginal, limited to occasional showing on cable television channels like HBO and video-cassette rental, points to the greater power of conservative ideology, channels of distribution and publicity, and hegemonic control of culture during the 1980s. The existence of films like *Independence Day*, however, show that strong feminist impulses are still alive in popular culture and constitute a perpetual threat to the conservative hegemony.

Negotiating Feminism: Terms of Endearment

 Terms of Endearment was one of the most popular Hollywood films released in 1983 and was awarded more Oscars than any other film that year. I shall argue that it can be read as a conservative response to feminism that takes primarily conservative positions toward the family, gender roles, abortion, and single women. Its ideological positions are sometimes blatantly proclaimed, sometimes more subtly, thus a close reading is necessary to bring out its conservative ideological problematics.

 Terms is entertaining and skillfully concocted, though I believe that its popularity derives from its cunning manipulation of real sexual conflicts and emotional problems that people are confronting today which it cleverly resolves through offering a traditional conservative agenda. Consequently, *Terms* combines a liberal openness to free sexual expression and an exploration of contemporary sexual politics with a conservative affirmation of the family and traditional gender roles. Part of the resurgence of melodrama in Hollywood cinema, it is one of the many recent films that show families undergoing crisis and potential disintegration. Unlike *Kramer vs. Kramer*, *Ordinary People, Author! Author!*, and many others which portray unfaithful or insensitive wives as wreckers of the family, and nurturing fathers as saviors, *Terms of Endearment* sympathizes with the wife and presents the husband in an extremely ambivalent light.[7] But on the whole *Terms* can be read as an attack on feminism and sexual liberalism.

 Terms is directed by James Brooks, a former TV director who was the creative force behind "The Mary Tyler Moore Show," "Rhonda," and "Taxi." The film combines codes of the TV situation comedy and TV movie melodrama to present a bourgeois morality tale in favor of the traditional family and traditional sex roles.[8] Although *Terms'* subject matter and melodramatic focus on family tragedy is related to the tradition of Hollywood "women's pictures" that flourished from the 1930s through Sirk's 50s family melodramas, its style and representational codes derive from TV and show a growing hybridization between film and television in the United States.[9]

Like an increasing number of television movies, it focuses on contemporary social problems and, stylistically, it quickly presents a situation of emotional intensity, and then cuts to another scene. This structure allows for little continuity, in-depth development of character, or serious discussion of the issues. The result is that everyday life is portrayed as a series of disconnected little dramas; this narrative strategy is evident in *Terms* which poses all significant life-choices around whether they preserve or threaten marriage/family. It concentrates almost exclusively on familial and sexual relationships and roles, and none of the main characters seem to have any outside interests or activities that transcend family or sexuality.

In the opening title sequence, a young mother, Aurora (Shirley MacLaine) anxiously bends over her daughter, afraid that the sleeping baby has stopped breathing. In the next episode, which follows the never depicted father's funeral, the lonely mother crawls into bed with her daughter. These interior scenes use soft muted lighting and romantically framed images of mother love, though they also seem to project a critical images of the overly doting U.S. mother (scathingly critiqued as "Momism" by Philip Wylie).[10] But by the end of the film mother love is strongly affirmed and redeemed, and the film as a whole demonstrates what are both proper and improper roles for wives, husbands, and parents.

The film then cuts to an exterior setting with the daughter Emma (Debra Winger) sitting on the front lawn with her skirt provocatively positioned over her knees as moving men leer at her while they carry the goods of a famous ex-astronaut to the house next door. Her blonde girl-friend Patsy leans over and pulls Emma's skirt down over her knees. The contrast between Emma's more open and expressive sexuality and Patsy's more conventional sexual role playing and behavior is maintained throughout the picture. In scene after scene, Emma's personality is sketched out and she is presented as a sympathetic vehicle for audience identification. On the night before her marriage, she is shown getting stoned with Patsy as they listen to Ethel Merman sing "Anything Goes." This scene presents Emma as sexy, feisty, slightly rebellious and blending the modern (smoking pot) with the traditional (getting married, listening to Ethel Merman). Although the melody of the pop song is traditional, its lyrics, "Anything Goes," suggest liberal openness and readiness for adventure. The song too thus blends the modern with the traditional and helps establish the framework for Emma's own character, although as the story proceeds, we shall see that "the modern" (i.e. sexual liberalism) is discredited and more traditional values and gender roles are ultimately affirmed.

Against her mother's advice, Emma marries Flap, a young English professor, whom her mother believes is too immature and not ambitious enough. Their early scenes together portray a strong mutual sexual attraction, and Emma is consistently associated with a provocative and procreative sexuality: she bears three children in less than ten years, and when she fears that her husband is having an affair, she takes on a lover herself. Although her depiction could be taken as a "progressive" and "modern" representation of a healthy woman who refuses to accept the traditional "double standard," in fact she is (symbolically) punished for her sexual transgressions. Moreover, confirmation of her husband's infidelity coincides with news of her cancer, so that a parallel is established between illness and sexual irresponsibility; the film's "message" ends up coming out that women (and married men) must carefully restrict their sexual activity or face the destruction of their marriage and thus lose the most enduring form of love and emotional support in the face of life's sufferings and tragedies.

The first two-thirds of the film focus on the mother-daughter relation and on problems of marriage and family. Like *Kramer vs. Kramer, Ordinary People, Shoot the Moon,* and other early 1980s family melodramas, nothing social or political intrudes from the outside to disturb the family drama. Though the film supposedly takes place within a thirty year period from the 50s to the present, no sixties politics are mentioned, no feminist issues are posed (except negative references to abortion), and the characters have no concern for politics or social life whatsoever. There are also no attempts to provide any historical context for the events, and though the action covers several decades, the only background changes are rather trivial, and not clearly defined changes of fashion. It is as if upper and middle-class everyday life were an eternal situation of unchanging personal conflicts and resolutions. In this life, there is no Society or History, but only Personal Relationships— in which the Family is shown to be the only trustworthy and enduring Form (capitals here signify present and absent archetypes of the films; in fact, *Terms of Endearment* is stylistically noteworthy for its adroit manipulation of stereotypes and clichés which make the mixture appear fresh and "modern").

Although the daughter Emma has a close girlfriend and the mother Aurora has several steady suitors, all their social activity is focused on the home; indeed, the scenes which show mothers, daughters, and the husband leaving the house to have affairs depict events that threaten home and family. During much of the film, *Terms* seems to defend more open and less constricted sex roles for women: Emma is sexually expressive and even rebellious, and Aurora too takes on a lover after resisting for years physical relationships with her Houston suitors. Aurora's recognition of the fleetingness of life results in her abandonment of a rather traditional refusal to enjoy life and to seek both passionate sex and intimacy with a male after her 50th birthday, and Emma also refuses to passively martyr herself. Thus *Terms* seems to point to a new latitude toward sexuality and a more independent stance of women toward men in contemporary U.S. culture, although more traditional gender roles are affirmed later in the film.

Consequently, *Terms of Endearment* seems to be a conflictual text with contending ideological tendencies, some patently conservative, others less easily assimilable to traditional morality. In fact, like many Hollywood films, it wants to have things both ways, presenting, on one hand, liberalized sexual values for the more "modern" audience and conservative values for more traditional folks. The ideological negotiation thus also ends up being a successful marketing strategy. But after seeming to take the side of sexual liberalism, *Terms* then advances a conservative model of the family and traditional U.S. values and gender roles against feminism and sexual liberalism.

Mothers, Daughters, and Men

Terms is distinguished by its focus on mother-daughter relationships and problems of single or widowed mothers, as well as by its treatment of contemporary sexual politics. Since most Hollywood films have been centering on father-children relationships, and problems of teen-age boys growing up, the emphasis on mother-daughter relationships seems to provide a feminist twist to the film. Its portrayal of the relationship is, however, ideologically ambiguous. On one hand, it realistically portrays the tendency of mothers to excessively dwell on their daughters and to live vicariously through their lives. And it depicts how some daughters remain overly dependent on their mothers for primary relationships and emotional support. As the film progresses, it depicts shifting and evolving relations between the mother and daughter and focuses on Aurora's growing ability to become a competent and loving mother.

At first, Aurora seems to be rather self-centered and does not seem to need the daughter. She does not go to Emma's wedding, is not close to Emma's friends, and does not seem to be particularly close and intimate with her daughter. However, they seem to draw closer together after Emma marries and leaves the house. The film plays here on anxieties that aging women face when their children leave home that they are no longer needed. *Terms* assuages this anxiety by showing a situation where the daughter increasingly needs her mother's advice, support, and love. It holds out the hope that single, middle-aged women can find love and purpose after raising their children. Although there are frequent conflicts between mother and daughter, ultimately they are resolved and the film suggests that mothers continue to have an important role to play in their daughter's lives, thus assuring mothers that they are still needed.

Terms also represents real conflicts between contemporary husbands and wives. The husband puts his career and other interests before his wife and never really gives her an opportunity to help decide if they should take new jobs and move or not. Though the real conflict between domesticity and career is portrayed, it is never really developed. Likewise, the crucial issues of birth control, choices concerning child-bearing, and abortion as a solution to unwanted pregnancies are not really posed though they hover in the background of the drama. At one point, Emma discovers that she is pregnant with her third child and the mother suggests abortion. Emma reacts with horror and anger and positions the audience to experience abortion negatively, but the film never debates the issue or presents any feminist options. It is significant here that it is the mother who suggests the abortion and the daughter who resists it; this generational twist shows younger women becoming more traditionalist and points to pro-life positions taking hold of contemporary women.

Most of the main characters, in fact, contain a contradictory mixture of "liberalism" and "conservatism," though traditionalist values and roles end up ultimately being affirmed. Debra Winger's portrayal of Emma, for instance, contains a contradictory mixture of representations of a new, more independent woman, and of a traditional loving daughter and mother. Winger has been consistently playing relatively strong women who end up submitting themselves completely to men in her 1980s films (*Urban Cowboy, Cannery Row, An Officer and a Gentleman.*) Her unrepressed sexuality and vitality in *Terms* is structured into a traditional wife/mother role and though her affair with the banker seems to indicate that her sexuality cannot be satisfied within the confines of marriage, in fact her husband's infidelity justifies her "transgressions" and makes the point that the family cannot survive with infidelity on the part of either husband or wife. Thus what seems to be affirmed (i.e. open marriage, transgression of "double standards") is ultimately discredited.[11]

Aurora too is initially portrayed as a mixture of "liberal" independence and attitudes, and traditional sexual conservatism in her relations with her "gentlemen" friends in Houston. Emma's girlfriend Patsy represents the independent working woman living the "fast life," though she is deeply attracted to Emma's daughter and wants to raise her when they discover that Emma is dying. Garrett and Flap both contain a mixture of likeable and unpleasant characteristics, though the audience is positioned to view Garrett's move toward a traditional husband/father role as a positive development, while Flap's failures as husband/father represent him in increasingly negative ways. He doesn't really seem emotionally wrought-up over Emma's death and is even shown in the hospital cafeteria at one point with a gigantic meal and a book which he is perusing, until he spots Aurora who then proceeds to tell him that under no circumstances will she permit him to raise the children.

Thus while Flap is initially portrayed sympathetically, he is shown to be too weak and irresponsible to assume the responsibilities of husband and father. It appears that Flap just drifts into affairs because he is naive and immature, rather than being actively sexually aggressive. Yet he is also selfish and manipulative, and always seems to be running off to the library (and other women), leaving his wife to do all of the domestic chores and caring for the children. Moreover, Emma never questions the traditional roles of domesticity and child-rearing, nor does she suggest that he play a role in these areas. But while *Terms* implicitly raises the issue of whether the wife should have sole responsibility for child-rearing, this issue is never really articulated and so no sharing of domestic labor is posited.

Although the reasons for *Terms*'s popularity with male audiences are "overdetermined," perhaps men identify with Flap's refusal to take more domestic responsibility and with the refusal of both Flap and the astronaut Garrett to commit themselves to monogamous relationships. Perhaps *Terms* also projects a subliminal male fantasy of the wife dying so that the male can pursue another love interest.[12] While Flap initially claims that he wants to raise the children after Emma's death, he surrenders them to Aurora without any real protest, admitting that he's not really suited to raise the children, and thus freeing himself from parental responsibilities. Consequently, although the theme of male flight from the family is not really developed, it does provide a subtext which may in part account for male attraction to the film.[13]

This theme is amplified through Jack Nicholson's astronaut character, Garrett, who shifts from portrayal as a dissolute and irresponsible bachelor into an acceptable father-figure and potential husband. At first, Garrett is portrayed as a rather vulgar, somewhat neurotic, playboy who is basically alone and slightly pathetic. When he enters into the relation with Aurora, he becomes temporarily transformed into a more charming and likeable fellow—until he tells Aurora that he cannot assume responsibility for a relationship. And then, as mentioned, he is redeemed and transformed when at the end he takes responsibility for the relation and even enters into a father role. The final scenes reinforce traditional gender and familial role models by showing Aurora assuming the mother role with Emma's daughter while Garrett walks away with the boy, with his hand over the boy's shoulder in a fatherly gesture.

Consequently, the film ends by reconstituting the family that had been destroyed by infidelity and the wife's ensuing illness and death. On the whole, *Terms of Endearment* suggests that without the bonds of matrimony, familial responsibility, and strong commitment, males will engage in rampant promiscuity. Consequently, the film advances the conservative anti-feminist argument that women's liberation and the ERA are bad because they would allow men to leave the family; it suggests that the only thing holding men back from incessant womanizing are the traditional familial bonds and roles. Any departure from this norm will wreck havoc and cause disaster.

Thus, *Terms* uses an engaging story line, appealing characters, real social problems and conflicts, and seemingly *realist* style to convey its conservative messages. Although it seems to affirm sexual liberalism and "modern" values as the daughter takes on a lover and the mother pursues sex in her fifties, the film ends by validating only certain sexual arrangements and attacking others. By shifting the focus on the mother Aurora and her astronaut lover during the second half of the film, the conflicts within Emma's family are displaced and attention focuses on whether Aurora will be able to humanize and domesticate the rather obnoxious astronaut. She does and by so doing the film suggests that the family and marriage provide the only real solution to the problem of single people. In fact, the mother and the astronaut are the only two characters who undergo significant transformations. The mother is frustrated and unhappy until she takes on a lover, and the astronaut is transformed from a dissolute Lothario into a "nice guy" when he assumes the husband/father role in the end. At first resisting any "commitment" to Aurora, he begins to redeem himself when he shows up at the hospital where Emma is dying, and becomes more "humanized" and sympathetic by the end when he assumes the father role with the daughter's bitter and emotionally closed son in the final funeral scene. The astronaut thus can finally realize the promise of his name: Garrett Breedlove. The film portrays his redemption through assuming the roles of husband and father, and thus privileges these roles as the "proper" functions for men. (This may also help explain the film's popularity with men: underneath the macho surface dwells a "nice guy"—a reassuring message for neurotic males who engage in sexually manipulative and irresponsible behavior who also want to feel good about themselves.).

Cancer, Death, and the Triumph of Conservatism

It is the cancer scenes, however, that function most centrally and probably effectively in conveying *Terms'* conservative sexual politics. When Emma's cancer is discovered, the family is reconstituted in the final scenes with shots of Emma's children with Aurora and Garrett together in family portrait scenes which legitimate the family as the most natural and sustaining institution and social arrangement. The scenes of Emma dying, surrounded by husband, children, mother, and friends call attention to what is lost through her disease (and what would have been lost if she and her husband continued to have affairs).

The scenes depicting Emma's unsuccessful fight against cancer use intense white lighting and the sterile hospital decor to dramatize the family's tragedy. The very length and emotional jabs of the cancer scenes remind the audience of how important family life is and what a mistake it was to look for love outside of the family. The scenes elicit morbid sympathy from the audience and position it to accept traditional sex roles and values. Its lengthy duration on screen is a correlative to the idea of endurance that it promotes, and the *"Love Story* with children" scenes showing all the family members pulling together to come to terms with their grief and love positively promotes certain role models and values, and shows others to be discredited and inauthentic. In fact, one of the film's many objectionable features is the use of a serious and deadly disease like cancer as a vehicle for pro-family ideologies. Rather than exploring how people cope with cancer (as in *Independence Day*), it is merely a plot device to focus sympathy on the wife and to enable the family to reconstitute itself.

Terms therefore ends up affirming "mid-American" and suburban values of marriage and family over more urban cosmopolitanism. In the grocery store scene where Emma meets her soon-to-be-lover, the mid-West banker tells the check-out girl that she is being extremely rude when Emma doesn't have enough money to pay the bill, and then says that she must be from New York (the audience with which I saw it broke out into laughter and applause). When the dying Emma travels to New York with a friend, the New York working women talk of their divorces, abortions, and herpes. In the New York scenes, the camera focuses on the faces of the working women, emphasizes their condenscending and pseudo-sophisticated ways of relating to Emma, and generally represents them negatively. Clearly, liberal cosmopolitanism is being rejected in favor of conservative, mid-American, family values. All working women, or independent women without men, are shown to be unhappy and frustrated. The proper role for women is to be faithful, nurturing wives and mothers. That is, of course, a conservative male fantasy. In this light, Andrew Sarris suggests that Emma is the "fantasy Nurturing Woman" projected by author Larry McMurtry, upon whose book the film is based; this same nurturing woman figure was previously embodied in other films based on McMurtry's novels in the characters of "Cloris Leachman's coach's wife in *The Last Picture Show*, and in Blythe Danner's *Loving Molly*."[14] *Terms* insinuates that transgressions of these norms lead to cancer, herpes, abortion, sexual frustration, and emotional incompleteness. Thus suffering and submissiveness are valorized as proper roles for women, and the "terms of endearment" turn out to be those familial ties, rituals, and love which provides a haven in an otherwise heartless world.

Thus, *Terms of Endearment* ends up advocating traditional gender roles and legitimates the family as the only institution capable of offering support and nurture in the face of life's hardships. Nurturing mothers and faithful/ responsible fathers are affirmed, and selfish and unfaithful mothers, and weak and irresponsible fathers are discredited. In the face of Emma's impending death, the characters and audience are taught the importance of family and the errors of sexual transgressions. Aurora has matured and learned what it means to be a proper mother in the course of the film, and the final scenes show the family being reconstituted with her assuming responsibility for the discipline and nurture of the children. And Garrett too seems to be maturing and becoming ready to take on the responsibilities of being a husband and a father. Consequently, in the last post-funeral scenes the family is reconstituted with Aurora and Garrett ready to be parents to Emma's children.

Term's popularity is a revealing indicator of the need that people have for emotional stability and security in a time of instability and insecurity. The whole cycle of family melodramas shows vast confusion concerning sexual roles and politics and the need for reassurance. While the cycle as a whole can be read as a symptom of the increasing self-concern of an ascendent white upper middle class that no longer wants to be bothered with questions of poverty or inequality, it can also be read as a sign of the crisis of values in U.S. institutions and the need for an alternative sexual politics that provides security, empathy, warmth, and love without the neurotic and oppressive forms of patriarchy and dependence in the traditional family. The popularity of such melodramatic family films thus provides a challenge to feminist and leftists to reflect on the confused state of interpersonal relations and everyday life in advanced capitalist societies and to provide meaningful alternatives to middle class life and values.

But *Terms* itself shows no viable alternatives. Patsy's desire to raise the daughter as a single mother is discredited when the dying Emma tells Patsy that the younger brother could not bear to have his sister taken away and that the children must remain together. Since the burning issues of contemporary sexual politics are displaced in the film, we are left with the traditional family as the only institution capable of supplying warmth, love, and nurture to children. Supplying alternatives requires both that we attempt to reshape our lives and relationships and that cultural workers attempt to represent alternatives to the traditional family in film and video work.

Liberal Feminism in Independence Day

An attractive alternative to patriarchal famialism is found in the excellent but little known film *Independence Day* (1982). The film was released without much fanfare and publicity and has received little critical attention. It was directed by Robert Mandel and is based on a script by novelist Alice Hoffman. Mandel had directed plays in New York and went to the American Film Institute to learn filmmaking in the late 1970s. His later films include *Touch and Go* and *F/X*, though neither attains the level of the earlier *Independence Day*, which might well be due in large part to the sensitive script by Hoffman.

The story focuses on a young woman photographer, Mary Ann Taylor, played by Kathleen Quinlan, who lives in a small town in the Southwest, who is struggling for independence within a conservative small town culture. The film uses the codes of realism to portray her relationships with her mother Clara (Francis Sternhagen) dying of cancer; her quiet and supportive father (Josef Sommer) who runs a diner in which she works; and her boyfriend Jack (David Keith) and his sister Nancy (Dianne Wiest) who is married to a husband Les (Cliff DeYoung) who brutalizes her. The film takes place in a working class milieu and is sensitive to the nuances of both gender and class.

On the whole, the film achieves a nice balance between family, sexuality, work, and aspirations for a more creative and fulfilling life. The young woman, Mary Ann, is an aspiring photographer who is constantly shown employing her craft. The film opens with shots of her and her camera capturing the ethos of the small town environment. Near the end of the film, she wins a scholarship to study photography in Los Angeles. With her dying mother's blessing, she leaves town, breaking away and gaining her independence. Her boyfriend Jack at first attempts to get her to stay, and then accepts her decision; at the end, he joins her in Los Angeles, showing that you can get your career goals and your boyfriend too—a concession to Hollywood romantic codes and the "happy ending" which is one of the few ideological limitations of the film. Still, even this somewhat corny and conventional ending subverts the code of the male-dominated romance which returned with a vengeance in the 1980s after having been challenged and somewhat undermined in films of the 1970s.

Indeed, the relationship itself is somewhat unconventional. The boyfriend, Jack, is, initially at least, shy and Mary Ann must make the first moves to initiate the relationship. She is portrayed as sexually open and assertive without falling into traditional sex object modes. Both Mary Ann and Jack seem to care for each other and both are sensitive to the other's needs and interests. The boyfriend is a mechanic who is not particularly educated or creative, though he is basically a decent fellow who embodies non-patriarchal male values and learns to come to respect and accept Mary Ann's independence.

Jack's father and brother-in-law by contrast represent patriarchal behavior at its worst. At the beginning of the film, the father berates Jack for failing in engineering school while praising the brother-in-law Les's success as a salesman. The father brutally dominates his wife and children who for the most part—except for Jack—accept his crude manners and domineering demeanor. Les is even a worse patriarch and brutalizer of his wife Nancy. He constantly insults her, plays vicious games with her, and beats her when she fails to obey his every arbitrary and often brutal whim.

Independence Day thus carries through a rather systematic indictment of patriarchy. It also contains a contrast between a non-patriarchal, loving and egalitarian family (Mary Ann's) and Jack's oppressive patriarchal familal structure and Les's highly pathological and violent patriarchal behavior. The film also presents a contrast between women who silently submit to even the worst patriarchal abuse and women who rebel against it. The film thus contains a sharp delineation between positive and negative role models for both men and women and sharp critical visions of patriarchal domination and abuse.

Another feminist aspect of the film, moreover, is constituted by the depiction of Mary Ann's relationships with her mother and her boyfriend's sister. The mother-daughter relationship is depicted with quiet and subtle sympathy and insight, in opposition to the melodramatic excess of *Terms.* Their modes of communication are open and loving and the suffering from the mother's cancer highlights their love and sympathy for each other, rather than dramatizing ideological points as in *Terms.* The key dramatic scenes involve conversations between Mary Ann and her mother and in all cases the mother is supportive and loving. The turning point of the film occurs when a photographer whom Mary Ann idolizes arrives to tell her that she has been accepted into photography school and that he thinks that her work is exceptional and is eager to work with her. Because of her love for her dying mother and wish to remain with her, Mary Ann rejects the scholarship offer. The mother then comes to her and gives her daughter an envelope of money, saved over the years by scrimping and saving, as a token of love and support for her daughter's endeavors. The mother explains that this was her "escape money" which she saved in case she wanted to leave town. She explains that she now wants to give it to Mary Ann so that she can realize her dreams. "You just go," her mother advises, handing her the money. While this might be read as an example of the self-sacrificing mothers beloved by classical Hollywood film, its inflection and contemporary character rather point to the impossibility of the mother's generation attaining a degree of liberation and an independent life that is now open to the daughter.

Mary Ann's relation with her boyfriend's sister Nancy is also depicted with sensitivity and awareness of women's relationships and modes of communication. The two women genuinely care for each other and attempt to communicate and understand each other. One afternoon Mary Ann visits Nancy and they make "grasshoppers." As she gets a bit drunk, Nancy opens up for the first time. The women are laughing and talking together when Les comes home; enraged that his dinner is not ready, he throws Mary Ann out. She helplessly watches Les beating his wife through the window and races to Jack who speeds over to his sister's house where he finds a badly bruised and beaten Nancy. Jack then drives to a local bar where he finds Les with his girlfriend and gives him a thrashing. Les returns to Nancy and tells him that he will get even with Jack while forcing Nancy to invite him over that night.

The film depicts Nancy as unable to leave the husband and gain independence. Earlier in the film she attempted suicide when she was unable to break away and eventually she chooses a violent resolution to her dilemma. The day when Les returns home to avenge himself on Jack, Nancy seals the windows and turns on the gas. Les arrives, sniffs the gas, and sees Nancy greet him with a smile as she lights the match to blow up the gas filled house. Earlier, Les had thrown lit matches at her as one of his sick games and the fatal match emerges as a symbol to resolve the problem of the (mismatched) marriage. The episode dramatizes the difficulty some women have in escaping from a bad marriage and the need for sisterhood and a strong feminist movement to help women in trouble.

Independence Day uses traditional Hollywood codes (romance, small town drama, family melodrama) to make its feminist points, some of which are made subtly and quietly while others are powerfully dramatized. While the film is engaging and has some intense dramatic conflicts, for the most part it is slowly paced and carefully explores the life and relationships of its protagonists. Mary Ann is an extremely positive role model of the young woman striving for independence who is shown to be autonomous, competent, loving, and creative. The camera generally presents her in relationships to other people and the environment, rarely fetishing her in close-ups or frames that would abstract her from everyday life relationships. Male hero films, by contrast, use framing, lighting, and camera angles to deify the male heroes, to make them appear larger than life, as when Indiana Jones or Sylvester Stallone characters are framed as quasi-gods who possess supernatural power and greatness. The only dramatic close-ups in *Independence Day*, however, take place in the key scene with Mary Ann and her mother that uses alternating close-ups (the famous suture effect this time employed for feminist purposes).

Independence Day by and large employs representational and narrative strategies which focus on the texture of everyday life and the importance of relationships to other people and one's environment. It manages to give each character life and individuality while also utilizing a feminist framework to present and analyze the different modes of male patriarchal and non-patriarchal behavior and of women submitting to domination or struggling for independence. The film thus exhibits a successful blend of feminism and realism and—against some avant-garde film theory—shows how the codes of realism can be used to make feminist points. Its limitations, on the other hand, are a perhaps too conservative use of Hollywood codes of romance which frame Mary Ann's actions. Heterosexual, monogamous romance and marriage and family are the unquestioned bedrocks of the film's conceptual framework which delineates good and bad models of these institutions without more radically attacking the institutions themselves.

Yet the film's attack on patriarchy is systematic and compelling and it provides an unusually strong liberal feminist view of independence, sisterhood, and solidarity. It thus goes about as far as liberal feminism and Hollywood can go without radically questioning the codes of Hollywood film and contemporary sexual politics. Consequently, while the film does not reach the level of a more radical feminism, it provides a good example of a liberal feminist intervention in the sexual politics of the 1980s.

Conclusion

Films dealing with sexual politics in the 1980s are thus best read as a response to feminism which either attempt to incorporate feminist positions or to attack them while defending counterpositions. While it has some "liberal" aspects, *Terms of Endearment* can be read as a conservative response to more feminist positions on abortion, marriage, the family, and gender roles. For *Terms*, women are primarily mothers—period. Its "terms of endearment" are the old terms of famialism and women's destiny and proper role as mothers. Mothering is privileged as the essential activity for women, while *Independence Day* stresses the importance of independence, creativity, and a wealth of social relationships. *Terms* avoids the problem of patriarchy altogether. It's men are at worst, weak, as when the uncommitted Garrett engages in pathetic womanizing or, unable to commit himself, pulls away from Aurora; Flap is simply weak, unable to avoid temptation and to be honest with Emma. *Independence Day*, by contrast, presents extremely critical perspectives on patriarchy and exhibits forms and mechanisms of patriarchal domination and women's submission.

Films are thus rhetorical constructs that take positions on key issues of the era. *Terms* reasserts motherhood, family, and women's destiny as mothers during a time when these prerogatives were being challenged. It explicitly opposes abortion and dramatizes the destructive aspects of adultery, of threatening the bonds of marriage with extra-marital affairs. In addition, Aurora and Emma in *Terms* have no interests outside of their family. Mary Ann, by contrast, is at least interested in pursuing a creative career and realizing personal dreams (while the career women in *Terms* are shown as uniformly miserable, denatured and alienated); characters in *Independence Day* are also shown concerned with people and events outside of the family— although neither film depicts people interested in politics or involved in political or social movements. Yet within the field of sexual politics,

Independence Day presents more liberal feminist takes on contemporary issues than *Terms*. Consequently, the field of sexual politics during the 1980s is best read as a contested terrain in which Hollywood film presents examples of liberal and conservative positions, with occasional more radical examples rising from the margins, mostly from the independent film movement.[15] Politically sensitive film criticism should thus read films relationally within the context of contemporary political struggles and discourses. In this way, political film criticism can depict the dominant struggles going on in society and the opposing positions with their strengths and limitations. Doing film criticism without political analysis is a problematical and blinkered undertaking in view of the highly charged politics of Hollywood film. This is especially true in the domain of sexual politics where contemporary struggles in politics and culture reveal that the issues posed by the movements of the 1960s have barely begun to be confronted; their resolution depends on future struggles, movements, and their cultural representations.

Notes

This article is based on work done with Michael Ryan on our book, *Camera Politica: The Politics and Ideologies of Contemporary Hollywood Film* (Bloomington, Indiana: Indiana University Press, 1988). An earlier version of the analysis of *Terms of Endearment* appeared in *Jump Cut*, 30 (1988) pp. 10-12. For helpful comments on this article, I would like to thank Ryan, Judith Burton, Esther Fuchs, Lisa Gornick, Flo Leibowitz, Dan Thibideoux, Paula Russell, and Laura Thielen and other *Jump Cut* editors for comments and provocative questions which helped with revision.

[1]On the relationships between women's films and the politics of the era, see Molly Haskell, *From Reverence to Rape* (Baltimore: Penquin Books, 1974); Joan Mellon, *Women and Their Sexuality in the Cinema* (New York: Dell, 1973); and Kellner-Ryan, ibid.

[2]On the cycle of New Left, black, counterculture, and women's films of the 1960s see Kellner-Ryan, ibid. On independent films of the era, see David James, *Allegories of Cinema: American Film in the 60s*. Princeton: Princeton University Press, 1989.

[3]On the cycle of women's films in the late 1970s, see Charlotte Brunston, "A Subject for the 70s," *Screen*, vol. 23, nrs. 3-4 (Sept-Oct 1982): 20-29 and Kellner-Ryan, ibid.

[4]On the "Right Turn" in U.S. politics, see Thomas Ferguson and Joel Rogers, *Right Turn* (New York: Hill and Wang, 1986). Kellner-Ryan, ibid, depicts the right turn and coming of Reaganism through the prism of the Hollywood films of the era.

[5]On the return of the male hero to centrality in Hollywood film after a brief cycle of anti-hero films in the late 1960s and 1970s, see Kellner/Ryan, ibid. On the hero myth in Hollywood films and U.S. popular culture, see Robert Jewett and John Lawrence, *The American Monomyth*: (University Press; 1988; second edition).

[6]A number of articles have criticized the scapegoating of women in films like *Kramer vs. Kramer, Ordinary People*, etc. which can be interpreted as attacks on feminism. See Thomas W. O'Brian, "Love and Death in the American Movie," *Journal*

of Popular Film and Television, Vol. IX, No. 2 (Summer 1980-81): 91-92; Elayne Rapping, "The View From Hollywood: The American Family and the American Dream," *Socialist Review* 67 (Jan-Febr 1983): 71-92; Molly Haskell, "Lights...Camera...Daddy!," *The Nation* (May 28, 1983): 673-675; and Kellner-Ryan, *Camera Politica*.

[7]None of the reviews of *Terms of Endearment* that I have found probed its sexual politics and when I discuss the film with students, they invariably describe it as "liberal," perhaps because of the explicit sexuality and presence of figures like Jack Nicholson, Shirley McLaine, and Debra Winger.

[8]On the codes of TV situation comedies as morality plays, see Douglas Kellner, "TV, Ideology, and Emancipatory Popular Culture," *Socialist Review* 45 (May-June 1979): 19-22.

[9]On the tradition of Hollywood women's films, see Haskell, *From Reverence to Rape*, ibid, and Marjorie Rosen, *Popcorn Venus* (New York: Avon, 1973).

[10]See Philip Wylie, *The Generation of Vipers* (New York: Pocket Books, 1958). *Terms of Endearment* begins with the stereotype of the selfish, needy, and domineering mother but shows her softening and humanized through the relationship with her lover and her assuming a more proper mother's role with her daughter as the years go by.

[11]The filmmakers cut out scenes portraying the fun, tenderness, and intensity of the love-making between Emma and the mid-western banker. See the article by John Lithgow who played the banker in *Film Comment* (Nov-Dec 1983), pp. 28-32, who details the cut scenes. Such deleted scenes would have gone too far in the direction of celebrating extra-marital sexuality while the filmmakers decided to firmly come down on the side of traditional morality.

[12]On the standard melodramatic formula of wives dying, or disappearing, so that the husband can pursue other love interests, see Charles Derry, "Incest, Bigamy, and Incurable Disease" and Ellen Seifer, "Men, Sex, and Money in Recent Family Melodramas," both in *Journal of University Film Association*, 1983.

[13]On male flight from the family, see Barbara Ehrenreich, *The Hearts of Men* (New York: Doubleday, 1983).

[14]Andrew Sarris, "The Topic of Cancer," *Village Voice* (Dec. 13, 1983): 72. Sarris also remarks: "To win an Oscar, actresses must be suffering and submissive creatures with excessively messy lives. This is both the message and the mechanism of *Terms of Endearment* as the most widely admired tearjerker of the year" (p. 28).

[15]On the more radical interventions from the independent film movement, see Kellner-Ryan, ibid, Chapter Ten.

Contributors

Bat-Ami Bar On is Associate Professor of Philosophy at the State University of New York College at Oswego. Her major area of philosophical investigation is violence. She is currently working on a book entitled *Everyday Violence*.

Gail Burns is a graduate student in the Department of Anthropology at Ohio State University. Her concentrations include American Studies and American History. She counts watching television as one of the greatest pleasures life offers.

Diane M. Calhoun-French is Dean of Academic Affairs at Jefferson Community College (Southwest Campus) in Louisville, Kentucky. She has been active in the Popular Culture Association for many years and currently serves on the Executive Board. She is also Executive Secretary of the Popular Culture Association in the South. Her research interests include popular romance and mystery fiction, daytime serials, and women in popular culture.

Robert Gooding-Williams is Associate Professor of Philosophy at Amherst College.

Sandra Y. Govan is Associate Professor at the University of North Carolina-Charlotte. Her primary interests are African-American literature and culture; American literature; Popular Culture, particularly science fiction; and women's literature. Most of her publications have been "scholarly" articles in the areas cited but she has lately begun to try her hand at creative writing.

Paul Gripp is a Ph.D. candidate in Literary and Cultural Studies at Carnegie-Mellon University—Pittsburgh, PA.

Minabere Ibelema is Assistant Professor of communication at Central State University, Wilberforce, Ohio. He holds a doctorate in mass communication from Ohio State University.

Cheryl Kader is a doctoral candidate in Modern Studies in the English Department at the University of Wisconsin-Milwaukee. Her dissertation is entitled, *Gendered Social Space: Feminism and The Production of Meaning.* In her dissertation, she theorizes the production of feminist space by examining a few of the numerous texts, practices, and figures that have contributed to a significant rewriting of the contemporary American cultural landscape.

Melinda Kanner a Ph.D. candidate in anthropology at Ohio State University, is completing her dissertation on the relationship between ethnopsychiatry and popular culture in the construction of women and alcoholism. She has published articles on the history of anthropology as well as critical studies.

Douglas Kellner is Professor of Philosophy at the University of Texas at Austin and is author of books on Karl Korsch, Herbert Marcuse, and (with Michael Ryan), *Camera Politica: The Politics and Ideology of Contemporary Hollywood Film*. He has just published *Critical Theory, Marxism, and Modernity* and *Jean Baudrillard: From Marxism to Postmodernism and Beyond*. Forthcoming books include (with Steven Best) *Postmodern Theory* and *Television and the Crisis of Democracy*.

Timothy W. Luke is Professor of Political Science at Virginia Polytechnic Institute and State University in Blacksburg, Virginia. His research interests include social theory, political communication, and the social effects of the mass media. His most recent book is *Screens of Power: Ideology, Domination, and Resistance in Informational Society* (Urbana: University of Illinois Press, 1989).

Ray Pratt is Associate Professor of Political Science at Montana State University, Bozeman. He is the author of *Rhythm and Resistance: Explorations in Political Uses of Popular Music* (Praeger, 1990). He has contributed chapters to *American Media and Mass Culture* (California, 1987) and other books and several articles to *Popular Music and Society*. He has published widely in the fields of political theory and comparative politics and political economy. He has been a college radio disc jockey for a dozen years.

Diane Raymond is Professor of Philosophy at Simmons College, Boston, MA.

Robin Roberts is Assistant Professor of English at Louisiana State University and she has published articles on popular culture in *Journal of Popular Culture, Extrapolation, Science-Fiction Studies*, and *National Women's Studies Association Journal*.

Kerry Shea is an Assistant Professor at Saint Michael's College in Vermont, where she teaches medieval literature, women's literature and film. She has just completed a study of voyeurism in Hartmann von Aue's 12th century Middle High German romance, *Der Arme Heinrich* and is currently working on an analysis of maternal ideology in the films of Percy Adlon.

Linda Singer is Associate Professor of Philosophy at Miami University, and writes regularly on popular culture. As a feminist, she is especially concerned with the power popular cultural artifacts and institutions enjoy in the construction and dissemination of gender, pleasure, and desire. Her interest in the genre of "panic sex" films is part of a larger project to be published by Routledge as part of its "Thinking Gender" series entitled *Erotic Welfare: Sexual Theory and Politics in the Age of Epidemic*.

Nancy M. Theriot is Associate Professor of History at the University of Louisville. She is author of *The Biosocial Construction of Femininity: Mothers and Daughters in Nineteenth-Century America*, and is currently working on a book manuscript on the medical discourse on female insanity in the nineteenth century.

Contributors 249

Suzanna Danuta Walters is Assistant Professor of sociology at The Colorado College, where she teaches courses in Feminist Theory, Popular Culture, and Women and Media. She recently received her doctorate in sociology from CUNY Graduate Center, where she wrote on the representation of mothers and daughters in popular culture, and is currently engaged with questions of female spectatorship and the politics of popular culture.

Cynthia Willett teaches in the Philosophy and Culture and History of Philosophy programs at LeMoyne College in Syracuse, New York. She writes on deconstruction, dialectic, comedy, and tragedy.

Judith Bryant Wittenberg is Associate Professor of English at Simmons College.